THE BLUE PAWN

A Memoir of an NYPD Foot Soldier

D.D. SIMPSON

NEWMAN SPRINGS PUBLISHING
320 Broad Street
Red Bank, NJ 07701

First originally published by Newman Springs Publishing 2018

ISBN 978-1-64096-036-7 (Paperback)
ISBN 978-1-64096-042-8 (Hardcover)
ISBN 978-1-64096-038-1 (Digital)

Printed in the United States of America

I dedicate this book to all the men and
women that keep the rest of us safe.
Thank you for your service.

Contents

Acknowledgments

This memoir was extracted from a journal that I began early on in my NYPD career. I decided to change many of the names in order to protect those that might wish to remain unknown. In some instances, I have melded a few individual stories in the hope of bringing a clearer, more concise theme to my work. However, when it comes to conveying my personal struggles, and of those that were killed in the line of duty, I made every effort to chronicle these events in the manner in which they occurred. I pray my recollection, notes, and research serves the memory of those that paid the ultimate sacrifice with the respect and honor they deserve.

Prologue

Joe DiMaggio thanked the good Lord for making him a Yankee. As for me, I thank God for letting me be born in Brooklyn.

The borough of homes and churches was my Mayberry. Most people outside New York don't realize that the Big Apple is simply a collection of little towns. The town I was from is named Bay Ridge.

While growing up in Bay Ridge, I was educated in a diverse collection of ethnic groups; Greek, Italian, Norwegian, Polish, German, and a lot of Irish to name a few. Going over to one of my friend's homes for dinner was like going to Epcot.

Yes, I'd been blessed many times over to have been born and raised in Brooklyn. However, it wasn't the great food that made my community special. It was the people.

Living directly across the street from my school/church, I was never without being cared for by those who truly loved me. My teachers and coaches would become my role models. Leading by example and strong Christian values, these men and women stressed how love conquers all.

Father Gerald was my mentor. He taught me how to shoot a jump shot, as well as how to divide compound fractions. Some years later, I did my first boiler maker with the clergymen and dared to question the existence of God in his presence. Not one to judge, Father Gerald remained my friend throughout my life, always making certain none of his sheep wondered too far.

At the age of eight, I started asking store owners in my neighborhood for a job. They all turned me down except for one—Joe Falcone. Joe, short for Giuseppe, owned the local produce store in my neighborhood. In his heavy, Northern Italian accent, Joe promised he'd hire me as soon as I was old enough. Not knowing exactly when that was, I hounded the respected merchant for a job at least once a week for the next two years. He finally relented and hired me at the ripe old age of ten.

For the first several months, I worked only Saturday mornings. He had me start by cleaning out the milk and soda cases. Then I would dust the can goods and restock if needed. My favorite part of the day was when the Rectory would call in their grocery order. Joe would give me the list and I'd go around the store filling the basket with the requested items. When I was done, I'd take the order over to the Rectory kitchen to the awaiting Ms. Strahan.

The senior, unofficial matriarch of the church, Mrs. Strahan was one of the most ingratiating people I ever had the pleasure of knowing. She was so involved with the day-to-day operations of the church that most people went to her for help before they'd go to one of the priests. Besides being the cook, Mrs. Strahan was the bookkeeper, the fund raiser chairperson, the head of every committee and responsible for just about everything under the church's roof—including us altar boys.

I worked for Joe for the next ten years. I continued to deliver the groceries to Mrs. Strahan and on many occasions, with a note from the diocese letterhead, made runs to the liquor store for the thirsty clergy. It was always explained to me that the liquor was only to help the men of the cloth sleep at night. With that much hooch, they must've all slept like babies.

Those early years working in the store prepared me for life. I learned responsibility, how to handle money and, most importantly, how to treat people. I truly loved working there and if not for another calling, I would've been more than content to remain at the Verrazano Food Market.

During the application process to become a New York City police officer, I was required to submit letters of recommendation. I asked my boss, Joe, and several of the priests if they'd be kind enough to write one on my behalf. Joe wrote a beautiful letter, going as far as to say I was like a son to him.

As for the priests, they put a letter together that looked like it came from the Vatican itself. They praised my leadership skills along with my character and integrity. All six priests and the Monsignor signed the letter on my behalf.

However, the letter that touched me the most was the one I hadn't asked for.

Mrs. Strahan, having heard I was in need of these letters, submitted one to the police department. In her letter, she wrote that the city would be a safer place to live and work with me as one of New York's Finest.

Not long after, I was accepted into the Police Academy and my career as a New York City Police Officer commenced. The year was 1987 and the city—a pre-9/11 City—was dealing with crack, AIDS, and a spike in violent crimes. Terrorism, as we know it today, wasn't on the radar yet.

One of the first questions I was asked by an instructor in the Police Academy was why I wanted to become a police officer? For me, it was a calling. Perhaps the same type of calling a person may have for wanting to climb Mount Everest, or when a young individual decides to join the military. One may not be able to fully explain the reason for their decision, or even appreciate the danger that surrounds it, but all the individual knows is that they must answer that call or they won't feel complete.

When the tragic events of September 11, 2001 occurred, it affected all Americans deeply. However, in the New York area the shock was more profound. We had direct and intimate connections to the people that perished and the buildings that fell. We didn't suffer simply as a city or a borough, but rather from block to block—congregation to congregation.

Following the aftermath of 9/11, the New York Police and Firemen received an outpouring of respect and appreciation throughout the country. The sacrifice for these departments came at a great cost of life. NYFD, 343 firefighters; NYPD, 23 officers; the Port Authority Police, 37 officers; and Emergency Medical Technicians/paramedics, 8.

These men and women are heroes, not because they perished, but because when everyone was trying to escape from the burning buildings, they stayed true to their calling and ran into them.

As New Yorkers, we knew firsthand that these heroic acts weren't isolated to simply one day, but take place every day throughout the city. Tragically, it took the events of 9/11 to show the rest of the world just how courageous our men and women in uniform truly are.

But time is moving on. Praise for our first responders has been replaced with complacency. Police have been targeted simply because of their uniform. A group that prides itself in caring shouts slogans to kill cops.

My father, a retired police officer, warned me of the dangers of being a cop. He compared it to being a lowly pawn in a chess match.

The word *pawn* is derived from the Latin word meaning foot soldier. This is the story of one such soldier.

CHAPTER 1

Graduation Day

December 24, 2001, 0500 hours

This will be my final entry.

Father Gerald paid me a visit tonight. I know he only wishes to help but what he doesn't understand is that I don't want to be helped.

It'll be thirteen years tomorrow that I made a decision that haunts me to my core. During that time, I've allowed myself to be distracted, so as not to have to deal with reality.

But the past several months has forced me to deal with death on a scale that makes it impossible for me to continue masking my disgrace. Due to the events of 9/11, I can no longer hide from my cowardice. I've attended twenty-three funerals in that time, always hoping the next would either be my last—or better yet, mine.

It's been almost four months since I watched the Broncos destroy my hometown team, The New York Giants. I watched the game that night at The Wicked Monk Pub with my fellow drunkard acquaintances. I was drunk then just like I am now. I drink heavily because I'm an alcoholic and have no reason to be otherwise. I don't remember much about that evening, but the next day I'll never forget. While I was sleeping off my inebriated state, my country was being attacked. Fewer than ten miles away from the comfort of my bed, people I called friends and brethren would perish in a horrific act of terror. When I finally did awake, both Towers had fallen along with nearly three thousand souls.

The thought of suicide doesn't scare me; however, living with my demons does. Because of this, I will now embark on two trips. One will be to fulfill a promise I made a long time ago, and the other to silence my pain. Neither should take very long.

My decision is made, the implementation near, and finally a feeling I haven't felt in a long time has come over me: peace.

> "God will not look you over for medals
> degrees or diplomas, but for scars."
> —Elbert Hubbard

My dad, James Simpson, was born in Brooklyn, New York, during the Great Depression. His parents had arrived from Dublin just prior to the market crash of 1929. During the processing on Ellis Island, my grandfather was asked by the immigration officer for his name. He responded, "Michael J. Stenson." The agent, having difficulty understanding grandfather's thick Irish brogue, heard "Simpson," and so it was.

My grandfather immediately took the mistake to be a bad omen and pondered the thought of returning back home, but my grandmother wouldn't hear of it. According to her, she hadn't made the trip to America so she can have a better life but rather for her children, and her children's children, to have a better life.

By the time my dad was a teenager, he had filled out his wiry six-foot-two frame and was soon able to find work at the Brooklyn Navy Yard. He said it was here on those cold, blistery winter days that he learned to keep his head down and his mouth shut. Even years later, one could still see the wear and tear he accumulated from those days working on the docks along the East River. His oversized hands were like two stones from the hardened callouses, while his face bore the scars from the unforgiving ocean spray.

Dad met my mother, Margaret O'Brien, at an Emerald Society dance in 1950. He described the first time he laid eyes on her from across the gymnasium, that it was like being struck with a bolt of lightning. "She looked like Rita Hayworth, but prettier," Dad would recall. Unfortunately, I never had the opportunity to hear Mom's recollection regarding seeing my dad for the first time. The good Lord took her before we could share such stories. I was seven.

Shortly after they started dating, Dad was drafted into the army for the Korean War, and the romance was put on hold. When he returned, he set two goals for himself: marry the love of his life and to become a police officer.

The newlyweds purchased a pre-World War II, semidetached, two-family house across the street from our church, Saint Patrick's in Bay Ridge. According to Dad, the house was a never-ending project. He enclosed under the staircase to make more storage space but as a child, I turned it into my secret fort. It was there that I'd listened to Dad through the drafty thin walls share his experiences as a New York City Police Officer with Mom. I couldn't have been more than five or six and didn't understand half of what he was saying, but from the excitement in his voice, I envisioned him looking over Gotham as a hybrid of Batman-Superman dressed in a police uniform. With stories of chasing down bad guys, delivering babies, and throwing mobsters in jail still ringing in my ears, it shouldn't have been a surprise to anyone when I decided to join New York's Finest.

The day was July 6, 1987, when I, Dean Simpson, graduated from the New York City Police Academy.

After graduation, Dad took me, along with my older brother Francis, to the Water Club Café on East Thirtieth Street. I knew the eatery was a special place for Dad, since it was here he proposed to mother. Dad did his best to keep Mom's memory and spirit alive with Francis and me. He'd stress the importance of doing the right thing because, as he put it, "Mom is watching."

While sitting there in my dress uniform, looking out the window at the strong currents of the East River hitting against the base of the Williamsburg Bridge, Dad ambushed me with a question I hadn't expected.

"So, why did you want to be a police officer?" he asked.

Six months earlier when I told him I was accepted into the Academy, he hadn't much to say. In fact, he just grunted. I didn't take his lack of support as a slight but rather a concern on his part for having another son on the job. Francis, being three years older, joined the department a few years prior.

Not wanting to give a serious answer, I used big brother as my scapegoat.

"Well, Dad, Francis told me the graft was pretty good, so I thought what the heck."

"You're not out of the Academy an hour and your cracking jokes like that? All right, wise guy, let's say you find a thousand dollars in cash on a DOA (dead on arrival), would you keep it?"

Having opened a door I now wished to close, I assured him I was only joking about the graft but he still insisted on an answer.

"No, I would voucher the money," I replied.

"What if it were two thousand or maybe even four thousand?"

"No, sir, I'd voucher it."

"How about five thousand, what then?"

"No, sir, I'd still voucher it."

"Francis, would you please explain to the rookie where he's gone wrong."

Francis, twenty-three, was built more like my dad then I was. Always taller and stronger than me, he constantly pushed my limits growing up to become a better athlete. Nobody looked after me more growing up than Francis.

"You get to keep the five-thousand," Francis said with his trademark carefree smirk. "Everyone knows IAD (Internal Affairs Division) aren't permitted to go that high in a sting operation."

The two shared a good laugh at my expense as I sat there shaking my head.

Francis told me not to feel bad. "He used the same joke on me the day I graduated from the Academy. Dad doesn't realize IAD has probably allocated more funds since he retired a hundred years ago, so be careful."

"All kidding aside, boys, don't ever let anyone buy your soul," Dad said in a more serious tone. "Five, ten, a hundred-thousand— doesn't matter. No amount of money can ever buy back your soul. Just ask Judas. So, getting back to my original question, why a copper?"

Having failed at humor to deflect the question, I decided this time to give a straight answer.

"It's because of you, Dad. You're my hero. I thought you would've known that all I ever wanted was to follow in your footsteps and to someday tell stories the way you once told Mom."

As much as Dad's question threw me off guard, my answer had apparently done the same to him. With a grin and a pat on my back, he began to choke up.

Francis, quick to catch on that I knew some of Dad's stories, was eager to hear one.

"What stories?" he asked. "I don't remember hearing Dad tell any stories to Mom."

Dad was skeptical for the moment, going as far as to say I was bluffing.

"All right, if I'm bluffing, how then would I know there's someone in Chinatown named after you?"

"Wow, that was a long time ago. I don't recall telling you about that. Well, go ahead, tell Francis about his stepbrother."

With that, I began to tell Francis the story of how Dad delivered a baby when he was a rookie.

"Well, if I'm not mistaken, Dad was assigned to a foot post on Canal Street that day. An Asian man was yelling out the window from one of the apartments above. Unable to understand what the guy was screaming, but instinctively knowing the individual needed immediate assistance, Officer Simpson ran up the five flights of stairs to investigate. When he entered the apartment, he could see a lady lying on the floor apparently in labor. Officer Simpson holstered his weapon and proceeded to assist in the delivery of a little baby boy. The husband was so thankful he named the child after Dad, James Michael Fung."

"Nice going, Officer Simpson," Francis said, complimenting Dad on a job well done.

Francis enjoyed the story about Baby Fung and was now asking me to hear another. I declined, deferring to the source himself, Dad.

I knew Dad wasn't one to tell stories of past glory. However, being that it was a special occasion, I thought he was ripe for persuading. Francis and I both looked over at him waiting for him to start.

"Sorry, boys, I don't remember any," he said, in an effort to convince both of us.

Trying to nudge him on, I reminded Dad about the night he missed Christmas Eve with Mom because he locked up a mobster.

With a perplexed look on his face, he questioned how I knew about these things since I wasn't even born yet.

"Never mind that," I told him. "One story and you're done... please."

In a weak attempt to get out of storytelling, Dad said to Francis and me that he didn't know if he remembered much about that night. So, I reminded him it was Christmas Eve and that he just made the biggest arrest of his young career.

Realizing he wasn't getting off the hook, the old school patrolman finally relented.

"All right, well, you were right about the day. It was Christmas Eve 1955 to be exact. My partner Lenny Kaplan and I were working the four-to-twelve shift out of the Fifth Precinct. The Fifth was a great place for two young cops to work. Lots of action and good arrests to be made. Plus, with Little Italy and Chinatown located within the confines of the command, we ate pretty well, too.

"Lenny and I knew each other from the Academy. When the time came and the opportunity presented itself, we agreed to be partners. You boys remember that choosing a partner is serious business. You have to be able to trust the other person. It's the one closest to you that can either save you or hurt you.

"With Lenny, it was a natural fit. We were both more interested in being good cops then getting rich—if you know what I mean.

"On that particular night, we had two goals; have a quiet Chinese dinner at Wo Hops, and to stay clear of anything that would extend our shift. We decided early on not to write any summonses. Most would have thought we were in the holiday spirit but the truth was we didn't want to risk pulling over some motorist without a license and getting into some quagmire. There'd be no summons, no arrests, and no seeking out bad guys on this night. Unless there was a dead body lying in the middle of Canal Street, sector Charlie of the 5th Precinct had its blinders on.

"The shift was going as planned. By the time we finished dinner all the shops along Canal Street were closed. The only places open were a few restaurants on Mulberry Street. About thirty minutes prior to our shift ending, I decided to drive over to a small section of Little Italy to see the decorative lights the merchants put up every Christmas. Lenny immediately didn't think it was a good idea. He explained to me that we should stay in our sector because there were still too many people out and about. On the other hand, Chinatown was pretty much a ghost town. Lenny stressed that the blinders worked best when there were less people around to see. I told him to stop worrying and enjoy the celebration of lights for Baby Jesus. Lenny was quick to remind me that he was Jewish, to which I responded, "Great, so was Jesus."

"While I continued down Mulberry Street I observed a few wise guys outside of a well-known mafia social club. Some of the gangsters, in their expensive suits and greased-back hair, gave a friendly wave in our direction. Although there was no love lost between us and the wise guys there was usually a mutual respect given to one another. However, if the mafia boys were caught breaking the law, they understood the consequences. It was a simple cat and mouse game.

"As I was almost done driving pass the social club, I made eye contact with one of the guys. The Capone wannabe raised up the glass of wine he was holding and made a toasting gesture towards Lenny and me. After I returned the wave I noticed the man next to him put his thumb in his mouth and flick it in my direction. This Sicilian gesture was equivalent to giving someone the middle finger.

"Blinders or not, I saw it and wasn't about to have some wise guy flip me off. I pulled over and slapped the cuffs on the punk. After putting him in the back of the squad car, the other wise guys pleaded with me to let him go. They tried explaining that he was drunk and promised they'd serve him an appropriate punishment for his disrespect. I wouldn't hear it, so it was back to the Command with the prisoner. Just one little problem—what was I going to charge him with?

"I could see Lenny was visibly upset. He thought I should've let the incident go but for me it was a matter of principal. I explained to him that it was important to let the bad guys know that the men in blue were still in charge.

"I didn't like the wise guys or their lifestyle, but I tolerated them. I knew the game and respected the rules. Once one of these grease balls crossed the line, I didn't hesitate to make an arrest—even if it was Christmas Eve and the most serious charge I could come up with thus far was public intoxication.

"After mulling over my options, I told Lenny I'd give the wise guy a summons back at the Precinct and we'd be done in ten minutes.

"On the ride back to the precinct, the perp was in the back seat sobbing and muttering in Italian that he wanted his mother. I told him to quiet down and that he'd be back at the club before Santa arrived. The mafia wise guy was acting more like a child than a gangster. Lenny thought it was the booze but I thought perhaps the guy was simply nuts. Either way in a few minutes we'd all be done and everyone would be going their own separate way."

The Fifth Precinct was located on Elizabeth Street just off Canal in Lower Manhattan. The nineteenth-century building had a white painted brick façade on the front side and was attached to a row of similar four-story buildings. A black metal fire escape ran down the entire front side of the dreary four-story structure. It looked more like a run-down apartment house than a police station. The cold Command was home to more rodents than cops—not the kind of place you'd want to spend Christmas.

"As I brought the intoxicated wise guy into the stationhouse the Lieutenant, sitting behind the elevated oak desk, didn't look pleased to see the three of us standing in front of him. It was the holidays and making collars for dis-con wasn't exactly considered good police work.

"After explaining the situation to my boss, I was sternly instructed to write the summons and then get the hell out.

"I emptied the perp's pockets looking for his identification. At this point, all I wanted to do was identify the guy, write the summons and, as the lieutenant instructed, get the hell out of there. While emptying the perp's coat pocket, I discovered a wad of small papers with numbers on them. Not knowing what they were, I tossed them on the desk and continued looking for his identification.

"In the meantime, word had traveled upstairs to the Detective Squad that two patrolmen just brought in a 'wise guy.'

"One of the detectives from the squad made his way down to the backroom to see what we had. That was the first time I met Tony.

"Tony Vella was what they called on the job a dinosaur. He had twenty-seven years on, and nearly all of them were spent in the Fifth Precinct Detective Squad. He could've retired after twenty years but chose to stay. Guys had different reasons for staying. For some, they'd be lost without the job; for others, they'd rather work than be home with their wives; and for guys like Tony, they simply loved the job.

"Tony was a legend in Little Italy. His reputation for being a straight shooter enabled him to earn respect from all sides; wise guys, street cops, and even the brass. Tony didn't have double standards. He treated the busboy at Angelo's Restaurant the same way he'd treat a "made guy"—both with respect.

"His gift was that he knew how to talk to people and, just as important, he knew how to get people to talk to him. At five-foot-ten, and built like a wrecking ball, Tony sported the same cus-tom-made suits the wise guys wore. He knew his role as a detective in the mafia-ridden Little Italy, and he played it to perfection.

"The detective asked me what I had and I told him it was noth-ing big, just a simple dis-con.

"While talking to Tony, I noticed he kept looking down at the slips of paper on the table. I informed him that I was having dif-ficulty identifying the bumbling idiot. Tony told me not to worry about the identification because he knew who the wise guy was.

"'This is Mr. Vincent Gigante', Tony announced loud enough to awaken the perp from his stupor.

"Tony then kicked the wise guy's chair and told him to sit up. The detective explained that Vincent, or better known as Vinny the Chin, liked to play stupid when he got in trouble—an old Sicilian trick.

"With a sheepish grin on his face, Vinny sat up and just like that, the improv was over. I couldn't believe the entire episode was an act. I thought to myself that the guy missed his calling; he should've been an actor.

"The mobster wished the Detective a Merry Christmas and asked how he was doing.

"Tony, sporting a big smile on his face, replied back, 'Better than you, schmuck.'

"Apparently, Tony knew the slips of paper on the table were betting slips and that each slip was a separate count. Tony explained to me what I had: over a hundred counts of illegal gambling and racketeering charges against Mr. Gigante, a small fish but a big collar.

"With that, the suddenly pale looking Vinny asked to talk to Tony alone for a minute. Tony asked Lenny and me if we could give him a moment with his new best friend. As I walked out of the back room, I noticed the lieutenant glaring at me while checking his Timex. However, my concern was more about what was going on in the back room than worrying about catching the lieutenant's wrath. Sure, the time was ticking, but now instead of writing a summons and being home with your mother in a half an hour, I was looking at the possibility of making the biggest collar in my young career.

"Less than two minutes later, Tony called for Lenny and me to come back in. As I entered the room, I noticed a stack of cash sitting on the table. Tony began to talk. 'Mr. Gigante would like to wish you and your partner a Merry Christmas and were wondering if you'd be so inclined to let the matter at hand disappear along with this.' He pointed toward the money. 'And then perhaps everyone could go their own separate, merry way.'

"I asked Tony where the money came from and he explained that Mr. Gigante had money belts strapped to each thigh, and now he wished to be relieved of their contents.

"There was over a year's salary for Lenny and me on the table, and a decision had to be made quickly.

"Lenny and I were clean cops but that didn't mean we were without temptation. We saw things around the command. It wasn't hard to figure out which cops were on the take. All one had to do was see the type of car each cop was driving to figure out who was clean and who wasn't. Lenny drove a beat-up Oldsmobile, while I drove a ten-year-old Studebaker clunker. On the other hand, Tony had a shiny, brand-new Cadillac Eldorado.

"Whether he was on the take or not was irrelevant. Things were different back then. Pretty much everyone was on the take to some degree. The question for most was what graft was taboo. Every cop had his own standards. For some, a hot stove wasn't safe; while for others, whatever they took in graft they'd give their church ten percent to ease their conscience. For Tony, it was about the three Ds: no drug money, no dead money, and no degrading money. The first two were fairly simple to follow, but the last 'D' was about not taking graft that didn't feel right with him. That's one of the ways Tony separated himself from the pack and gained the respect of the wise guys. He was fair but firm. He'd take money to quash a gambling rap or to look the other way if some expensive fur coats happened to fall off the back of a truck. But if a wise guy was caught killing someone or pushing dope, no money in the world could buy Tony to look the other way.

"For the record, not all of Tony's graft went toward expensive suits and cars. The truth is a lot of that money was used to grease guys for information on bigger cases.

"I understand a cop on the take is dirty regardless of the circumstances, but try to remember things were different back then. I, for one, am glad the department cleaned up its act but back in the '50s, '60s and '70s, there was systemic corruption throughout the department. Prior to the Knapp Commission of the early '70s, the brass had their own blinders on and these blinders prevented them from seeing anything that would disturb their gravy train."

Under media scrutiny and tremendous public pressure, the Knapp Commission was formed. In 1972, Mayor Lindsay assembled the Commission to investigate police corruption. The Commission uncovered what everyone else in the Police Department already knew: that the police were paid 'protection money' by organized crime members in order to preserve the underworld's interest in prostitution, gambling, and narcotics. Because of the corruption scandal, Mayor Lindsay's political career was all but over.

"During this period, every cop had to make his own peace with how they'd deal with the graft. Tony had his three *D*s, and as for Lenny and I, we'd soon be facing our own decision that would test which way our moral compass pointed."

"As partners, we had discussed many different scenarios. However, this hadn't been one of them. We discussed things like if one of us was ever being held hostage for the other guy to not hesitate and take the shot. We had hand signals as well. If one rubbed his shield, it meant that whatever the situation was, they thought it to be good. If one were to rub the butt of the gun, they thought it to be bad.

"As I looked over at Lenny, I noticed his right hand down by the side of his .38 caliber Smith and Wesson service revolver—he was gently rubbing the butt of his gun. The decision was easy—no deal!

"I informed Tony of my decision and thanked him for his help. I appreciated that Tony didn't try to bully two rookies into a more favorable decision for the mobster; or worse, attempt to take the collar and money for himself. But I would learn that wasn't Tony's style.

"Tony wished us all a Merry Christmas and told me if I needed any help with the collar to give him a yell upstairs.

"Now I had to tell Lew there was a change in plans and that we weren't going to be done by midnight. I walked to the front and saw that there was a new lieutenant on duty. Without noticing, midnight had come and gone, and the changing of the shift had already taken place. I gave a run down on what I had to the new desk officer. The lieutenant told me to take my time with the paper work, and to make certain it was all done properly.

"To my relief, I was no longer being rushed out of the command. The lieutenant wished me a Merry Christmas and congratulated me on a solid collar. That's when I realized I wasn't going to make it home to be with your mother on Christmas Eve.

"I told Lenny to take off, but he refused. We were partners and he insisted on helping me with the booking. I felt bad because I knew he had plans with his wife, a tough Italian Catholic girl from Canarsie. We made a compromise; Lenny would help voucher the money into evidence and be on his way within the hour.

"Before heading down to Central Booking, I decided to stop upstairs to see Tony and thank him for his help. I knew I owed the veteran Detective a bit of gratitude for enlightening me that I had something more than a simple dis-con. He congratulated me on a solid collar and said something prophetic. He told me he looked forward to someday working with me in the squad, and sure enough, in time, we did just that."

*****

I was grateful to Dad, an individual who rationed his words carefully, to be willing to open up to Francis and me. The man with the sad, dark eyes was old school, which meant no tattoos, no facial hair and certainly no boasting of past accolades.

In the hope of having him continue, I asked him about the fate of Gigante.

"In regards to the charges, I never heard anything from the DA's office," Dad went on to say. "Maybe he took a plea or maybe his money found its way to a more willing recipient. Either way, I didn't care. I did my job. As for 'The Chin' himself, every now and again there'd be an article in the paper about him. Some guys have a way of finding trouble and he was one of them. A few years after I locked him up, I heard he failed in an assassination attempt on mobster Frank Costello. While serving time for the botched attempt, he shared a cell with mob boss Vito Genovese. Through his new connection into the Genovese family, Gigante would get his own crew and eventually work his way to the top—the Godfather himself. But he never did stop playing the role of the bumbling idiot. With his stained robe and worn out slippers, the character actor walked the streets of Greenwich Village to the delight of the media. He was a shrewd businessman that used his 'act' in an attempt to keep the Fed's off his back and his ass out of prison. However, his acting career finally ended when he died in the place he was trying so desperately to avoid: prison."

Francis seemed less interested in what happened to the mafia boss than he did about finding out how much trouble Dad was in for standing Mom up.

"Your mom was an understanding person," Dad recalled. "She knew my responsibilities as a police officer and was aware that things may unexpectedly come up. However, Father Gerald wasn't as understanding for missing his midnight mass."

While Francis and I sat there listening to Dad tell the story, I once again envisioned him as a superhero. Not because he threw a bad guy in jail, but because he never stopped being our dad. I can't imagine how difficult it was for him to be a widower with two young boys to raise, but he did it. According to Dad, he attributed his faith in God for giving him the strength to get through his most difficult times.

After finishing our lunch, I thanked Dad for making the day special for me. Looking at me as a proud father concerned with my future, he squeezed in some last-minute advice. He urged me to do two things while I was a police officer. First, he emphasized how important it was to be prepared. "Preparation and smart decision making go hand in hand," he stressed. Second, he wanted me to start a journal while I was a police officer. He told me that not keeping one himself was one of his biggest regrets.

He told me that time was going to go by faster than I could ever imagine. "When you look back, twenty years will feel like twenty minutes. Experiences you thought you'd never forget become distant memories."

The next day I was to report to my new command—Midtown South Precinct. My career, as well as my journal, would soon start its first chapter together.

CHAPTER 2

Hello NYPD

To find out what one is fitted to do, and to secure an
opportunity to do it, is the key to happiness.

—John Dewey

Mother, Margaret O'Brien, was born in Ireland in 1935. When she was five, my grandfather, Frank O'Brien, having some ongoing "issues" with the local authorities in their Northern Ireland hometown of Crossmaglen, thought it be best to move him and his family to America. The young Irish family, which included mother's younger sister, Grace, settled in Flatbush, Brooklyn.

Regrettably, I struggle with my memories of my mom. If not for the picture I keep in my wallet, I'm certain I would've forgotten what she looked like by now. She spoke softly, still with a hint of her native brogue present. I don't recall her ever raising her voice or getting upset. However, I don't remember her smiling or laughing either. It's the silly things I remember like her ironing Francis's and my school uniform every evening by the kitchen counter, or how she used a ton of hair tonic before I left for school to help keep my crop in place.

One of the more vivid memories I have of my mother is the morning she walked me to my first day of school. I was reluctant letting go of her hand that morning. Sensing my displeasure, she assured me everything would be fine. She said, "Dean, the first day in anything is always the scariest because we don't know what to expect.

But then we somehow get through it, make friends and our life is better for it. Try to remember the other children are nervous too, so be nice to them and they will be nice to you."

Every time I started something new, I thought of Mom and the words she shared with me on that day. Unfortunately, she was no longer around to hold my hand and give me similar words of encouragement, but the essence of what she told me was still with me.

The day after lunch with Dad and Francis, I reported to the Midtown South Precinct for orientation. I packed a bag with my uniform and gun belt and took the "R" train into Manhattan. On the ride into the city, I started to get butterflies in my stomach. I was excited to get started but also very nervous. The words mother used to comfort me years earlier on my first day of kindergarten, those same words that I'd recall on my first day of high school, were now echoing in my head as I walked the two blocks from Penn Station to my new command on West Thirty-Fifth Street. Today was officially my first day as a New York City Police Officer. I had no idea what to expect, but thanks to Mom, I knew the toughest part would soon be over.

When I walked into the Midtown South Precinct, there were two things that immediately stood out to me; the pictures of the fallen heroes the command had lost in the line of duty over the years, and the banner that hung above the front desk, "Midtown South— The Busiest Precinct in the World."

For as long as I could remember, all I ever wanted was to follow in my dad's footsteps. But for the first time, as I stood there reading the banner, I wondered if I was ready. There'd be no place to hide for a police officer in the heart of Midtown. Soon, people were going to look to me to have every answer to every question. I thought to myself, *Good luck*.

I'd be assigned to "The South" for the next six months as part of my probation period. As a rookie, I'd be working alongside other newbies with added supervision in the form of sergeants. In previous years, the department used detectives to train the rookies. However, the brass soon realized using the older more disgruntled detectives, nicknamed "hag-bags," didn't make for a positive influence on the young impressionable rookies.

The proper police jargon is actually "hair bags," but as a child listening to father's stories, I always thought he was saying hag-bags. Shortly after being on the job, I soon realized I was mispronouncing the word that described the older, sloppier officers. But since they mostly acted like a bunch of old hags, I felt my term, *hag-bag*, better described these useless, deadbeat officers.

There'd be twenty rookies reporting to the South that morning. All those fortunate to get into the Third Division detail did so via a hook, including me. A hook was a contact, a connection, somebody who knew someone. The call was made, and if your hook was big enough, your first pick on your wish list came to fruition. Rookie cops didn't just accidently or by chance get assigned to the Third Division. The jewel of the city was saved for the rookies with the biggest hooks.

My hook was Dad. His hook was his former partner Lenny Kaplan, now Chief Kaplan. Dad made sure I was going to be in the heart of the city and not in some godawful place like Bedford Stuyvesant. Or worse yet, Staten Island counting sheep.

Dad didn't have to tell me how fortunate I was to be assigned to the prestigious division. I knew I was given a tremendous opportunity, but it was still up to me to make the most of it. But prior to solving all the city's crime problems, I would first need to attend orientation.

After changing into my uniform, I reported to the muster room where the orientation would take place. Similar to the children on the first day of kindergarten, all the rookies stood around quietly, sporting a worrisome look on their face. Being one that wanted to get the awkwardness out of the way as quickly as possible, I already decided prior to entering the room to introduce myself to the first person I saw. That person was Officer Eddie Byrne.

After introducing myself to Eddie, I asked him if he had done anything special after graduation. He explained to me that he was a rollover from the transit PD and had graduated the Academy the previous year. Now that his transfer finally went through, he was happy to be working above ground for a change.

Eddie and I were situated by the front door of the muster room. As more rookies entered, I decided to introduce Eddie and myself to them. In less than ten minutes, the once quiet, apprehensive room was now buzzing and full of excited chitchat. The first step on the first day was officially over.

At around 0800 hours, four sergeants and one very tough looking Lieutenant came walking into the back room. The lieutenant introduced himself as Lieutenant Higgins. He reminded me of my maternal grandfather with his white hair and strong jaw line. He struck me as a no-nonsense kind of guy.

After introducing the four sergeants with him, Lieutenant Higgins went over what they'd be doing with us during orientation. It sounded like we'd be filling out a lot of paperwork; payroll, firearm information, life insurance policy (in case one of us was killed in the line of duty), and lots of other clerical forms.

Lieutenant Higgins informed the squad that the Third Division Commander, Inspector Moretti, would be stopping by later to say a few words. He reminded us to stand at attention when the inspector entered the room.

Lew then turned and pointed to the four sergeants and told us that they were our supervisors. He explained how they'd be hands on and would not only supervise, but teach us things we didn't learn the previous six months in the Academy.

"These guys have seen a lot of action," the lieutenant said. "Keep your eyes open and you may actually learn something over the next six months. However, if by chance anyone of you should do something stupid to jam up one of my bosses, I promise, you won't make it through probation. I will now leave you in the hands of my sergeants."

Next to the podium was a seasoned looking sergeant sporting a pair of thick, grayish sideburns and a mustache. While the solid-built supervisor stood there glancing over the room, I noticed his impressive rack of medals displayed over his sergeant's shield. This sergeant was no desk jockey. Only someone that had spent significant time on the streets would be able to accumulate such an impressive rack. I was familiar with the medal he displayed on the top of his shield holder; it was the Combat Cross. The second most prestigious medal in the department was only awarded to those members that exemplified above and beyond courage while under fire. Dad was awarded his after he foiled a botched, armed bank robbery. As for the department's most prestigious award, Dad had one of those as well: The Medal of Honor.

In a deep, baritone voice, the boss introduced himself as Sergeant Ryen and welcomed the squad by letting us know exactly how he felt about the Third Division. "This is the best of the best. I know it's not by chance you fell onto our lap here. You all have a hook and your hook happened to be bigger than the other hundred or so other hooks that were trying to get their golden child in here. For the record, your hook's influence ended at the door. I don't care if you're the Police Commissioner's favorite nephew, you'll be judged on merit, not by nepotism. You're going to be working in the heart of the greatest city in the world. You'll be assigned posts in Times Square, Saint Patrick's Cathedral, Rockefeller Center, Radio City Music Hall, the Theater District, and all over beautiful Midtown Manhattan. We're going to have a lot fun out there. You're going to learn a lot, do a lot, and in the process, keep this great city safe."

There was a true passion in Sergeant Ryen's voice. One could tell he loved the city and wanted us to love it as much as he did. I knew from the moment Ryen introduced himself that I was going to enjoy working with him.

My feelings went against what Dad warned me about regarding the brass. As he described them, they were like sharks, feeding off the weak while trolling their egos through the department. When it came to the department's brass, Dad didn't hide his disdain for what he considered "bullies with rank." According to him, "The higher up the ladder the brass went, the bigger the ego." There were two things that could get Dad's blood pressure up: a neighbor not curbing his dog in front of our house, and discussing the brass in the NYPD.

I heard someone yell, "Attention!"

The squad as one jumped to our feet as the inspector entered the room. I was somewhat familiar with Inspector Moretti, the Third Division commander, having seen him several times giving interviews on the local news. Dad believed there wasn't a camera the inspector didn't like or a microphone he wouldn't stop to talk into. At five-foot-four, the inspector was short on height but not on attitude, and certainly not on ego.

"My name is Inspector Moretti," his eminence proclaimed in a high, squeaky voice, while standing in front of a podium meant for someone taller. "I'm the commander of the Third Division. If anyone calls me a guinea bastard, I'll kick their ass. Now sit your dumb asses down," he barked to the group.

The words "Hail Caesar" came to mind. I thought the inspector had some serious issues coming in here and starting off with that bizarre statement. I was quite certain no one in their right mind was going to call the commander of the Third Division a guinea bastard, so I didn't understand why the little man had to emphasize what he'd do if we did. Maybe the arrogant jackass simply wanted to flex his brass muscles knowing we had to sit there and take it. I doubted he ever walked into a City Council meeting or a Community Board hearing and opened with that line of crap. But we were nothing but little peons in his eyes, and he wanted to let us know it.

The inspector spoke for five minutes, throwing around a lot of threats; "If you smash a squad car in a pursuit… you're fired! If you lose your firearm while on probation… you're fired!" After about the fourth, "You're fired," I started to tune him out. My attention began to focus more on the four Sergeants behind him. I wasn't an expert on body language, but looking at some of their reactions, I think they may have felt the same way about the inspector as I had. After the inspector finished his rendition of Karl Malden's preacher character from *Pollyanna*, with his fire and brimstone sermon, he exited the muster room.

The next person to speak was a burly Irishman in his early thirties. He didn't have as many medals over his shield as Ryen but his display was respectable none the less. The Sergeant waited for the inspector to leave the room prior to speaking.

"Well, I think the inspector has made it clear about the don'ts, so maybe it's time to go over some of the do's. By the way, I'm Sergeant Denny, and I'll be your babysitter for the next six months and I hate being a baby sitter," the sergeant growled.

The group let out a much-needed laugh after the doom and gloom speech we all just listened to from the inspector. The sergeant's timing for a bit of levity seemed to help relax the group. He went on to explain how things were going to work in the detail and exactly what was to be expected from us.

The rules were fairly simple; don't get hurt and, especially, don't get killed. Denny told us the paper work for the sergeants would be excruciating. This brought another laugh from the group and removed any reminisce of tension left behind by the inspector.

Denny went on to explain that our primary goal was going to be cleaning up Forty-Second Street, nicknamed "The Deuce."

In 1987, Forty-Second Street was a cesspool. All the old beautiful marquis theaters that housed the great plays of the '30s and '40s was now replaced with sex shows and smoke shops (stores that sold drug paraphernalia).

I knew the block well from when I was a high school teenager. My buddy, Ronnie Jordan, and me would take the train into Manhattan and pick up supplies for a fake ID business we'd hatched. There were stores along Forty-Second Street that sold the supplies we needed. I used Dad's typewriter to type in the information on the fake ID, paste the customers picture (a fellow underage high school student), and use a hot iron to laminate it all together. To make one ID cost approximately $2 dollars. We sold them for $50. Ronnie was the brains of the operation and, according to him, I was the muscle.

At five-foot-six and weighing 110 pounds, Ronnie was an easy target for bullies at our Fort Hamilton High School in Bay Ridge. One day, I was outside waiting for my next class when I saw some kids pushing Ronnie around. I didn't know who Ronnie was, but that didn't stop me from going over to tell the punks to cool it. That's when one of the punks proceeded to sucker punch me in the side of the head. I went down like "Frasier." Ronnie and I were friends from that point on.

The entrepreneurial Ronnie had a job in a bagel store close to the school. In the spirit of Adam Smith, Ronnie used his business skills to work out a deal between the teachers and the owner of the store to deliver coffee and bagels every morning at a discounted rate. He became a big hit amongst the teachers, so much that the other students knew not to mess with him anymore. The breakfast orders started to become so big that he was given permission for an assistant—me. For my effort, I was given a free bagel every morning with the added bonus of not having to report to my first period homeroom class.

The first time Ronnie took me to Forty-Second Street, I was scared and excited at the same time. It was kind of like a roller coaster ride—it was fun to be scared but it would suck if the cart came off of the tracks and I was killed.

I found myself in one of the most dangerous areas in NYC. I was fourteen, six feet tall and weighed a feathery one hundred thirty pounds. I'd been on school trips to the Planetarium and New York Stock Exchange, but I'd never visited Manhattan on my own before. I was a nervous wreck, but as for Ronnie, he had a certain swagger in his walk as we exited the subway station. He was confident, and confidence in the city can make up for a lot of shortcomings. He was absolutely fearless as he walked Forty-Second Street. Nobody bothered us as we went from shop to shop picking up supplies. All the workers seemed to know Ronnie and, to a degree, showed the vertically-challenged teen some respect. On the other hand, they didn't even look at me. It was as if I didn't exist.

While walking Forty-Second Street, I couldn't help but notice all the adult theaters. Ronnie noticed me looking and started teasing me. Truth was I never saw a naked woman before, and just from the risqué pictures on the outside of the buildings, I was more than just a little curious. Ronnie asked me if I wanted to go into one, but I was too scared. We finished our business and were back on the "R" train heading home to Brooklyn.

I experienced the Deuce firsthand and concluded it was an unholy place, a modern-day Sodom & Gomorra. I thought it was disgusting, filthy, and filled with Satan worshipers. However, I knew

I'd be back. The adrenalin rush of walking Forty-Second Street was too much to only do once. Over the next few years, Ronnie and I would make the trip several more times to the hedonistic strip. I even got up the nerve to visit one of those adult theaters. It was definitely an eye-opener.

It was now six years later and Sergeant Denny was telling the group that cleaning up the Deuce was priority number one. The Sergeant explained that robberies and drug trafficking were on the rise on the historic block. We were going to be assigned the task of deterring crime before it happened, and when it did, make the necessary arrests. The thought of seeing a lot of action really had my adrenalin pumping. I couldn't wait to get started.

There were two other sergeants that were assigned to the squad, but they didn't speak at orientation. When introduced by Denny, the two, Marks and Gooden, simply waved to the group. I think many of us in the room would've preferred if they addressed the squad, if for no other reason than to see if they were amiable like Denny and Ryen, or if they were demented like Moretti.

The long day of filling out paperwork and listening to the do's and don'ts had finally come to an end. Ryen told us to report the next day at 0700 hours and to be ready to hit the streets.

My squad consisted of the four sergeants, four female rookies, and sixteen male rookies. Each shift, the sergeants would choose two rookies to ride in the patrol car with them. The rest would be assigned foot post around Midtown. The squad car assignments would rotate every shift, allowing all of the rookies to take turns in the RMP (radio mobile patrol).

I was hoping to work with Eddie when assignments were handed out for the squad car, but since the sergeants went in alphabetical order, it would be unlikely. Eddie had previous experience and seemed to have a solid head start on being a police officer. Whoever was fortunate to work with Eddie was going to have a partner ready to go.

The next day, I was given my first assignment, a foot post outside the Port Authority Bus Terminal along Eighth Avenue, adjacent to the Deuce. Being in front of the Port Authority building made me nothing more than a human information booth, except without the booth.

In my first twenty minutes as a New York City Police Officer, I was asked everything from where the Empire State building was to directions to Central Park. I was asked directions to places that I'd never heard of before, such as Saks Fifth Avenue and FAO Schwartz. I was embarrassed and frustrated in my inability to assist people. In twenty minutes, I was asked over thirty questions and didn't have an answer for any of them except, "Sorry, I'm not sure." The only person I helped was someone looking for the bus station—if I didn't get that one, shame on me. People were looking to me for leadership, and it turned out I was as lost as they were. So much for honoring Dad's wish regarding being prepared. It was time for me to do something about my ignorance.

I walked across the street to a souvenir shop and purchased a tourist map of the city. With a view of the map, I could see how the city was laid out and where many of the important tourist destinations where located.

Manhattan is shaped like a football field. Toward the southern end is lower Manhattan; Wall Street, the World Trade Center Towers, Chinatown, and Little Italy. As one travels north, the island gets wider. Fifth Avenue is the dividing point for east and west. There's an eight-block difference between 428 West Forty-Second Street and 428 East Forty-Second Street. This being the case, it would behoove me to learn exactly where the hell I was in case I needed to call for help. Central Park was just north of Midtown. I hadn't realized how much the park encompassed the city until I looked at the map. The park ran north of 59th Street to 110th Street, from 5th Avenue to Central Park West.

My impromptu crash course in map reading enabled me to get a better grasp of the city. Except for those treks to Forty-Second Street with Ronnie years earlier, I was clueless when it came to Manhattan. For the moment, I was saved thanks to a $2.99 tourist map.

My first lesson as a police officer was embarrassing. I was ill-prepared when I stepped onto my foot post. Six months in the Academy and a day of orientation didn't prepare me for twenty minutes on patrol in Midtown Manhattan. I promised myself I'd never embarrass myself like that again. Before I stepped onto a post, or entered a squad car, or took on any other police assignment, I'd be better prepared. I would know the addresses surrounding my assignment, the stores, banks, nearest hospital, or any other information needed to ensure that I didn't get caught looking like a baboon again.

Besides helping tourists with directions and assisting them with taking group photos, my first shift as a New York City Police Officer was uneventful. Excluding my earlier faux pas, I was overall pleased with my first day and looked forward to hearing about everyone else's back at the command.

In the locker-room, all the rookies were abuzz discussing their first day on patrol. Eddie asked how my day went, and I told him I felt more like a tour guide than a police officer. I was too embarrassed to mention that I bought a map of the city, so I kept that little secret to myself. While I was talking with Eddie, I could hear one of the guys in the locker-room making a lot of noise about his day. The cocky rookie was Michael Burke. Mike was tall with a solid build and was well aware of his good looks. He was boasting about how he wrote ten parking summonses and wrote an additional five moving violation citations. I assumed he was in one of the squad cars with a sergeant, but as it turned out, he was doing all this from his foot post. It hadn't occurred to me to pull over vehicles from a foot post but it did to Mike. It would've been easy to dislike Mike, but he was so full of himself that I thought him to be more comical than arrogant. In a good way, Mike was setting the bar for the rest of us. I'd be sure to write some summonses the following day.

The next morning, I was assigned a foot post on the Deuce. Unlike the previous day, I had other members of the squad assigned to the post with me. The block was geographically a large area to cover, and at any time could have several officers on foot patrol and an additional RMP assigned to it.

One of the other officers assigned to the Deuce with me was Sharlene Williams. Sharlene was a black female officer who seemed extremely shy. After I introduced myself to her, I tried to make small talk. I asked her where she was from and she told me Bedford Stuyvesant.

Bedford Stuyvesant, also known as Bed-Sty, was known for being a very rough area in Brooklyn. Every year, the Seventy-Fifth Precinct, which encompassed the neighborhood, led the city in homicides.

I told her my class was 87–18 ('*87* was the year and *18* was the class number). In the '87 Academy class, there were forty classes and over one-thousand recruits. Because the class was so big, I didn't know any of the other nineteen rookies assigned to the Third Division while I was in the Academy.

When I asked what her Academy class was, she told me 86–23. I thought she made a mistake, but before I could question her she repeated, "It's 86–23."

She explained to me that after graduating from the Academy the previous year, she was assigned to the Third Division. The sergeants gave her a "below standard" on her evaluation, so she was not permitted to move on to her permanent command. Furthermore, she had to remain on probation and if she received another below standard evaluation, she'd be dismissed from the department.

I felt bad for Sharlene's woes, but for some reason she didn't seem overly concerned about the possibility of being terminated. On the other hand, I started to worry about my future and whether or not I could be in a similar position as Sharlene six months from now. The last thing I wanted was to have a subpar evaluation and be held back—or worse, dismissed.

I asked her if she had written many summonses or made any arrests while assigned to the division. She told me she wrote some, but again, not enough to please the sergeants; and as for making any arrests, she said that she hadn't made any yet. With that, I suggested we make some car stops and produce some activity. She seemed a little apprehensive, but agreed. We began by taking turns pulling cars over while the other gave backup.

I went first and pulled over my first car. The back taillight was out and I told the driver to pull to the curb. I was so nervous. I could hear my voice crack when I asked the driver for his license, registration, and insurance card. After retrieving the items, I walked to the back of the car to write the summons. Sharlene must've seen how nervous I was because she told me to take my time.

After I finished writing the citation, I asked Sharlene if she'd look it over for me. She agreed and proceeded to find several errors. I'll never forget how kind and patient she was with me that day. She didn't judge me or make me feel like an idiot. She had knowledge and was willing to share it with me. I was grateful to have her as my partner.

By lunch time, we both had eight summonses each. She told me she never wrote more than ten in a month. I could see her confidence starting to rise. It was as if I started the shift with one person and a completely different person emerged. After our meal, we went back to doing car stops.

I was up next. The afternoon traffic was fairly heavy on the Deuce. This made it easier since we could walk in-between the cars while they were waiting for the traffic light to change—looking for violations such as expired tags/inspections, equipment violations, or anything else we could find.

I noticed an '85 Buick Regal with dice hanging from the rear-view mirror. This infraction is found in our moving violation bible, the VTL (Vehicular Traffic Law). The code was 375:30, *Obstructing Drivers View*. Not exactly a big infraction but enough to pull the car over.

I knocked on the driver's window and pointed for him to pull to the curb. The driver, a white male teenager, ignored me at first, so I knocked a second time to get his attention. When the traffic light changed from red to green, the driver slammed on the gas pedal and hit the car in front of him. Sharlene, realizing the driver was trying to get away, ran and stopped the vehicles in front of the Regal. Now the car was blocked in. With my gun drawn, I told the suspect to shutoff the ignition. To my astonishment, the driver listened. In retrospect, I guess being trapped and looking down the barrel of a .38 Caliber Ruger didn't give him much of a choice but to comply. I then gave him instructions to get out of the car and get on the ground. After cuffing him, I called the dispatcher on my radio and requested the Third Division Supervisor to respond. My first collar!

Sergeant Ryen was on the scene before I could catch my breath. "What do you have, kid?" he asked.

I explained to the sergeant that when I instructed the driver to pull over, he attempted to pull away and in the process, struck another vehicle.

The sergeant immediately called in the plate number. The dispatcher came back with, "Ten-sixteen," stolen vehicle. The charge was grand theft auto, a felony. Two days on the job, and I already had my first collar—and a felony at that!

Earlier in the shift, I was so nervous I could barely ask a motorist for his credentials without stuttering, but during this car stop, I hadn't been nervous at all. I felt in complete control of the situation.

Ryen, all smiles after one of his guys made a solid collar, gave me a pat on the back and told me, "Nice job, kid."

Up until that point, I had forgotten all about Sharlene. She was off to the side as if she was one of the onlookers. She'd gone back into her shell.

When I was an altar boy at Saint Patrick's, Father Gerald would mentor me. He'd tell me about life, the good, the evil, and everything in between. He would stress the importance of character and decision making. He'd tell me the two went hand in hand. The better the decision process, the wiser the individual. The more selfish the decision, the more unhappiness the individual would reap. He'd remind me that my reputation was based on what I did in public, and my character based on what I did in private. Thanks to Father Gerald and his words of wisdom, I knew what the right thing to do was.

I told Ryen that the collar belonged to Sharlene, that it had been her car stop. Ryen pretended not to hear me. For whatever reason, he wasn't pleased that she was about to get credit for the arrest.

I put the suspect in the squad car and then quickly walked over to Sharlene. I leaned over and told her that this was her collar. Sharlene had her first arrest. The smile came back to her face. This was her day—my day would come soon enough.

Sergeant Ryen was already in the squad car when Sharlene got in the back seat with the prisoner. Ryen gave a shrug of the shoulders and then drove off.

It didn't matter that I wasn't getting credit for the arrest. I knew I did the right thing and because of my decision, along with the arrest itself, I felt an amazing sense of accomplishment.

At the end of my shift, I went back to the command to sign out. When I entered the locker room, Eddie had heard about the collar and congratulated me. I explained to Eddie that I simply assisted in the arrest and that the collar belonged to Sharlene.

Mike then interrupted and asked how I could give up such a collar.

I didn't like the tone of Mike's rhetorical question, and I certainly didn't like having to explain myself to anyone, so I repeated what I had just told Eddie but this time with a little edge to my voice.

"Like I said, I assisted, car recovered—bad guy in jail."

I started to get changed when one of the other rookies came in the locker room and told me that Ryen wanted to see me in his office asap.

I went upstairs and knocked on the open office door. Ryen was on the phone, so he motioned for me to come in and pointed to a chair to sit in.

The office had several desks, one for each sergeant, and in the back of the room, a door leading to the lieutenant's office. The boys weren't the tidiest of fellas. Files and papers were all over the place. I noticed a dart board with the Ayatollah Khomeini's picture hung on it and some empty beer cans on top of the filing cabinets. The sergeant was sitting at his desk still wearing his uniform pants and a white tee shirt. Besides the fact that he wanted to see me, he looked done for the day.

Ryen finished his call and then directed his attention toward me.

He got right to the point. "You like giving collars away?"

"Sir, I haven't made any arrests yet to give away."

Ryen kept looking at me, his eyes piercing through mine. I wasn't sure if he was waiting for me to say something or if he was trying to get a read on me. He then finally spoke. "You want a cold beer?"

I hadn't expected the offer but graciously accepted.

Ryen grabbed a Bud out of the dorm-size refrigerator next to his desk and tossed it to me.

After thanking him for the beer, he proceeded to calmly talk.

"I knew your dad. He was in the Detective Squad when I was a rookie in the Fifth. Our paths didn't cross much, but everyone knew your father was one of the good guys in a time when a hot stove wasn't safe. I doubt he'd remember, but he once helped me with a burglary collar down on Mott Street. A couple of wise guys caught with their hands in the cookie jar. I was working the night your dad's partner was killed—bad night. I'll never forget it. I never in my life saw it rain so hard as it did that night. I thought we were going to have to build an ark. Detective Tony Falcone, he was my first police funeral. Sad to say, but he wasn't my last. Anyway, a piece of advice for you, don't give up collars."

I tried explaining to the sergeant I hadn't. "It was her car stop and I was just there assisting."

With that, Ryen reached into his desk drawer and proceeded to throw my handcuffs on the desk.

"I believe these belong to you," he said. "Funny how your handcuffs got on her perp. Listen, I have no personal issues with the girl, but I don't think she's fit to be a police officer. She's too timid. She doesn't want to get involved. I don't know if she's afraid or not, but eventually she's going to get hurt—or worse, she's going to get someone else hurt. So, if you're thinking the collar helped her cause, it didn't."

I tried one last time to convince him. "Boss, honestly, it was her quick thinking that enabled me to catch the guy."

Ryen was kind enough to listen as he sipped his beer, but I think the decision had already been made; Sharlene wasn't going to make it past probation.

After a few weeks, the squad of rookies started to gel as a unit. The group started socializing after work. Friendships, and in some cases, romances started to bloom.

Mike started seeing one of the female rookies, Beth Fey. Her father was Chief of Detectives Chief Fey. Not easy to hide that hook, but she tried her best to do so. No one was surprised that Mike and Beth, or should I say "Ken & Barbie," became an item. Both were young, good looking, and seemed to make a nice couple. Although Mike was cocky, I learned it was more show than anything else. As for Beth, she was well-grounded for someone with her pedigree. However, I didn't think it was a good idea to be dating someone in the work place. If things went south, which they often did, it would make for an awkward situation. But, for the time being, the love birds seemed happy.

One afternoon after finishing a day shift, I went to pick up my paycheck. While I waited in line with Beth, I asked if her and Mike were stopping by the pub for a cold one later. She told me that Mike took the day off and that she'd like to go but didn't have a ride. I offered to take her and she accepted.

It was generally understood among the squad, including the sergeants, to meet at The Irish Pub on paydays. The Pub was across from Carnegie Deli on Fifty-Fifth Street and Seventh Avenue. I enjoyed the camaraderie amongst the group. I loved how everyone tried to embellish their war stories only to be blown out of the water by one of the sergeant's stories, especially the ones told by Ryen. I enjoyed the perfectly poured Guinness by the bartender, Bill O'Malley. It's fair to say I thoroughly enjoyed every bit of my downtime at The Irish Pub.

As Beth and I drove over to the pub, she discussed her frustration about being one of the few that hadn't made an arrest yet. In an attempt to make her feel better, I told her I hadn't made one yet either. When we arrived at the watering hole, a few of the guys from the squad were already there. I ordered a pint and asked Beth what she'd have, and she replied, "Wild Turkey and coke." She didn't look much like a bourbon drinker to me. In fact, the feather-weight, strawberry-blonde didn't look like a drinker, period. But I'd be wrong about that. I was still waiting for my Guinness to be poured when she was already ordering a second drink. For me, I liked things a bit slower. I was in the habit of nursing my pints knowing we were still under our boss's watchful eyes. I wasn't about to get sloppy in front of them. For Beth, she came to drink and so she did. In less than hour, the sub-one-hundred-pound female was toast. I pulled her into a booth and asked her if she was all right.

That's when she began to tell me more than I wanted to know.

"It's over between Mike and me," she confessed. "Dean, I told him I like someone else and he's not taking it too well. I can't hide my feelings anymore. That's why he took off today."

I didn't know why Beth was opening up to me, but I was curious who the other guy was. I had a sneaky suspicion it was Sergeant Gooden. I had seen the two on several occasions laughing and giggling like two high-school teens. I could understand Beth being easily impressed since we were newbie's and he was a sergeant.

Beth asked if I wanted to know who it was she was referring to. Although I was curious, I told to her that it wasn't my business and I should probably stay out of it. She looked at me with her glassy, blue eyes and said, "Well, it is your business because it's you."

For a second I thought she was joking, but then I could see that wasn't the case.

"Beth, please tell me you didn't tell Mike this?"

Beth nodded her head that she indeed had.

This was not good. I walked away leaving Beth in the booth and decided to forgo having another pint. I decided it was time to leave. I walked out of the bar toward my car to go home when Beth came from behind and asked if I'd give her a ride home.

I'd like to say I did the right thing, that I told Beth I considered Mike a friend and friends didn't do that to one another; or that I was thinking of Dad's warning about the toxic combination of women and booze and how I should stay away. However, on this particular evening, lust won over loyalty, as stupidity reigned over wisdom.

The next morning, when I showed up at the precinct, I didn't know what to expect. With Mike's locker situated next to mine, I was praying when I walked in that he wouldn't be there. Unfortunately, as I turned the corner, there he was. The always grinning, cocky jokester looked anything but. His head was down, his shoulders slouched, and he had a look on his face of pure despair. He looked up and saw me staring at him. In a low, somber voice, he said, "Hey Dean, I guess you heard."

My stomach sank. Before I could tell him how sorry I was for what I did, he told me they were probably going to take all his vacation days away for a year (twenty in all) and extend his probation period another six months. I hadn't a clue what he was talking about but realized he was still in the dark about Beth and I, so I asked him what was going on.

He told me that the day before, while his on his way to work, he left his bag on top of the roof of his car.

"I had my gun and shield inside the bag," Mike explained. "By the time I realized my mistake, the bag had flown off of the car—somewhere between my house and the Long Island Expressway."

I knew the severity of the situation and tried reassuring the dejected rookie that everything would be okay.

"It's not your fault. I'm the idiot that left the bag on top of the car. I'm surprised you didn't hear about it. I called Beth and told her what was going on yesterday. Didn't you see her?"

With guilt running through my veins, I told him that I did see her (certainly more than he probably would've appreciated) but she hadn't mentioned the incident to me.

The two of us finished getting dressed and then headed upstairs for muster. As we walked out of the locker room together, I was left asking myself what the hell just happened.

Mike and I entered the muster room and there was Beth. He walked up to her and the two love birds were back to being Ken & Barbie. She didn't even look my way.

The foot post for my shift that day was on Thirty-Third Street and Sixth Avenue. I would've much rather been assigned to the Deuce or Times Square, but we all had to take turns at different locations and tonight was my turn to be posted in front of the decrepit Hotel Martinique.

During the '70s and '80s, the hotel was used as short-term shelter for families on public aid. They were often referred to as "welfare hotels." Squalor didn't begin to describe the condition of the place.

The previous week, when I was assigned to the squad car with Sergeant Ryen, we had a radio call to one of the rooms for suspected child neglect. As Sergeant Ryen and I entered the room, I nearly lost my breakfast. The stench of urine and human feces was overwhelming. The mother, a black woman in her early twenties, was crammed along with her three children, aged two, four, and five, into an area smaller than my dad's den. The children had no clothes on and were sitting in their own waste. The strung-out mother was apparently a drug addict. There was a mattress without a box spring lying on the floor in the middle of what was once a hotel room. The mother was laying on it in the fetal position shaking like a leaf.

Without hesitation, Sergeant Ryen took control of the situation. He called for Child Services and immediately removed the children from the home. While I stood there watching him take charge, I felt something crawling up my leg under my trousers. I banged my foot on the floor and several roaches came falling out. That was it—goodbye, breakfast.

The only bathroom available was down the hall for the entire floor to share. There was no way I was going to make it, so the next closest place for me was the mini-kitchen sink. I let go of my breakfast, rinsed some water on my face, and continued with the police work at hand. Ryen acted as if nothing happened and continued the process of removing the children.

I wish I didn't get sick, but I did. I figured in time I'd build up a tolerance for such things and keep my breakfast where it belonged.

After we finished, Ryen and I walked through the lobby. I looked around and said to him, "What a shithole this place is."

The sergeant stopped me in my tracks and told me to look around. "Really look, Dean," he said. "Can you see it? Can you see what this place used to be? Look at the spiral, marble staircase, the carved architecture around the lobby, the copper punched tin on the ceiling. You're missing what's here. The hotel is beautiful, full of history and culture, and was once the place to be seen. No, it's not the hotel's fault; it's the people occupying the hotel that's the problem, along with the politicians that look for a quick fix by putting them here."

I realized I touched a nerve with the sergeant. I felt bad and wanted to apologize but thought it was best for me to just keep quiet. However, his point was not lost on me. I needed to open my eyes and see more of my surroundings. Another day, another lesson learned.

Now that I was assigned to a foot post in front of the Martinique, I thought it might be a good idea to know what was in proximity to the hotel. I still had my trusted tourist map and could see that next to the hotel was the PATH Station. The bustling station is a hub for commuters between New York and New Jersey. The Empire State Building was located one block east on Fifth Avenue, and the largest department store in the world, Macy's, was one block north on Thirty-Fourth Street. Madison Square Garden was just west of where I was by two blocks. Of course, now that I was prepared to give people directions, nobody asked.

The shift was mostly uneventful. I wrote a few summonses, filled out an accident report for a fender bender that occurred on the corner of my post, and posed for a few pictures with tourists. Just before my shift was to end, there was a radio call from the dispatcher of a possible domestic dispute at the Martinique Hotel. I immediately went over the radio to inform the dispatcher that I was on the scene and would handle the job. I heard Sergeant Ryen go over the radio to notify the dispatcher that he was on his way.

Domestic disputes could be anything from a simple argument to a homicide. Being that emotions usually ran high with those individuals involved, it was taught in the Academy to tread cautiously when dealing with these potentially volatile situations.

The room number was 432. As I entered the lobby, I could hear the couple arguing all the way up on the fourth floor. I ran up the stairs, and as I stood in front of the partially opened door, I could see a black couple going nose to nose in a heated argument. I pushed opened the door and stayed in the hallway.

In a calm voice, I asked, "Excuse me, is everything all right here?"

The women began screaming that she had a restraining order against the man and wanted him arrested. She ran into the hallway to show me the paperwork.

The Order of Protection was current. It was issued by a family court judge and clearly stated that the man involved was not permitted at the address given or within five hundred feet of the Martinique. In a situation such as this, the responding officer must arrest the violator of the Order of Protection. The courts rightfully took away the discretion of the police regarding whether to make an arrest or not. All too often after the police would leave the scene, the violence would immediately start right back up again, many times with tragic consequences. If someone was in violation of a court order, they had to be arrested—it was that simple.

I asked the male to step outside into the hallway so I could speak with him. He responded to me with, "Fuck you, pig."

I could see that the individual was extremely upset. I needed to take control of the situation before it escalated. The male in front of me was at least three inches taller and carried a good fifty pounds more muscle on his frame than I. The last thing I wanted to do was attempt to physically remove him from the room. However, there were two young children in the small apartment in harm's way. Something had to give. I thought it best to try and reason with him first. As long as things didn't escalate, we could at least talk.

"Sir, I've done nothing to disrespect you. I'm asking you as a gentleman to come outside the room so we can talk. Sir, there are children present. I'm sure you don't want them listening to your business. Please, come out here so I get your side of the story."

His response did nothing to defuse the situation. "Copper, this is my home, that's my bitch, and those are my kids, and no judge and no pig is gonna tell me what the fuck I can and cannot do."

"Sir, I'm trying to show you respect and handle this so no one gets hurt or traumatized," as I pointed to his two children shaking in the corner. "Please sir, look at your children. You don't want this. Come out here and talk to me. Please, sir. You're a big guy. I don't feel like rolling around with you. I just want to talk. Come out here away from your kids and give me your side. You don't think I know firsthand how much of a pain in the ass these women can be."

I sensed from the dirty look the victim was giving me that she wasn't pleased with my last comment. However, I needed to get this individual out of that room without incident, and if by me showing him some empathy did the trick, then so be it.

"You don't understand. She's a fucking ho," he exclaimed.

I pleaded with him again, "Please, sir, come out here so we can talk like gentlemen."

I was stalling. I knew this guy was going to jail once she showed the Order of Protection. What I wanted now was to defuse his anger and wait for the cavalry to arrive.

Finally, I was able to convince him to come and speak with me in the hallway.

"What's your name, sir?" I asked.

"James Love, and I ain't going to no jail copper," he told me.

"My father's name is James, a good Christian name. Do you read the Bible, James?"

I could tell the question caught him off guard. He put his head down without answering.

"James, I'm not here to preach to you or tell you how to live your life. For me, reading the Bible is like food for the soul. When I'm angry, it calms me down, and when I'm sad, it lifts me up. Maybe you want to try it sometime. Now, let's get back to the matter at hand. You know the rules when it comes to an Order of Protection. I have zero discretion. I have to take you in but how we do it is up to you. My guys are downstairs waiting for us." I was bluffing, of course. "We can walk down like men or we can go like screaming babies. Your kids will be watching. I promise I won't put the cuffs on you until were in the squad car. I don't want your kids to see their father like that. I just need to check you for weapons, okay?"

I somehow was able to get through to the herculean James and he allowed me to search him. The situation was calming down.

"Dude, this is bullshit," he said. "She lied to the judge to get that restraining order."

The last thing I wanted to see was James get riled up again.

"James, stay with me. Don't let her get the better of you. If you act like this is no big deal, she'll be disappointed and you'll win. Believe me, I know how these women lie and manipulate to get what they want." I said this as I thought about Beth. "You think you're the only guy that's ever dealt with a crazy woman?"

As we walked down the stairs, I quietly asked the dispatcher for an ETA (estimated time of arrival) for the Third Division Supervisor. Ryen went over the radio to advise me that he was handling a multi 10-53 (car accident) at Fifty-Fourth and Broadway and that he wouldn't be able to respond.

I advised the dispatcher that I didn't need the supervisor and would be going to the South on administrative business.

I was only three blocks from the stationhouse and decided a walk might do James some good. While we walked, James told me he was a Vietnam veteran.

"I'm angry all the time and don't know why. I lost my job a month ago. I was in jail for a week because she told the cops I hit her, but I didn't. If I hit that bitch, she'd be dead. She lied to the cops and then to the judge. He signed the order without ever getting my side. I lost my job because I was in jail, and now I can't see my kids."

I didn't know if James was telling the truth regarding not hitting his estranged wife, but I did agree that if a guy that size hit someone, he very well may kill the person. He no doubt had a temper but as he calmed down, I could see he was not an evil man.

I bought a couple of hotdogs and soft drinks from a street vendor for James and me in front of Madison Square Garden. James looked over at the Garden Marquis and asked if I liked the Knicks. I told him that I didn't have a choice in the matter since my dad was a huge Dave Debusschere fan. For the next several minutes, while we ate our hotdogs and talked sports, I took the opportunity to make a suggestion to James.

"James, you seem like a good person and a caring father. If you want to have a relationship with those kids, you're going to have to figure out a way to deal with their mother without the anger. Get some counseling. Anytime I had an issue that I didn't think I could handle on my own, I'd talk to my priest."

James thanked me for the advice and then apologized for some of the things he said back at the apartment. I used a basketball analogy to explain my feelings on what transpired. "No harm, no foul."

Just prior to entering the precinct, I put the handcuffs on James and proceeded to the front desk. I told the lieutenant on duty what I had. He pointed me to the cells where I'd have two hours to process the arrest. Two hours may sound like a lot, but since I never made an arrest before, I knew I needed more time than that.

I put James in the holding cell and started to gather all the paperwork I'd need to process the collar, including the four sets of fingerprint cards. I never did fingerprints before. I was way over my head and needed help fast.

While sitting behind a metal desk in the arrest room, I looked over all the papers I had to fill out and felt completely overwhelmed. I put my hands over my face and said a quick prayer. When I removed my hands from my face, my prayer was answered. Standing in front of me was my brother Francis and his partner Chuck Summers.

Chuck had been Francis's partner the past two years. He reminded me of the character on the cleaning bottle, Mr. Clean. Chuck was an amateur bodybuilder that sported a handle bar mustache and a shaved head. He was a serious individual with a reputation for being a good cop. Seeing the two of them in front of me was a welcoming sight.

Francis looked at me with a stupid, silly grin and said, "Looks like you could use some help, rookie."

In a conciliatory voice, I agreed.

"Don't worry about the prints, Chuck is the best print man there is," Francis assured me. "I'll type-up the arrest reports and notify warrants, just in case there's a hit."

I asked Francis what I should do.

Francis, in a very serious voice, told me to get a piece of paper and pen and to get ready to start writing. Once I was ready, Francis told me to pay very close attention and then proceeded to give me their lunch order. The facetious Francis knew he had me over a barrel, and the truth was I was more than happy to buy them lunch; but I could've done without being strung along by my big brother.

After taking their order, I went down the block to get their sandwiches. By the time I came back with their food, the two of them were almost done processing the collar.

In my youth, Francis had always been there for me. After Mom died, he instinctively took on a more guardian role when it came to watching over me—he was only ten. During his teens, he started to rebel. He was constantly getting into fights and, on occasion, escorted home by the police for mischief in the neighborhood. Dad tried his best to beat the devil out of him but nothing seemed to faze Francis. All our relatives were surprised when he joined the police department. Francis's outlook was the old "If you can't beat 'em, join 'em" motto.

All the prints and paperwork were done except for the Complaint Report. Francis thought I should do a little something for my first collar, and I agreed. The two of them did ninety-nine percent of the processing in less than forty minutes—well under the allotted time of two hours.

Before Francis left the Arrest Processing Room, I asked him how he knew I had a collar. He told me he heard my "nervous ass voice" over the radio when I called for the sergeant, so he decided to take a spin over on his meal hour to see if I needed a hand. Once again, my big brother was looking out for me.

As the two walked out of the room with their hot roast beef on rye sandwiches at a cost of ten-bucks a piece, I told them to enjoy their lunch and sincerely thanked them for all their help.

A few minutes after Francis and Chuck left, Sergeant Ryen came barging through the door with Mike and Eddie.

"Sorry, kid, we got tied up in a pile-up but don't worry, the cavalry is here to help. We still have plenty of time to get everything done. What are you up to?" he asked.

"Sarge, I'm almost done with the 61 (complaint report)."

"Great, we'll help with the other paper work and then we'll get the prints going and then notify…"

I interrupted the sergeant in midsentence to let him know everything else was done.

"Sarge, I just have to finish the 61 and I think I'm finished," I told the skeptical Ryen.

He then asked to see the print cards. While looking over the four sets of fingerprints, I could see his wheels turning and his eyes surveying around the arrest room as if to see if there was anyone else in there that could've helped me. I noticed Mike and Eddie looking on in amazement. They both already made collars and came close to going over the two-hour time limit.

"The desk officer says you came in here less than an hour ago, and you got all this done by yourself?" Ryen asked.

I was all set to tell my boss about how my brother and partner gave me a hand but when I opened my mouth the words, "Yeah, not a problem," came out. I knew better than to lie, but at that moment I liked the idea of impressing my boss and peers more than worrying about my credibility.

Ryen walked over a few feet to the holding cell where James, the only prisoner, was being held.

Ryen then asked him, "You look familiar. When's the last time you were in here?"

"Last month."

"Maybe it would be better for all concerned if you'd stop breaking the law and follow the court order," Ryen said to James while glancing over my paperwork.

James gave a nod of the head to my boss's advice and then Ryen asked him one last question. "By the way, did you cooperate with your arresting officer when he took your prints or did you give him a hard time?"

The inquisition by Ryen had its purpose. It wasn't about advising the prisoner to stop violating his wife's Order of Protection but rather to find out if I was the one who actually did his prints.

James smiled at Ryen and then told him that he fully cooperated with the arresting officer.

James didn't say a lot but it was enough to cover my butt. My first collar was in the books and James and I had our own little secret. As for Sergeant Ryen, he looked over the paperwork one more time, shook his head some more, and then left the room with the other two rookies. I was never one to be comfortable telling a lie, but I figured this little white lie was one of those "no harm, no foul" kind of things. Unfortunately, I'd be wrong.

Every Monday started a new week for the squad. The only change would be whether we were working the day shift (seven-to-three) or the evening shift (four-to-twelve).

This particular week, we were doing four-to-twelve's. I loved the shift. There was more action at night than in the day, and the chance of making a quality collar drastically increased.

As I stood at muster waiting to hear my assignment for the evening, I was surprised not to hear my name called. After everyone cleared the muster area, I approached Sergeant Ryen and informed him of the oversight. The sergeant told me it wasn't an oversight and not to worry. He explained that he wanted to talk to me about my new assignment.

"What new assignment?" I asked.

Ryen went on to explain that for every group that comes through, the sergeants handpick one or two rookies to assist with the administrative duties.

"Simple stuff for you and me but for a lot of these other guys, not so much. See, by you helping the others process arrests, vouchering property and other clerical type duties, it allows us sergeants to stay out on patrol. It usually takes us a while to pick someone that we're all completely confident in, but after I told the other bosses about your arrest on Friday, we all agreed that you're our new corporal."

I'm thinking this would be a good time to come clean, to tell Ryen I had two other veteran officers assist me with processing the arrest in record time, and how it was my brother's partner that was the fingerprint master—not me. That all I did was run and get two roast beef sandwiches on rye with extra Russian dressing. *Holy crap, what just happened? No harm, no foul—my ass!*

Of course, I didn't come clean. My credibility would've been trashed. But I wasn't without a plan.

Ryen brought me upstairs to their office and showed me my desk. I kept on thinking to myself that this was not happening. All the guys were out there making collars, writing summonses, being cops and I, with one-month police experience, had been promoted to desk duty. *No way, time to get out of this mess right now.*

"Hey, Sarge, I'm honored, but I don't want to be behind a desk just yet."

"No, you won't be. You'll be splitting the duty with Eddie. He had previous experience in Transit and knows what to do, too. You guys will rotate being our assistant."

I asked Ryen what I was supposed to do.

"Simple. Just listen to the radio and if you hear any of our guys coming in with a collar or some administrative stuff, go downstairs and help. You'll be our gopher; otherwise, the rest of the time is yours."

As I sat at my desk with my heart racing and my stomach flipping, I started to think real fast. I had nothing to do and decided to go to the Arrest Processing Room hoping there'd be some prisoners I could print. I grabbed a radio and headed to the cells.

When I entered the room, I noticed the cells were filled with female prisoners. There happened to be a prostitute sweep along the westside and they all needed to be processed. I offered the arrest team to help with the fingerprints and they gladly accepted.

For the better part of the shift, I listened to my radio, praying no one in the squad would make a collar, and fingerprinted the girls. The first few I did I had to do over because the ink smudged. Finally, one of the female prisoners showed me how to hold the knuckles and roll the tips of the fingers so as not to smudge. Obviously having been through the system many times before, she had more experience than I when it came to fingerprinting. It took several hours but I was starting to get the hang of it. Thankfully, the girls were patient with me. They must've known I was a rookie and didn't seem to mind when I screwed up. Everything was going smoothly until one of the female prisoners asked me if I had a girlfriend. In retrospect, I should've answered yes because when I told her I didn't, all hell broke loose. Simultaneously, I had over twenty prostitutes whistling and yelling at me.

"Hey, baby, I'll be your girlfriend."

"Sugar, I like that white ass of yours."

"Honey, I'll make your world spin and your toes curl."

The girls were getting louder as they were sensing how uncomfortable the ordeal was making me. They started dancing in the cells provocatively, asking me if I like what I saw.

One of the arresting officers came back to see what all the noise was about.

"What the hell is going on back here?" the officer barked.

When he saw the girls dancing in the cells with their tops off, he told me to get them under control and then walked out.

I started pleading with the girls to quiet down and put their tops on, but they ignored my request. Finally, in desperation, and before a boss came in, I told them if they'd settle down, I'd buy them all McDonald's.

Twenty Happy Meals later, I was able to regain control of the room.

I spent my first shift as the "Arrest Processing Officer" doing fingerprints and running to McDonald's. I didn't have a lot of options, since I needed to somehow encapsulate the skills of a seasoned veteran in just a few hours. Maybe I was kidding myself and eventually Ryen would expose me for the fraud I was, but until then, I was going to have to pretend I actually knew what the hell I was doing.

As for the girls, after the dancing, laughing, and flirting, they had their burgers and were on their way to Central Booking. I appreciated their patience in regards to me printing them. These ladies-of-the-night made me laugh and taught me how to do prints at the same time. That alone was worth the fifty bucks I spent on Happy Meals.

The only question I had now was how long I'd be able to keep up the charade. Thanks to a slow day on patrol, and nobody coming in with any collars, I was at least able to make it through day one without being exposed.

CHAPTER 3

Carnival

Only a life lived for others is a life worthwhile.

—Albert Einstein

Not everyone on the job had someone they could confide in the way I could with my dad. On the rare occasion one of the guys did try to open up about their feelings, it was usually followed with a peanut gallery audience made up of unsympathetic, wise-cracking cops. I was fortunate to have Dad nearby whenever I needed a compassionate sounding board. He had the amazing ability to know when it was time to listen and when it was time to give advice. What I didn't know, and was too naive to realize it at the time, was the fact that my best friend wasn't always going to be around for me to lean on.

I confided in my dad about my new experiences on the job. I told him how Miss Lunatic was, well, a lunatic and about Francis coming through for me in a big way by assisting me on my first collar. I explained to him how on every shift there was something new and exciting to learn. I then told him about my favorite boss, Sergeant Ryen, and how he knew of him and Tony back in the Fifth Precinct.

"Legends on the job," I told Dad on how Ryen described the dynamic duo.

"I was fortunate to have good partners, first Lenny then Tony," Dad said as he began to reflect back. "Like any good relationship, it came down to trust and respect—can't have one without the other. All this stuff you're going through right now is part of the maturation process. At times, it can be fun, and at other times it can be stressful. The idea is not to add to the stress with bad decision making. Be careful who you let close to you, especially when it comes to choosing a partner. Remember, it's the ones closest to you that can hurt you the most. Just be careful, trust your instincts and you'll be fine."

I always had a lot of questions for Dad regarding his time on the job, but instinctively knew it was never a good time to ask. However, now that I was wearing the same shield as he once had, I hoped the man that thought having to answer "paper or plastic" at the grocery store to be an intrusive question, would now allow me some insight into his experiences. Feeling the timing was finally right, I decided to ask how his partner was killed.

Dad sighed, took a long pause, and then went on to explain the events of his partner's death that fateful, tragic night.

"Sometimes you can do everything right and things still go wrong. All the training in the world is no match for bad luck. Tony and I were partners for five years. He had more than enough time on the job to retire, but he'd tell me, "Retiring to Florida would be nothing more than relocating to a waiting room to die." The job had become his life, his identity. He was an important person in Little Italy. Take that away and he was afraid he'd be another lost soul just waiting to checkout. I learned a lot from him. He taught me how to interview suspects and decipher between the truth and bullshit. Not with a fist or intimidation, but with respect. Most of the bad guys didn't want to live with the guilt that goes along with their lifestyle. They want to be free of it and it was our job to play the role of a priest and listen to their confessions. The kind of respect that Tony received was because he was truly one of the good guys. He was a straight shooter, one of a kind.

"The night he was murdered I was supposed to go with him to serve an arrest warrant on a low life petty thief named Terry Jackson. Just before we left the squad room, the phone rang. To this day I wish I never answered that phone. I told Tony something came up and to get one of the other guys to help him serve the warrant.

"We served dozens of these warrants without incident. How was I to know this one would be different?

"That phone call was the first piece of bad luck. I can remember as I drove back to Brooklyn in the rain that night, the uneasy feeling inside me. I can't explain it. I just knew I shouldn't have left, but I ignored my instincts.

"Jackson lived in a walkup on Baxter Street. From what I was told, when they went to his apartment, his mother said to Tony and his partner that her son was downstairs in the bar. She said he'd been down there all afternoon drinking and to please be careful with her little boy. Evidently, he was crossed and wasn't happy about the idea of going back to Sing Sing Prison.

"When Tony went downstairs to the bar, the other detective stayed upstairs going through Jackson's room. Why? Only God knows. I would've been at Tony's side in the bar.

"Tony being stuck with an incompetent partner was the second piece of bad luck that night. There's no way that punk would've got to him if I was there.

"Jackson had seen the two detectives go upstairs to his apartment. He told the bartender if they came in the bar to arrest him, he'd waste them both. The bartender thought it was just the booze talking, so he didn't take the wiry, little drunk serious.

"When Tony entered the bar, Jackson charged at him with a knife. According to the bartender, as Tony tried to get out of the way of the oncoming Jackson, he slipped and fell toward the perp and his knife. The bartender said because of the rain, the entrance way was wet and slippery. The knife was a three-inch buck knife. If this drunk stabs Tony virtually anywhere else, he lives. If he slips in any other direction, he lives. If it didn't rain, he lives. If I stayed to execute the warrant with him, he lives. I lost count on how many things had to go perfectly wrong in order for things to turn out the way they did. That's how most tragic events unfold: a perfect sequence of awful events.

"As for Jackson, he took off running. After sobering up the next day, his mother convinced her son to turn himself in. I was the one that had to process the arrest. I had thoughts go through my head of what I wanted to do to this guy. I knew if I hit him just once, I wouldn't have been able to stop, so I did my job and processed him for the murder of my partner. A few of the other detectives in the squad room had other ideas. They wanted to go into the cell and dole out some street justice on the cop killer, but I told them if I wasn't doling out punishment today, neither would they.

"If I hadn't received that call, if only I stayed with Tony, he'd still be alive."

I listened intently to every word Dad had to say. I could see the pain in his face and how that night still haunted him.

I didn't ask but assumed the phone call that sent him back to Brooklyn must've had something to do with mother and her health issues.

My mom was constantly in and out of the hospital when I was young. I can remember the ambulance coming so much that the paramedics knew me by name.

I knew there were some things Dad wasn't ready to discuss. I was grateful he opened up to me about Tony, but my instincts told me he wasn't ready to do the same when it came to discussing Mom.

However, since he was willing to discuss the old days, I thought it'd be a good time to ask him something else I didn't know about: how he made detective.

Dad seemed much more at ease discussing this part of his past.

"My big break was, of course, the Vinny 'The Chin' collar. Luck runs both ways and I guess that was my piece of good luck. After the arrest, I was offered a position in Public Morals. The detail was a pathway to the gold shield. However, it usually would take about three years of dealing with the scum of the earth before finally making it into a detective squad. I received mine in less than three months.

"Public Morals in Manhattan was a cesspool of crap back then. The detail was designed to crack down on public moral offenses: gambling, prostitution, and illegal social clubs. The truth is it was a cash cow for cops and bosses alike willing to look the other way by accepting payoffs for protection. There was only one other place in the department where the corruption was worse and that was the

Narcotics Division. Both details were a pathway to the gold shield, but very few people went through the gauntlet without getting dirty.

"I knew if I stayed long enough, I'd be no better than the prostitutes we locked up. It got to a point that I couldn't tell the good guys from the bad guys. I was just about to put my transfer in to go back to patrol, which meant no detective shield, when a stroke of luck fell on my lap.

"It was the night my squad raided a bath house in Greenwich Village. Back in the '50s and '60s, these bath houses were illegal and were considered a public health hazard. More accurately, they were simply another way for the brass to harass the homosexuals. There were two things the brass disliked immensely: not getting their cut of the graft and homosexuals.

"As I was rounding up the perps in the bath house one of them pulled me on the side.

'Hey officer, I'm on the job. I'm a lieutenant down at One Police Plaza, you've gotta get me out of here.'

"I really grew to hate those four words: 'I'm on the job.' A lot of guys thought their shield, and the four magic words that went along with it, gave them immunity for just about anything. I'd pull over a guy for driving like a maniac on the Belt Parkway only to have him flash his tin, utter the phrase, 'I'm on the job,' and then burn rubber in my face as he drove off.

"However, this particular incident was a bit more serious than a traffic stop. The lieutenant was John Anderson, the Commanding Officer of Public Information Bureau for the NYPD. Basically, the lieutenant had a cushy detail being the liaison between the department and the local news media. It's safe to say if word got out about the captain's extracurricular activities, his career would've been over.

"At first, I was irritated when the lieutenant uttered the magic words to me, but while Anderson stood there in nothing more than a bath towel and a whole lot of baby oil dripping from his body, I thought maybe this could be an opportunity.

"I had the lieutenant quickly gather his belongings, and then I escorted him out the back door. Still wearing nothing more than his towel, I hailed a cab and sent the commander on his way. As luck would have it, the following week I was transferred back to the Fifth Precinct. However, I didn't return as a patrolman but as Third Grade Detective Simpson. And that's how I received my gold shield and eventually became partners with Tony."

"Did you ever see the lieutenant again?" I asked.

Dad nodded his head and said, "Oh yeah, years later. But that's a story for another day."

Monday I was back at work. Eddie and I were still splitting the responsibilities of "corporal-gofer-arrest processing officer." My skills must've improved enough because the bosses never did call me out for my little white lie. I was getting in a good groove in the Midtown Command. I was making quality arrests when on patrol and making good use of my time when I was assigned to the office.

My squad was almost at the halfway point before we'd be transferred to our permanent commands. It was then I realized time was going by way too fast. I loved every minute and wasn't looking forward to the inevitable change. I loved what I was doing so much that one day, when I was with Eddie on the Deuce, I told him I'd work the job for nothing. He thought I was crazy, but that's how much I loved it.

When the sergeants had some down time, they would study for their upcoming promotional exam. I would hear them ask each other questions trying to trip each other up. That's when I came up with the idea to start studying for the sergeant's exam.

While assigned to the office, my bosses mostly ignored my presence. My desk was all the way in the back next to the lieutenant's office. They stayed in the front unless they had to get something from one of the filing cabinets back by me. I always had the police radio tuned into the Third Division, listening for anything that I might need to bring to the boss's attention.

One afternoon, Ryen came to the back of the office to where I was studying. He saw me reading the Patrol Guide and sarcastically quipped, "Enjoying some light reading?"

"Boss, I'm just following the lead from you, guys."

Then Ryen said something that caught me off guard.

"Not me. No more promotional exams for this dinosaur. In less than a year, I'll have my twenty in and then I'm out of here."

I told him his was too young to retire, and then asked what his future plans were.

In a half-hearted voice, the sergeant replied, "I'm going fishing. Twenty years is enough for me. I've seen a lot and not all of it good. I want to leave while I still have all my faculties, especially when it comes to caring. It's easy to fall into the trap of a nasty old hair bag. I don't want to get to that point. Coming here to the Third Division actually helped extend me a few years. You young whippersnappers helped recharge my batteries."

By the time the sergeant finished, I wasn't sure how to respond. From the trepidation in his voice, I didn't know whether to offer him my congratulations or my condolences on his upcoming retirement. So, after a brief moment of silence, I began telling him about my research project.

"I forgot to tell you I visited the New York City Public Library on Fifth Avenue last week. Did you know there are a lot of books in that place?" I could see Ryen look over his reading glasses with a puzzled look on his face. "Turns out they even had some reading material about that old beat up Martinique place. Did you know back in the '20s they use to host film premiers at the hotel? In fact, there was a silent film actor named Harry Young, also known as 'The Human Fly,' who thought it would be a good idea to scale the outside of the hotel to help promote his new movie. The Human Fly lost his grip and plunged nine floors to his death. Imagine all the paper work that poor patrol sergeant had to do that day. And, since you might be doing some golf in between your fishing, you'd be interested to know that it was none other than the Martinique Hotel that hosted the meeting to create the Professional Golfers Association (PGA). A guy by the name of Wanabaker had an office in the building and invited dozens of professional golfers to help put the group together."

With a look of approval on his face, Ryen thanked me for the history lesson and then proceeded to correct me.

"The guy's name was Wanamaker, not Wanabaker, you dumbass."

I laughingly responded, "Yes, sir."

I knew the field trip to the library was not lost on my mentor. He wanted me to open my eyes, so that's what I began to do. Everywhere I went in the city—every park, building, museum and statue—I looked at differently now. I wanted to learn more about things I never knew I cared about. I knew all these places had a story to tell, but like most people in the city, I used to walk right on by without taking the time to see the true meaning and beauty of these landmarks.

After thanking my boss for correcting me on Mr. Wanamaker's name, I then, in the spirit of keeping the banter going, asked him what was up with his sideburns.

Ryen sported a heavy thick pair of sideburns that had been out of style since the early 1970s.

Ryen laughed and then asked if I knew where the term originated from. Of course, not having a clue, Ryen told me I had my next research project. He did give me a hint by telling me it had something to do with the Civil War. In less than an enthusiastic voice, I responded, "Wonderful."

The recent week felt different from the fast-paced summer days I'd been accustomed to around midtown. The Deuce had been uncharacteristically quiet. Ryen had explained it was actually par for the course that the last week of August to be this tranquil in the city. According to him, a lot of people that work in Manhattan take off prior to Labor Day weekend in order to extend their holiday. Less people in the city meant less crime.

That Friday, the unit was notified we'd be working the West Indian Day parade that upcoming Monday, Labor Day. All vacation days were rescinded and we were to report directly to Brooklyn.

Mike, who was standing next to me at muster, laughed and said he needn't worry since all his vacation days were already rescinded. I felt bad for my coworker. The official word came down that week: all his vacation days would be forfeited and his probation period would be extended an additional six months. In a way, he was fortunate because losing one's firearm while on probation could've been grounds for dismissal. All the sergeants went to bat for him and sent letters to the disciplinary board before their final decision. Apparently, the letters carried some weight and Mike's job was saved. I was happy for him because I knew he was a good cop and deserved the boss's going the extra mile for him. The only reservation I had was if the sergeants would've done the same if it was Sharlene that lost her firearm. I think the answer to that one was pretty obvious.

On Monday, I, along with the rest of the squad, reported to Brooklyn. A temporary headquarters had been set up for our muster area. Sergeant Denny was in front of the group giving us our assignments. The normally jolly sergeant was anything but on this particularly hot summer day. He was sweating profusely and his voice kept cracking while reading the assignments. There were none of his usual dry jokes to help calm the air. I could see the other sergeants off to the side talking with each other in a low voice with their hands over their mouths. There was something going on, but I was unaware of what it could be.

During the course of the summer, our division worked several parades and details throughout Manhattan. This was our first one outside our home borough. The previous details had been fun and uneventful. I hadn't any reason to think this would be different.

We were to be broken up into four teams, each assigned to a sergeant. I was hoping I'd be assigned to Ryen, but when my name was called, I was with Sergeant Gooden's group.

I hadn't worked much with the young sergeant since being assigned to the Third Division. I knew he had a good reputation amongst the other rookies. My only concern was his lack of experience. The other sergeants were all seasoned veterans, while Gooden looked more like one of us rookies.

The Asian-American sergeant was one of the few members of the service that were fortunate enough to have been eligible to take the promotional exam soon after graduating the Academy. The city gave the exams so sporadically that many deemed it to be more of a crap shoot than an actual promotional exam. There were guys on the job for ten years before they had their first crack at the civil service test. Then there were guys like Gooden who had no more than a year's experience on the job, and were fortunate enough to hit things just right. The city didn't give much thought to the fairness of the process, but then again, a department that promotes only on the merits of an exam shows how detached they were from a truly fair process.

This was one of many reasons Dad disdained the bosses on the job. He'd say, "How can you promote someone that hadn't made an arrest or didn't do any real police work in their entire career?"

While I was in the Academy, there were police officers instructing classes that never spent a day on patrol. Their sole purpose was to be assigned to the Academy in order to allow themselves the extra time to study for the promotional exam. This is why Dad felt the upper brass had zero regard for the street cop.

"Having never walked a day in their shoes, how can these pricks have any compassion or empathy for what the street cop goes through on a daily basis?" Dad would protest. With their college degrees in hand, being a street cop was beneath them. They were going to be the ones to tell the cops how to do their job while they sat on their pampered asses hiding behind a desk somewhere.

Of course, not every boss falls into this category. Bosses like Sergeant Ryen earned their stripes by learning the job from working the street and by the book. But the reality was until the department put more of an emphasis on a patrolman's performance, there'd always be book-smart supervisors without real police experience.

Sergeant Denny emphasized how this parade was very different from the other details we'd previously worked before in Manhattan. According to him, the West Indian Carnival wasn't exactly the Macy's Thanksgiving Day parade. He explained how each year there were several shootings and stabbings along the Eastern Parkway parade route. He stressed one last time, before dismissing us to our groups, to be safe.

After Denny's instructions, we reported to our assigned sergeant. As I walked over to where Sergeant Gooden was standing, I noticed that Mike was assigned to Ryen, Ed to Sergeant Denny, and most of the female officers were with Sergeant Marks, except for Sharlene, who was with me in Gooden's group.

Sergeant Marks was the least popular sergeant among us rookies. At six-foot-three, Martin bore a striking resemblance to Tom Selleck. Selleck, an actor who played a private investigator on a popular television series during the '80s, was tall, good looking, and had a thick black mustache, just like Marks. Somebody must've told Marks he looked like the actor because he always came to work wearing the same type of Hawaiian shirts the character wore on the show.

Unlike the likeable Magnum character, Marks came across as arrogant and aloof. Maybe he thought being a sergeant in the NYPD was beneath him. He rarely ever smiled or said a kind word. If he was forced to tell one of us to do something, it was always with a bit of an edge to it. However, around any attractive female officers, he was Mr. Personality. Mark's unfriendly attitude wasn't saved just for the male rookies in the squad, but also for his fellow sergeants. He was always off to the side while the other sergeants stood together. It seemed as though if there wasn't a female around, he was bored. I thought it was a good thing I didn't have boobs; otherwise, I might've been assigned to his group.

Gooden gathered our squad and began to go over our assignments. At twenty-five, Gooden was only a few years older than most of the guys he was supervising. His father was stationed in Vietnam during the war and married his Vietnamese mother. The thin built sergeant's jet-black hair was longer than the department's regulation allowed. I'm not certain how he was able to get away with it, but I assumed being a boss in the Third Division probably came with some perks; and letting one's hair grow must've been one of them. His very cool-looking Fu Manchu mustache wasn't exactly in line with department's regs either.

Gooden looked like a Kung Fu fighter with the hair, the mustache, and his natural Asian complexion; but it was how he wore his service revolver that made him look like a real badass. He wore his gun belt low and at an angle, resembling the old gun slingers of the West. I don't know if it gave him any tactical advantage, but he sure did look cool.

Unlike Marks, Gooden seemed to relish being a boss. He was always smiling and pleasant to deal with. The composed sergeant began going over the day's assignment with the group. "Gentlemen, and oh, Sharlene," he started to say, "our number one objective is to go home tonight in one piece. As Sergeant Denny explained to you before, this carnival can get a bit hairy. Do not, I say again, do not do anything to incite these people. There are going to be agitators out there hoping they can provoke you into a confrontation—do not take the bait. If someone blows cannabis smoke in your face, ignore it. If someone jumps on a squad car and yells, 'Die, you mother fuck-ing pigs,' I want you to look the other way. You're going to put your blinders on. No one will be arrested for anything other than a serious felony today. Do not come to me with some dis-con, urinating in public, or pot smoking nonsense. Not today. Your first responsibility is to protect yourself. Your second is to protect your fellow officers and your third is to please, not put me, as your supervisor, in harm's way—any questions?"

The sergeant couldn't have been clearer in his instructions to us, but of course there's always someone that wants to feel important, so they have to ask a stupid question. And, yes, there is such a thing as a stupid question. Today's "Mr. Inquisitive" was Officer Frank Strange.

I disliked Strange from the moment I worked with him in the squad car with Sergeant Ryen. For the entire tour, he ran his mouth and asked one question after another. Sometimes he'd ask a question just so he could answer it. He was a squirmy, little know-it-all with bad breath—perfect brass material.

"Um, Sarge, I have a question," Strange uttered in his high-pitched, squeaky voice, while adjusting his coke bottle glasses. "What should we consider to be a serious felony over a non-serious felony?"

Gooden responded, "Hey, guys, we're talking about guns and knives—life or death situations. Otherwise, I don't want you taking police action without checking with me or one of the other bosses first, okay?"

"Well, what if someone's drunk and..."

Before Strange could finish his hypothetical scenario, Gooden interrupted him but with a much more serious edge in his voice, and repeated himself, "Life or death situations guys. Let's be smart out here and use common sense, as well as a lot of discretion—got it?"

The concept was simple: get out of there in one piece and prevent any riots in the process.

So, before Strange could ask another brilliant question, Gooden told everyone to pair-off. He told us it didn't matter who was with who because we'd be rotating partners throughout the day.

I turned to Sharlene and gave her a nod, and we teamed up. Two of the other officers teamed together and that left Gooden with Strange. As we started to walk to our assigned spots along the parade route, I could see Gooden wasn't happy with whom he was left with and reminded the group that the pairings were temporary and would be rotated.

Gooden had the group take our positions along the police barricades. As I looked up and down Eastern Parkway, I observed a major police presence as far as the eye could see. For a moment, I wasn't sure if we were getting ready for a parade or a riot.

I grew up in Brooklyn my entire life but never heard of the carnival before. When I asked Sharlene if she was familiar with the parade, she proudly declared to me that she'd been a participant in the festivities as a baton twirler as a youngster.

The normally timid Sharlene was openly proud of her West Indian heritage and seemed to enjoy sharing the details of the carnival with me. She explained how the West Indian Day parade attracted well over two million people every year, and that several of the Caribbean Islands were to be represented in the procession, including her native country, Jamaica.

"I know the parade has a bad reputation for violence, but it's caused by a few trouble makers," she said. "The vast majority of the party goers come here to peacefully enjoy the festivities. It's truly an amazing spectacle of colors, costumes, performers and celebration of West Indian culture."

I enjoyed listening to Sharlene as she pridefully spoke of her culture. I liked Sharlene from the first day we worked together. We couldn't have come from more different backgrounds. She was born in Jamaica, I was born in Brooklyn. I was raised by my father; her father was in prison for manslaughter. I never saw a dead body prior to my Academy class trip to the morgue; she witnessed her mother being killed when she was twelve. I'm white and she's black.

Growing up in Bay Ridge, I didn't know any black people. The neighborhood was a melting pot of different white ethnic groups, but none from Africa. The first time I had any interaction with black people was when I was in eighth grade and took the "R" train to DeKalb Avenue. I was going to Brooklyn Tech to take their high school entrance exam. I never made it to the school that day.

When I walked up the stairs of the DeKalb station, there were several black, male teens blocking the exit. They looked at me and said that I was in the wrong neighborhood—if I wanted to pass, I would have to pay a toll. The four teens were bigger and obviously stronger than I was; however, I was faster. I ran back down the stairs and found another exit. Once I was able to get to the street, I continued running as fast as I could down DeKalb Avenue, never looking back. I lost the four teens and in the process found myself lost. I could see people in the neighborhood looking at me funny. I clearly stood out. I was too naive to be scared, which in retrospect was probably a good thing. All I wanted was to find my way back home. On the next corner, I saw a police car. I walked over to the vehicle and asked the officers where the closest subway station was. The one officer pointed back to where I just came from. After explaining my reason for not wanting to return to that location, the officers were kind enough to drive me to a different subway station.

The experience didn't influence me negatively toward black people. I was harassed by a lot more Irish and Italian punks in my neighborhood, but that didn't make me hate their ethnicity. What the experience did do was make me more aware that I didn't belong in some areas of the city, the same way I'm certain many young blacks felt about coming into white neighborhoods.

For the longest time, I viewed myself as a good Christian. I believed I wasn't prejudiced toward anyone's race or religion. It wasn't until I met Sharlene that I became aware that I was indeed prejudiced. I knew this because I had feelings for Sharlene but chose not to act on them for fear of what others might think.

The truth is Sharlene was different. She came from a different part of the city than the rest of the members in the squad, and she had a different upbringing as well. But these differences weren't the reason for her being ostracized from the rest of the squad. The biggest difference was as clear as the color of her skin: she was black and we were white.

While I stood there in front of the police barricades listening to Sharlene, I made the decision that after the shift, I would let her know my feelings toward her.

The parade finally began around eleven. I watched the floats go by with the exotic costumes and performers and told Sharlene that she was right about the parade being amazing. The crowd was in high spirits while they enjoyed the music of the West Indies. We were warned by our bosses that this was going to be a long day, but thus far, all was going well.

I kept my eye on the crowd while glancing at the floats that passed by. Sharlene had a laugh at my expense when she caught me glimpsing a bit too much at some of the female dancers. I told her it was difficult not to be distracted by some of their costumes. Many of the female dancers had nothing more on than a thong bikini bottom along with some strategically placed feathers to cover their chests—very erotic.

The day was moving along without incident. Besides the occasional smell of cannabis in the air, the spectators had been fine. I observed Lieutenant Higgins going from sergeant to sergeant to ensure all was going as planned with their groups. I asked Sharlene what time the parade was over and she told me around four. It was as if Sharlene was reading my mind because I no sooner asked the question when she reminded me that this was going to be a long day. I asked her if the parade was over, and there were no more floats or performers, what need would there be for the police to stay around?

That's when Sharlene enlightened me that the real parties didn't begin until the parade ended and the sun went down. I was still hopeful that this year would be different. Maybe the party goers would want to go home early and none of those impromptu block parties off Eastern Parkway would break out.

When four o'clock approached, the parade procession began winding down just as Sharlene had predicted. I convinced myself things would be different this year and soon we'd all be on our way home. I observed the crowds get thinner, and by the time the last floats went by, the crowd had nearly completely dispersed.

Soon after, Gooden announced that we were done and to follow him back to the temporary headquarters.

I was right! I knew it. There was no way the city was going to pay for overtime if there was nothing going on. The parade was over and it was time to go home. I might've been a rookie, but my instincts were of a seasoned veteran.

When we arrived at the temporary HQ, I could see all the other officers and sergeants just standing around. I figured our bosses were waiting to get the official dismissal time before letting us go.

Not long after, we were instructed to muster up along with the other divisions. I thought this to be odd because when we were finished at other similar details, the sergeants would simply give us our dismissal time and we'd be on our way.

While standing in formation, I started to hear the other officers murmur that we weren't going anywhere. The whisperers were saying that we were to be reassigned to the side streets in case a block party started up. I turned to the one officer that was doing most of the talking and asked how he was so certain. He told me he heard the orders come over the lieutenant's radio. Apparently, we weren't going anywhere.

Finally, the orders came down for us to start securing the side streets. So much for having the instincts of a veteran.

Block parties, and the shutting down of a street, are permitted throughout the city but require a permit. In this case, no permits were issued. However, that wasn't going to stop the party goers from doing what they pleased. Our job, as the police, was to babysit. In other words, we were to stand there like *piñatas* or better yet, like fish in a barrel, and do absolutely nothing while groups of people indiscriminately took over a block.

While walking to our assigned block, I could see Sergeant Ryen looking as if he was going to explode, and finally he did.

"Have we not learned that appeasement never works?" Ryen said to anyone who'd listen. "Is there one time in history that backing down to bullies didn't require a stronger reaction later on? How did appeasement work for Chamberlin when dealing with Hitler? If they don't have a permit—close the bastards down! This gutless department is run by a bunch of squat-peeing cowards just like Chamberlin. What an absolute disgrace."

I assumed the boss's frustration was one of the reasons why he was getting ready to hand in his retirement papers; but as for me, like a good lamb I kept quiet and followed my shepherd.

When we arrived on the block, Sergeant Denny instructed us to remain with our assigned supervisor from earlier. I started walking toward Gooden when I noticed Ryen looking at me and pointing toward the sky.

"These bastards love throwing shit from rooftops, be careful."

I could sense the seriousness of the situation in his voice. I now had a better understanding why the bosses had been on edge throughout the day.

When the six of us arrived to our assigned block, I quickly surveyed the area. I took note that there were probably a hundred or so party goers, but the vehicular traffic was still passable. I noticed there weren't any cars parked along either side of the street. According to Gooden, in previous years, there were many vehicles damaged and set ablaze from the party goers. The significance of this detail meant we had little cover.

The attached, six-story apartment houses ran the length of both sides of the street. As I looked down the other end of the block, I could see a green construction dumpster located just off the sidewalk. The dumpster was about a football field away, but I could tell it was one of the bigger ones—a thirty or forty-yard container. In case things started falling out of the sky, this was the cover we needed.

As I assessed the situation, I couldn't help but have an uneasy feeling about our current assignment. Being at street level was like being in a valley with the bad guys having the higher ground. To make things worse, our group was standing so close to each other I could reach out and touch the other five officers. I thought we were an easy target for someone to throw a bottle in our direction and hit one of us even if their aim wasn't that good.

I wanted to talk to Gooden, but I didn't want to do it in front of the others. I didn't think it would be a good idea for a rookie to be telling the sergeant we were standing too close together and oh, by the way, there was a dumpster down the block that would solve our biggest issue—cover.

I walked a few feet away from the group and then turned back and casually asked Gooden, "Hey, boss, do you have a second?" Without hesitation, Gooden started to walk over. I'm guessing he was assessing our situation as well and was open to hear what I had to say.

While being assigned to the office, I prided myself on not disturbing the bosses and to only speak when spoken to. Gooden had a fairly good idea I wasn't calling him over to ask him his views on the weather.

While Gooden was making his way toward me, I couldn't help but notice he had a shadow. It was Officer Strange. Most people would've had the common sense to know I wanted to talk to the sergeant alone, but not Strange. Gooden, noticing I was looking at something behind him, stopped and turned to see what it was.

"What the hell are you doing, Strange?" Gooden asked in a not so pleasant tone. "I feel like you're my own personal proctologist. Go keep the others company."

To my surprise, Strange didn't say a word and walked straight back to the group. Gooden, still a little hot with his personal proctologist, abruptly asked me what was up. I told him I didn't think standing down on this end of the block holding hands with each other was such a good idea. I pointed to the dumpster down at the other end and asked him what he thought about relocating. Besides my explanation regarding the cover it offered, I brought to his attention how the street light above the dumpster wasn't working. I figured what the bad guys couldn't see, they couldn't hit.

I wasn't sure how Gooden was going to react to my suggestion. I'm just a rookie, and although he was a young boss, he was still a seasoned veteran. Some guys might say no, even if it was a good idea in order to protect their ego; but not Gooden.

"Outstanding, out... bloody... standing," he said with full enthusiasm. He looked over to the group and told them, "Guys, let's go."

The six of us began our walk to the other end of the block, with Gooden and me leading the way. I told him what Ryen warned me about earlier regarding bottles being thrown off the roof tops in our direction. Gooden laughed and said that Ryen was putting it mildly.

"These bastards were throwing bricks at us last year," Gooden said. "They'd break them off from the sides of the buildings and hurl them down at us from the roof. Fortunately, the cars took the damage, not us. They got smart this year and relocated their vehicles. Thank God for the dumpster. Great call, Dean, seriously great call."

The sergeant's words meant a lot to me. I told Gooden it would've been just a matter of time before he saw the big green dumpster and came up with the idea himself. That's when Gooden told me something that just about scared the hell out of me. He explained to me that he had terrible eyesight and would've never seen the dumpster. I thought to myself how the sergeant must've had one hell of a hook to pass the department's eye exam.

In the short-time it took us to get to the other end of the block, I noticed the crowd had nearly doubled in size. The partygoers had taken over the street, forcing vehicular traffic to seek an alternate route. I kept looking up at the rooftops, but so far all was clear.

When we reached the far end of the block, Gooden had us spread out around the dumpster and reminded us to keep our eyes open. As the others walked away to get in position, Gooden held me back and then said, "You're my eyes tonight, don't drift too far away from me."

By now it was dark, and the street light that earlier wasn't working, was beginning to flicker on and off. The crowd had swelled to an unmanageable size for six officers to handle. The people in the street pretended we weren't even there. They were smoking pot and drinking alcohol in open containers as though they hadn't a care in the world. They stayed far enough away from us, not because they were afraid we'd arrest them, but because they didn't want to accidently get hit by any flying debris intended for us coppers.

I wasn't scared but I definitely felt uneasy. I started to wonder if this was how Custer felt right before the Battle of the Little Big Horn.

I could tell the sergeant was a bit anxious about our current situation. He kept reminding me if I saw anything to let him know. I jokingly replied that he'd be the first one I'd tell when I was interrupted by a burst of gunfire. I wasn't certain where the shots were coming from, but I knew they were intended for us. I instinctively grabbed Gooden and pushed him up and over into the dumpster and then I followed. When the shots subsided, I took a glimpse to see if I could make out anything but it was too dark. Gooden was yelling at the other officers to get in the dumpster when another hail of shots rang out. All the other officers jumped in the dumpster except for Sharlene. I peeked over the top of the dumpster to see her standing there as if she was frozen. Gooden yelled for Sharlene to get in but she didn't move. Without much thought, I jumped out of the dumpster, grabbed Sharlene and pulled her over toward Gooden. He then reached over the side and pulled her in.

The gunfire seemed to be coming from the roof tops across the street. I could hear some of the rounds spraying the outside of the metal dumpster. We were trapped and simply had to wait it out. After what seemed like an eternity, but was probably less than twenty seconds, the shots finally stopped.

Someone in the apartment house must've called 911 because within a minute, the block was full of police vehicles and personnel. Several older women came out of their apartments to see if we were all right. One of them was so angry she started yelling toward the roof tops for the boys to start acting like men and not thugs. She looked like a sweet old grandmother but acted more like a field general.

After getting out of the dumpster, the elderly women came over to ask if we were all right. Being the one closest to her, I told her we were okay and thanked her for her concern. Then, in a heavy Jamaican accent, the plus-sized grandmother said, "You, the crazy one. I saw you from my window—pointing to the first-floor apartment across from the dumpster. You jumped out of that thing to go help that girl—you either stupid brave or stupid crazy."

I knew the good citizen wasn't trying to be comical, but at the moment, that's exactly how I took her commentary. So, as I had a good laugh, the strong-spirited women glared at me and said, "Oh, I get it, you just stupid."

"No argument here, ma'am," I replied, while the Good Samaritan walked away shaking her head.

The other sergeants and the rest of the squad were all now on the scene, along with ESU (Emergency Service Unit).

ESU is NYPD's equivalent to a SWAT unit. As the saying goes, "When people get in trouble they call the police—when the police get in trouble, they call ESU." The cavalry arrived and the block and rooftops were now secured.

Of course, the thugs were long gone, but thankfully, at least, the unlawful block party was officially over.

The bosses told us to start heading back to the temporary head-quarters but this time it was for dismissal—thank God!

During the walk back, Gooden caught up to me.

"That was a bit insane," the sergeant excitedly expressed. "I'm glad I had you with me tonight."

With the adrenalin still freshly pumping through my veins, I simply nodded my head and continued walking without saying any-thing. I was still in disbelief on what just transpired, and although the sergeant kept on talking, I wasn't able to focus on what he was saying. The only thing I could think of was getting out of there.

Back at the temporary headquarters, I felt someone touch my shoulder. It was Sharlene.

With her head down, she began to say, "I don't know what hap-pened back there. I just couldn't move. I could've gotten you hurt. I'm sorry."

I hadn't given much thought to the peril Sharlene put Gooden and me in. I knew her actions weren't intentional and after all, no one was hurt. So, having just finished working the Labor Day from hell, I suggested to Sharlene to simply buy me a drink and we'd be even. However, Sharlene seemed less than receptive to my idea. In fact, my offer seemed to offend her. With her apology behind her, she quickly responded in an agitated tone.

"Dean, we've been working together for a couple of months now. Why is it you're asking me tonight?"

I started by telling her how I felt about her and how I was hoping we could start seeing each other. I then addressed her question.

"I'm sorry I hadn't invited you out prior. I'm not proud of the fact that I allowed myself to worry about what others might think. But the fact that I'm asking you now hopefully shows you something."

By the time I was done, I could see by Sharlene's body language that any chance I might've had, had long passed. She wasn't blind to the squad's socializing or immune to the effects of being left out.

She was kind with her words, telling me she was attracted to me, but the fact remained she was hurt by being ostracized by her fellow officers, which included me. In the end, she let me down easy by saying it simply wasn't good timing. She felt that her life and career were at a crossroads and she didn't want to complicate things further by starting a relationship. I felt helpless because I knew her decision was unwavering.

After getting dismissed by our lieutenant, the squad was discussing where to meet for a drink. Ryen suggested that since we were already in Brooklyn to head over to his cousin's bar in my neck of the woods—Bay Ridge. I was happy with the choice because the bar was close to my home, and after having to dive in the filthy dumpster, a hot shower was in order.

Now that the craziest shift in my young career was officially over, it was time to relax with my squad and suck down a few pints.

Halleujah!

CHAPTER 4

Fallen Hero

I'm trusting in the Lord and a good lawyer.
—Oliver North

In the spring of 1969, Dad had decided it was time to leave the Fifth Precinct Detective Squad. Reporting to the command had simply become too difficult in the days following the tragic death of his partner.

As luck would have it, a memo came down from the Intelligence Division that they were seeking detectives with special skills. Unlike me, Dad didn't have the luxury of a hook to help him with his transfer request. However, his skills as a military reporter while in the army during the Korean Conflict gave him something the brass were seeking; an MOS with foreign affairs experience, along with accredited writing skills. Shortly after submitting his application, he was called for an interview and subsequently selected into the prestigious detail.

The Intelligence Division was located on Vesey Street in Lower Manhattan. The detail would entail the young detective working with diplomats, foreign dignitaries, and local government officials. Although there wasn't any promotion or pay increases with the transfer, being selected for the assignment allowed Dad the change of venue he was hoping for. Another important factor for him was that the detail was clean—no graft. He always felt it was a matter of time before the department cleaned up the corruption, and he didn't want to be scooped up in the net when it came down.

Dad was but a baby in his new surroundings, but he'd learn quickly what was expected of him; nitty-gritty investigations, accumulating information on people of interest and creating detailed dossiers. All the information was collected and either acted upon or saved for future use. There always seemed to be some group demonstrating in front of the United Nations or a Foreign Embassy in Manhattan for one reason or another. Having an understanding of the protestors and their agenda helped Intel better prepare itself.

According to Dad, the securing and escorting of VIPs around the city was the easy, more enjoyable part of the detail. The real grunt work came with the meticulous, time-consuming collection of intelligence through interviews and research.

The professional atmosphere at Intel brought back a sense of pride to the Third Grade Detective's work. No longer was he sneaking out greased up captains from bathhouses or worrying about how not to get tangled up in the nickel-dime graft of the Detective Squad. This was clean police work with professional detectives leading the way. Each detective had his own niche. Whether it was having foreign language skills or an expertise regarding a particular region, each detective was assigned accordingly. For Dad, because he spent three miserable years in Korea reporting on the war for the army press, he became the Far East liaison.

He knew from dealing with the Chinese while in the Fifth Precinct that they were an overwhelmingly, law-abiding group of people that respected the police. However, by the late '60s there'd been a migration of young Chinese gang members from Southeast Asia arriving into the States and causing havoc for local businesses. Intelligence was gathered, investigations conducted and when warranted, arrests were made.

Although the detectives had their individual responsibilities, when it came time to escorting diplomats and VIP's, the group worked as a team. The subject, along with the level of security risk, would determine the amount of personnel assigned to any given detail. The detectives in Intel would recon all necessary locations (i.e., hotels, restaurants, parking garages) and go through the proper channels in securing these locations. Since, these operations usually dealt with diplomats and heads of state, the State Department personnel would work jointly with Intel in securing the subject.

In the spring of 1970, word came down that the recently appointed vice premier of the Republic of China, Chiang Ching-kuo, would be visiting New York City in late April. Since the subject fell under Dad's geographical area of responsibility, he'd take the lead in organizing the visit and begin investigating any opposition groups that may pose a security risk.

After researching any possible agitators, the Detective discovered a group that went by the name of WUFI—World United Formosans for Independence. The group aggressively opposed the current regime in China headed by Chang Kai-shek, the father of Vice Premier Chiang-kuo. The members of WUFI strongly voiced their collective concern that the vice premier would continue in his father's totalitarian footsteps when the time came for him to take over as leader.

WUFI had applied for, and received, a permit to demonstrate the vice premier's visit to New York City. After looking into the group further, Dad discovered that WUFI consisted mostly of professors throughout the United States hoping for political and social changes in their countries of origin: Taiwan and China. On the surface, the group didn't seem to pose any major threats to the vice premier. So, after all the intelligence was gathered, it was determined by the commander of Intel to assign the minimum of two detectives to the seemingly low risk, security detail.

In his words, my dad, Detective Simpson, recounts the events of that day and the aftermath that followed:
On the day of the event, April 24, 1970, everything was going accordingly. The heavy morning rain that covered the city didn't seem to deter the WUFI demonstrators from attending. The local command had set up a barricaded pen directly across the street from the main entrance to help in containing those that wished to protest the vice premier's arrival, which was set for noon.

Since the subject was from the Far East, I was the lead detective. There were four State Department Officers assigned to the detail and only one other guy from my office, Detective Hank Suarez. Uniformed personnel were taking care of crowd control outside, so all we had to do was get the subject in the Plaza Hotel safely and the rest would be relatively simple. Although, there's always the possibility of a threat while guarding a high-profile subject, there wasn't anything specific to indicate this escort would warrant any extra concern. As for the demonstrators that were already in attendance, they seemed to be cooperative as they awaited the vice premier's arrival.

The vice premier and his delegation were being given an escort from the NYPD's Highway Patrol from Kennedy Airport to the Plaza Hotel. I stayed back with the two other State Department guys to go over the last-minute details. One very important detail I was sure never to overlook at these assignments was the menu for the luncheon. Good food in fancy places was a great perk in working at Intel.

I was going over the menu when the call came over the radio that the subject was two minutes out. I went back outside and positioned myself in front of the Fifth Avenue entrance and awaited the arrival of the motorcade.

The main entrance of the historic hotel is a magnificent display of architectural beauty and class. The sidewalk directly in front of the entrance is laid in a diamond shape, black and white granite stones. The stairs, made of cut granite, is partially covered in a crimson red rug with brass railings along each side that lead up to the three brass revolving doors. The sides and area above these doors are covered in rich black wood, with a gold leaf border. The veranda is supported by six oversized marble columns where several flags are displayed, including the US, Canada, and the Plaza's. Above the transom is the Plaza's trademark crest, etched in the golden stained glass.

As the motorcade turned onto Fifth Avenue, I could hear the crowd of a hundred or so demonstrators get significantly louder. This was the first time I realized this unassuming, peaceful protest might be anything but. I didn't understand exactly what they were screaming in Mandarin, but I didn't exactly need an interpreter to appreciate that these people were really upset. In fact, the energy level given off by the protestors was equivalent to crowd five times its size. With my senses now on full alert, I was no longer thinking about the London broil I'd be having at lunch but rather if someone might actually try and take this guy out.

I positioned myself slightly behind Vice Premier Chiang-kuo as he exited the limousine. There were only a few feet between the curb and the carpeted staircase. After that, were eight steps leading up to the brass, revolving doors and finally into the sanctuary of the lobby. Maybe it was because of the hysteria of the crowd or the fact that I simply wanted to get the subject in the hotel as quickly as possible, but it seemed as though it took forever for the well able-bodied vice premier to navigate each step. If I were him, I would've been moving with a purpose, but for whatever reason, the vice premier didn't seem daunted by the incensed crowd.

As the vice premier reached the first step one of the demonstrators from across the street broke from the barricaded pen and started to create a ruckus. The distraction had everyone in the detail looking in that direction—to my right. Call it luck, instincts, or good training—maybe a combination of all three—but I was looking in the other direction. Sprinting toward the subject and me from our blindside was an Asian man with a black, automatic Beretta pointing directly at the vice premier. With less than a second to react, I reached out and was able to grab the would-be assassin's hand, and in the process, deflected a shot that was meant for the subject. The deflected round harmlessly embedded itself in the wood above the revolving glass doors.

The subject was rushed into the Plaza by the State Department guys without further incident. However, for me, I still had my hands on the gun, as did the assailant, but now it was jammed in my stomach. My hand was wrapped around his and my finger was on his trigger finger—holding the trigger in the down position as to not allow another shot to go off. I yelled as loud as I could, "Don't jump on—nobody touches us!" There were a few motorcycle cops that were big boys and I was afraid if one of them did something, I'd lose my grip on the gun and another shot would go off, but this time in my belly.

At that point, I was more afraid of my own guys than the gunman. But for the grace of God, everyone stayed back while I tried to get control of the gun. After a brief struggle and a short roll down the stairs, I was able to dislodge his hand from the gun. I yell, "Okay, I got it," and then the motorcycle cops pounce on the perp and cuff him.

The gunman, Peter Huang, was charged and convicted of attempted murder of a diplomat, as was the decoy, Huang's brother-in-law, TT Deh.

A few months later, I was awarded the department's highest medal: The Medal of Honor. I was one of just a few in the department's long history to have received the Medal non-posthumously. I was proud I was able to thwart the assassination attempt and thanked the good Lord for no one being injured that day. I was on the news and in all the papers. My family, my neighbors and fellow parishioners all went out of their way to congratulate me on being a hero. Yes, I was a hero—an NYPD hero—but sad to say, only a dead hero is safe from the wrath of the brass in the NYPD.

During my time on patrol I was awarded several medals including the Combat Cross. I never displayed the department's second highest honor because a life, as justified as it was, had to be taken by my hand. However, receiving the Medal of Honor was different. By saving a life without having to take one in the process, I decided to wear my medal with honor and distinction. I was proud of my actions but due to the grief of a few jealous pricks, I wish I never had accepted the hunk of medal.

After receiving the Medal of Honor, everyone seemed to treat me differently. My peers looked at me as if I were a living legend, which I didn't feel comfortable with, while the brass leered at me with contempt.

Not long after receiving the medal, an inspector walked over to my desk at Intel and asked me if I was the Medal of Honor recipient, Jim Simpson. I respectfully responded back to the inspector that I was. I thought perhaps the boss wanted to congratulate me on a job well done or something along those lines, but I'd be wrong.

The inspector, with a look of disbelief on his face and complete disgust in his voice said to me, "You know it makes me sick to think that you'll get the same inspector's funeral as me one day."

I couldn't comprehend what I just heard. Was this imbecile serious? I stood up from my desk and told the inspector that he was welcome to have my inspector's funeral at any time and the sooner the better. I excused myself and went to the men's room and began to cry.

Up to that point, I hadn't really reflected on the assassination attempt or the actual peril I faced. I could've been killed and had my inspector's funeral already. The inspector's comment triggered something inside me that, in retrospect, was probably a good thing. The release of emotions was well overdue and helped calm my nerves. But while sitting in the stall, I wondered how this person could be so detached from humanity. He was incensed that a mere detective should be entitled to the same ceremonial honors normally reserved for an inspector. What an absolute asshole—what an absolute prick.

Prior to the discussion with the inspector, I was unaware of the added privilege bestowed upon me for receiving the distinguished medal. The Ceremonial Unit for the NYPD was only used at funerals for members killed in the line of duty, rank of inspector or higher; and to my surprise, Medal of Honor recipients. However, years later, the brass had been so annoyed with sharing the special ceremonial detail with anyone other than themselves that they finally discontinued the service for Medal of Honor recipients. I'm thinking brass in Latin must translate to mean "petty little pricks."

Besides the medal bestowing me with a wonderful inspector's funeral to look forward to one day—one in which I could give a rat's ass about—there was a real perk that did unexpectedly come my way.

I guess from all the media attention that I garnered, I caught someone's eye in the governor's office. I was told that I was permanently reassigned to guard the governor of New York State, Nelson Rockefeller.

My new assignment was pure gold. Although I was still technically assigned to Intel, I rarely needed to report to the Vesey Street office. The governor's chief of staff, Chuck Nagel, made it clear on day one that I answered only to him and the governor. Both men were gentlemen and treated me extremely well—nothing like the NYPD brass.

The Governor spent most of his time at his office in Midtown Manhattan. When he did have to go to Albany—the state's capital—I was allowed to report to his office on West Fifty-Fifth Street and be kept on standby. In reality, all I had to do is call into the governor's secretary, Megan, and she'd keep me posted on the governor's travel plans.

I was in my own little cocoon and virtually untouchable from the department while I was assigned to the governor—or at least I thought so.

It was now the spring of 1973, and I'd been with the governor for over two years. On occasion, a newspaper reporter or a local news outlet would contact me for an interview regarding the assassination attempt at the Plaza Hotel. Usually, it was because they were doing a related story on the Far East or something along those lines. Most of the interviews came the first year and the requests quieted down after that.

In March 1973, there was an assassination attempt halfway around the world in Sydney, Australia, on Prince Phillip, the Duke of Edinburgh. The bombs that were to be used were discovered prior to being detonated, and the plot was foiled.

It was speculated that the explosives planted at the hotel where the Duke was staying were in retaliation for the "Bloody Sunday" massacre that occurred the previous year in Northern Ireland. The massacre outrage stemmed from British soldiers shooting twenty-eight unarmed civilians, killing fourteen of them. The Irish Republican Army was now suspected of the assassination attempt on the Duke.

CBS News was looking to do a story on the incident and wanted my professional insight on how best to prevent these types of acts. In the interview, I gave the same song-and-dance I had dozens of times before, explaining how important the preparation work was prior to such high-profile escorts, and how to expect the unexpected once the subject is in motion.

The day after the interview broadcasted, I was notified to report back to the Intelligence Unit on Vesey Street. Call it denial or stupidity, but at the time I didn't realize I was being called back because of the interview I gave to CBS.

The Department has guidelines regarding a MOS speaking with the media. One must go through the chain of command and wait until written consent is given by the brass. After the assassination attempt at the Plaza, I'd given loads of interviews without the departments consent and no one ever said a word.

I no sooner walked in the front door of the unit, when the lieutenant began yelling from across the open bay for me to get in his, as he put it, "goddamn office."

I was ten years older than this little prick, had twice the time on the job as him, but because he had a brass-colored bar on both of his collars, he was going to let everyone that was present know he was the boss and I wasn't.

If I walked any slower to the lieutenant's, office I'd be in reverse. I stopped at the cooler to get a sip of water—greeted a few of my coworkers at their desk—and then unhurriedly entered the little prick's office.

"Yes, Lew, did you need me for something?" I politely asked.

The twenty-something little college boy was about to have a meltdown. He started to hyperventilate and couldn't get out what he wanted to say. When he finally caught his breath, he told me I was off the governor's detail.

"How dare you give interviews without my fucking consent," the lieutenant yelled. "Who the hell do you think you are? I am your Commanding Officer; you can't take a shit without my permission. My dinner was interrupted last night because Chief Johnson called me wanting to know who the fuck allowed this moron from Intel permission to give an interview to CBS. Who the fuck do you think you are, Mister? You're done, no more Governor assignment for you. For now on, you report here. Understood—Mister?"

I knew it would be futile to discuss the issue with the prick, so I didn't say a word. Even if I wanted to answer one of his questions, he'd be sure to interrupt me. As far as the lieutenant was concerned, he achieved his goal of reasserting the food chain—he was the boss and I was the piss ant.

I gave a nod of the head and proceeded to walk out the little prick's office the same way I entered it; slowly, with my head held high. The lieutenant was purposely yelling loud enough in order for the entire office to hear. He hoped to humiliate me in front of my colleagues, but instead showed how petty and unprofessional the department's brass truly is. I would've liked to give the adolescent lieutenant a good ass whipping but I'd be throwing away my career, along with my pension. It's not to say I wasn't tempted.

All I could think about as I walked out of his office was how many more months until I hit my retirement date—fifteen to be exact. It always puzzled me why my friends in the NYFD would stay past their twentieth year and not retire. They'd explain to me it was because the men on their job were an extension of their family, bosses included. They all looked out for one another, unlike the NYPD.

I had no intention on finishing my shift, so I banged out a personal day and left. I decided to drive up to the governor's office to say my goodbyes and to thank Chuck and Megan. Both had been very kind to me over the years and were supportive when Margaret passed away.

As I made the drive uptown, I wasn't upset. I knew it had to come to an end someday. I felt fortunate to have been a part of the governor's detail. I met great people and experienced more than I ever thought possible. By the time I arrived at Rocky's office, I was at peace.

When I went upstairs, I saw Chuck talking to Megan at her desk. The full figure, forty-something year-old blond was always in good spirits and was blessed with a great personality. As for Chuck, he was significantly less pleasing on the eyes and could explode like a volcano at his subordinates without a moment's notice. Always wearing the same wrinkled suit and sporting a mad-scientist hairdo, the chief-of-staff to the governor seemed always to be hard at work.

I was glad the two were together. It would make it easier informing them I wouldn't be reporting to the office any longer. After giving them the news, along with a brief explanation to what transpired, Chuck looked at me in disbelief and then asked, "Jim, are you not happy here?"

I explained to Chuck that I was extremely honored to have served the governor and loved every minute of my time with the entire office. I went on to explain that my commander at Intel was calling the shots and that I'd no longer be able to continue in the detail. Chuck, a man I never saw crack a smile, started to laugh and then asked me if I wanted to stay with the governor. I explained to him that I would love to, but I was being reprimanded for violating a departmental policy and it would be impossible for me to stay.

"Jim, do you realize who we work for?" Chuck rhetorically asked. "We work for Nelson Aldrich Rockefeller—Roc-ke-fel-ler. This is his office and I'm his chief. That makes me a very powerful man in my own right. Do you think you would've lasted this long with the governor if we both didn't trust you with his life? The old man likes you—I like you—Megan wants to make babies with you. I'll see you here tomorrow, understood?"

I shook Chuck's hand and thanked him for his support and kind words. With a grin, I then added that I was unaware of Megan's true intentions, which brought a hearty laugh from all those present.

I was amazed that in less than an hour I went from being treated like dog meat to having someone reassure me that humanity still existed. I don't ever remember somebody going to bat for me the way Chuck did that afternoon.

There was one thing I had no way of knowing at the time, but in the not-too-distant future, the governor's office would once again come to my rescue when it came to fending-off the brass.

The call went out and from then on, I answered only to the governor's office—nobody else. For as long as Rocky was governor, I'd be protected from little prick's like the lieutenant.

I'd always be grateful to Chuck, but his strong-arm tactics rubbed some down at One Police Plaza—the NYPD's main head-quarters and refuge to most of the brass, aka pricks—the wrong way. Thanks to the protection of the governor's office, I was safe for the time being.

I made the decision I'd still retire the following year. Rocky still had two years left in his term, so I figured I had nothing to worry about. That is until six months later when the governor announced he was resigning. He made some lame excuse for his departure, but everyone knew it was because he wanted to spend more time preparing for a presidential run. I respected his decision because a lot of politicians would've held onto their office while dedicating their time to another cause—but not Rocky. He was a man completely dedicated to whatever he was undertaking. If he couldn't give a hundred percent, then it was time to leave. A person's name and money can open a lot of doors, but I doubt he would've been elected governor of New York State an unprecedented four times if not for his unwavering commitment to public service. I believed he'd make a great president. But for obvious, selfish reasons, I wished he would've stayed on as governor for just a little while longer.

The department didn't waste any time calling me back to the Vesey Street office. The last time I was at the Intel Unit, I was being publicly stripped down by a pygmy with the rank of lieutenant. I wasn't sure what to expect. But one thing I did know was that I no longer had the protection of the governor's office.

As I walked in the front door, I was greeted by a new commander, Lieutenant Jose Vinals. The lieutenant extended his hand as he introduced himself. Since the last commander I dealt with wanted to tar and feather me, I was waiting for this one to turn into a terrier at any moment, but he didn't.

"Jim, I'd like to talk to you in my office," the lieutenant cordially instructed. "Why don't you grab a cup of coffee and meet me in there after you get settled?"

After saying hello to some of the guys and getting my coffee, I made my way over to the commander. When I walked into his office, I began fantasizing about beating the crap out of the previous brass-bar displaying imbecile. However, I quickly snapped myself back to reality and made a mental note to keep my composure regardless of what the lieutenant had to say.

The youthful lieutenant with the military style hair-cut began the conversation. After offering me a seat, he then asked me how my time was with the governor. I told him it was a great experience but then I lied by adding that I was glad to be back at Intel. I explained how the long hours were taking a toll, since after all, "I wasn't getting any younger."

I didn't want anyone to know how much I loved being part of the governor's detail. I wanted everyone to think I was happy to be back, but the truth of the matter was I was counting down the days until retirement.

"Well, Jim, I'm glad you're here with us at Intel. I went over your record and it's impressive to say the least—very impressive. If there's anything I can do to make the transition back at Intel easier please, just let me know."

"Well, there is one thing. I'm retiring next year and could use any sanctioned overtime that might be available."

"Jim, you know the city is in a financial crisis, but I promise any overtime that comes across my desk, I will give to you first. You have my word."

I wasn't concerned about the overtime but simply wanted to see how the lieutenant reacted to it. Nothing gets the brass more in a tizzy than guys trying to balloon their final year by working extra hours to help increase their pension. I respected the lieutenant's reaction and believed he was being sincere. I thanked him and left his office.

I was relieved that my first day back in the office was significantly better than the last time I was there. All I wanted now was to finish my time without incident and retire. I had accumulated a ton of vacation days while on the governor's detail, so I figured I'd be off nearly half of the remaining year before I needed to put my retirement papers in.

Over the next several weeks I dove back into doing some investigations, putting together some dossiers and doing follow-ups on persons of interest. One night, I was working late on a case when my old partner, Lenny Kaplan, came walking through the door.

Now a chief in the department, Lenny came into the squad room inconspicuously—no uniform and without displaying his shield.

Although we kept in touch over the years, we slowly drifted apart. The last time I saw Lenny was at Margaret's funeral, nearly two years earlier. I was happy to see my old friend.

"Lenny, you SOB, how the hell are you?"

"Jim, it's good to see you. It's been too long. How are things going for you here?"

I told him everything was going well, but I couldn't help but sense his visit wasn't to catch-up on old times. I noticed Lenny kept looking around the office while we spoke, making certain he wasn't detected.

The two of us worked several years together in the black and white squad car. There were weeks when I spent more time with him than Margaret. Once you get to know someone's habits and mannerisms, it's easier to read their minds. After spending all that time with Lenny, I knew he had something bad to tell me. My only question was how serious it was going to be. After a few more pleasantries, my old partner finally made the purpose for his visit clear.

"Jim, I wasn't here tonight." I knew whatever was coming next wasn't going to be good. "We both know One Police Plaza is a collection of jealous, white hair scumbags that don't like it when one of their pawns gets bigger than them. The Medal of Honor, the media attention, having the governor's office override a chief's decision—this is all enough to give one of these vindictive bastards a coronary. I hear things in the hallway and around the building downtown that you're on their radar. That's not a good thing. Be careful. Watch your back and do everything by the book."

"Lenny, I've been a choir boy since I left Public Morals. They can't have anything on me because I haven't done anything."

"You know they don't need much in order to twist your nuts in a vise. Just be careful and keep a low profile till you put your papers in."

I thanked my old partner for the heads-up and after a quick embrace and a pat on the back, the chief was on his way.

At first, I wasn't overly concerned with my ex-partner's visit. My retirement date was approaching and the detail I was in was clean. However, I started to become more worrisome when I played Lenny's words back in my head regarding "putting my papers in." I believed he was not only warning me about the brass, but letting me know to get out of the NYPD asap—evidently, the pricks were coming for me.

After driving myself crazy thinking about the meeting with Lenny, I decided to put my worries to rest. I decided to be a good little boy for the next several months and then retire as planned.

The next few months went by without incident. Lieutenant Vinals was making good on his promise, offering any sanctioned overtime to me first. I appreciated having a good boss for a change. It only took over nineteen years for me to find one. The guys in the office were less in awe and more relaxed with me than they were when I first received the Medal of Honor. I was enjoying my last days on the job but was still looking forward to my retirement date. Everything was going well—maybe too well.

I was at my desk one afternoon when the phone rang. On the other end of the line was Jerry Dematteo. Jerry was one of my Confidential Informants (CI) when I was in the Fifth Detective Squad. He had a heroin addiction that would continuously get him in trouble. So, every time he'd get pinched, I'd get a call to bail him out of jail. I'd save his ass and in return, he'd give up somebody doing something they shouldn't have been doing in the first place. With Jerry's inside connections in Little Italy, I was able to close out a lot of 61s (open complaints). I personally didn't like Jerry, but in terms of a CI, there was no one better. I hadn't heard from the junkie since I left the Fifth Squad and was now wondering the purpose for his call.

"Jimmy, what's up bro? It's your boy De-mat-te-oh."

"Who's this?"

I knew who it was, but I wanted the junkie to think I'd forgotten about him.

"Jimmy, it's your bro, Jerry, Jerry Dematteo. Don't tell me you forgot the guy that helped you clean up Mott Street?"

"Oh, Jerry, I thought you were dead. What rock have you been hiding under?"

"No, I've been around Jimmy. You know, busy trying to make a buck."

I was very concerned that the junkie had my direct line. I asked him how he was able to track me down. He gave me a bullshit answer about how he had a cousin working down in the police personnel department and that he had to call in a favor to get my number. Normally, I'd give out the dispatch number and have the calls transferred. This made it easier for me to screen incoming calls. Only a handful of people knew my direct line—I didn't like that he was now one of them.

I had no desire to small talk with Jerry, so I asked him what he needed. He told me he was having a problem with his old lady. She was screwing some wannabe wise guy in Brooklyn and he wanted some more information on the character. Without me asking, Jerry offered up one of the captains in the Genovese family for my help. He told me the capo was a big player when it came to heroin trafficking and that he could provide dates, times, and locations for major deliveries.

I knew Jerry a long time. Scum like that didn't change their habits. First, in all the years I used him as a CI, he never called unless he was arrested. Second, he never offered me anything in return. I always had to be the one to initiate what I wanted for helping him. And third, he never gave up "made guys." Now, after all these years, he's offering to set up a capo for some information on a guy that he could find out about on the streets. Something wasn't kosher, but maybe there was a big collar to be made here. I figured I had nothing to lose by playing along. If I was able to get some solid intelligence on this capo, maybe the department could uncover another "French Connection." I figured whatever information I'd get from Jerry I was going to put into an Intelligence Report and pass it along to the Narcotics Division. So, I decided to see where the rabbit hole would lead me.

I took down the guys information that Jerry wanted me to check on and then told him to meet me at McSorley's in the East Village the next evening at eight o'clock.

Without getting any information on Jerry's guy, I met him the next night at the bar. I figured before I lifted a finger, I wanted to find out more about the carrot he was dangling in front of my face.

I picked McSorley's because I had access to an office across the way on East Seventh Street that overlooked the bar's entrance. I wanted to see if he'd come alone, which he did. I arrived a few minutes after and sat down at the bar next to him.

"Hey Jim, good to see you," the strung-out junkie uttered.

I immediately asked who the capo was. Jerry started twitching as if he was being administered electric shock treatment.

"Jimmy, what about the guy I asked you to do a check on?"

"Asshole, the guys a mad guy, stay the fuck away. Now who's the capo?"

Of course, I was bluffing. I knew nothing about the guy banging his old-lady and had no intention in finding out anything until I knew if Jerry really had something to offer. What came out of his mouth next sent alarm bells off in my head.

"Jim, thanks, you always did look out for me. You know I always took care of you guys back in the day. I have some new snow tires in the car I want you to have for old time sake."

I came down here to see if I could get intelligence on a capo in the Genovese family and this guy is offering me snow tires in return for giving him classified information. I immediately smelled a rat. I grabbed Jerry by his jacket and told him to shove the tires up his ass. While grabbing him, I felt for a wire. Maybe I was paranoid, but I felt the entire thing was a setup. I didn't want anything more to do with the charade, and told him to either divulge the capo's entire heroin operation or fuck off. He began stuttering to a point that I couldn't understand a word he was saying. I'd seen enough. After grabbing him one more time to check for a wire, I got up and headed for the door. That's when the junkie pleaded with me one last time to take the tires. I'd seen that look of desperation in Jerry's eyes before.

Without exception, I'd always make the incogitant junkie sweat before I'd accept a deal from him. I was always able to make him give up more because I knew how desperate he was for another "fix" and/ or "get out of jail free card." Now, he had that same look of despair, but this time I wondered if there was someone behind the scenes squeezing Jerry to try and set me up.

There's a motto at McSorley's Old Ale House—"Be Good or Be Gone"—nothing good was becoming of this, so I was gone.

On the ride home, I played the initial phone call I had with Jerry and the meeting in the bar over and over again in my head. I assured myself that I did nothing wrong. Eventually, I convinced myself I was only being paranoid because of Lenny's visit.

Three weeks later, I was called into the lieutenant's office. Vinals instructed me that a notification came down for me to report to the Internal Affairs Division (IAD) the next day.

Vinals had been a straight shooter with me since my return. I could tell he was uncomfortable with having to give me the notification. I appreciated the commander's concern but I never had an issue with IAD before and truly believed I wasn't having one now.

The next morning, I reported to the Internal Affairs Office in Brooklyn. After signing in, I was told to have a seat in the waiting area. Finally, a sergeant in plain clothes came out and asked if I was Detective Simpson. I replied I was and started to get up. The sergeant abruptly told me to sit back down, telling me they weren't ready for me yet. As I sat back down, I could feel my blood rush from my head. I thought I was going to faint. I wasn't nervous and I had nothing to hide, so the dizzy spell came as a bit of a surprise to me.

I decided to take my Bible out and I began to read. The pocket-sized Bible was a wedding gift from Margaret. Since her passing, I had many difficult days and found that reading the Good Book put me at peace.

I was reading Proverbs when the sergeant opened the door again. He motioned for me to come in. As I started walking to the door, the sergeant put up his hand for me to stop and started talking to someone on the other side of the partition that I couldn't see. "No, we're not ready for you, sit back down," the sergeant barked while slamming the door in my face for a second time.

I returned to my seat and continued reading the Book of Wisdom—"The fear of the Lord is the beginning of knowledge." I reminded myself "fear of the Lord"—not the fear of men. The men on the other side of that door wanted me to be paralyzed from their fear, not God's. I put my trust in the Lord, and dismissed the powers of Satan.

I could see that I was to be treated like a dog. Over nineteen years of service, hundreds of arrests, dozens of medals, zero previous infractions, a detective shield—and now this is how the mighty brass would treat their lowly, blue pawn. I calmly sat back down and looked at my watch. I had been sitting like a child in timeout for the past hour and forty-five minutes. I once again opened my Bible and began to feed my soul with the word of God. The more I read, the stronger the Holy Spirit was with me. The delay tactic by the brass was used to make me weak, but it only helped strengthen my resolve.

A period of time had passed when the sergeant opened the door a third time. I was so entirely engrossed in reading the Bible that I hadn't noticed he was standing in the doorway waiting for me. After a brief moment, the sergeant raised his voice in annoyance and told me to get up. I continued to read while the sergeant became increasingly frustrated with my lack of obedience toward him. I blocked him out until I finished reading the final verse of Proverbs:

"Honor her for all that her hands have done, and
let her works bring her praise at the city gate."

God and Margaret were now by my side. I closed my Bible and entered the room.

Upon entering, I could immediately sense the hostility in the air. The three men, all in dress uniform with shiny brass plated insignias, peered over in my direction with hate in their eyes and judgment clearly already rendered. The fact that I did nothing wrong was irrelevant.

One of the pricks began reading off the charges I was facing: "Detective James Simpson shield number 2621 you are hereby accused of Bribery, Possession of Stolen Property, and Official Misconduct. Prior to these charges being forwarded to the Manhattan's District Attorney's Office, do you have anything to say in your defense?"

I truly believe if I hadn't read the Bible prior to my entering the room, I would've collapsed. But with my newfound strength I answered in a strong firm voice.

"I need not defend myself against these concocted charges. Would you be defensive if someone accused your mother of being a prostitute? Or would the accusation be so absurd that any response to such a charge would only tarnish an otherwise unblemished reputation?"

These little men hoped I'd panic. They tried to sweat me by making me wait in their oxygen-starved reception room for over two hours. They tried to intimidate me by leveling felonies charges. They tried to disgrace me, but all they did was disgrace themselves. I didn't give them the satisfaction of seeing me break down—but I did get to imply their mothers could possibly be a bunch of whores.

"Detective Simpson, you are hereby indefinitely suspended without pay," another of the pricks uttered. "Leave your gun and shield on the desk, you're dismissed."

As I walked out of the building, I felt a sense of calmness come over me.

Since Margaret's passing, I hadn't allowed myself to mourn. The governor's detail, and the laborious hours that went along with it, had become a welcoming distraction. I knew the drink had taken a hold of her long before she took her last breath, but what was I to do? I tried to help but I failed. Now it was me that needed help and I found it in the spirit of Margaret. I know it may sound crazy, but I felt her with me today. How else can I explain the reason for taking along the Bible she gave me or the calmness I now felt? I didn't know how things were going to turn out, but I did know I'd never be without that Bible or Margaret again.

It was obvious I was going to be in for a fight. I had God and Margaret with me, but since neither was licensed to practice law in the State of New York, it was time to get a good lawyer.

My first phone call was to my union representative, John Harper, of the Detective Endowment Association (DEA). I needed to know my rights and start planning a course of action. After contacting John, I set up a meeting in his office for the following day.

The next morning when I arrived, I was surprised to notice that several of the other DEA trustees where waiting for me in John's office. One by one, they shook my hand and stressed how this entire episode was nothing more than a political witch hunt. After five minutes of introductions and praise for my service to the department, we finally sat down to discuss my situation.

First to speak was John. The well-dressed, mid-thirty-year-old, was polished from head to toe. One thing I knew about these hybrid cops/union reps was that they were nothing more than politicians at the end of the day. However, without many options at my disposal, it was time for me to listen to what these guys had to say.

"Jim, I made some calls and pulled some strings to find out where this train wreck is heading. The DA's office has put the case in front of the Grand Jury already. So, forget this bullshit that they're just now going to forward these charges to the District Attorney's Office. They want you to think you have time—you don't. Unless I'm mistaken, an indictment will be handed down any day. I haven't seen or read a thing about your case but we both know if the DA wants to indict a ham sandwich, they can. I want you to be prepared because once the indictment is handed down, they're going to request you to surrender yourself."

"Arrested?" I asked in disbelief.

"Yes, Jim. But don't worry Joe (Joe Butler, another DEA trustee) and I have a strategy for that, but let's take this one step at a time. Do you have legal counsel yet?" I told him I hadn't. "Jim, the Union can provide counseling free of charge or you can get an attorney on your own. This is your life were talking about, your freedom, your reputation and your pension. You came here for advice and that's what we're going to give you. But at the end of the day, you'll be the one making all the decisions. Your first one is retaining counsel. Allow me to introduce Joe to go over some options."

Evidently, the trustees all went to the same expensive tailor. If not for the different size diamond-set in their pinky rings, it would've been difficult to differentiate one from the other.

"Jim, let me start by saying it's an honor to finally meet you, I just wish it was under better circumstances. Here's my advice in a nutshell. Don't discuss anything with anybody, including us. Except for your attorney, you're a mute. From the little info that's seeped out, my guess is you rubbed a few guys the wrong way down at the 'Palace' (One Police Plaza) and now they want to make your life a living hell. We have some good attorneys that work for us. But we're all in agreement, you need the best—and that's Will Serrano. He's expensive. Since he's not an official DEA attorney, there's going to be some out-of-pocket expense. If you go that route, we'll throw a 10-13 racket to raise some money for you. But, depending how long this gets dragged out, I want you to prepare yourself for a financial crunch."

I listened for about ten minutes to both trustees and then made the relatively easy decision to go with the high-priced attorney. I had some savings and thought I could always take a second mortgage out on the house, if necessary.

I asked Joe how to get in touch with the attorney. He smiled, got up from his seat, along with the other men in the office, and left. There was one man remaining.

The immaculately-dressed individual with the slick back grey hair had been quietly sitting in the corner, puffing away on a Cuban cigar. He introduced himself as Will Serrano. I could see that his shoes were more expensive than my entire wardrobe.

When I was in the Fifth dealing with a lot of wise guys on Mulberry Street, I noticed some of them tried to pretend they were a player by wearing expensive clothes. This wasn't the case with this guy; he was the real deal—a high priced, big shot, New York City attorney.

But something wasn't adding up. This guy was too big of a player to be sitting in an office listening to my case. The distinguished-looking gentlemen removed his thick, black-framed glasses and began to fill in some of the missing pieces to the puzzle.

"Jim, I'm here because a mutual friend of ours wants to make sure you're in good hands. Those guys (referring to the DEA representatives) don't know about our "friend," so let's keep it that way. Discretion is very important in matters like these. If my instincts are right, you'll never see a bill from my office. I apologize for sitting in unannounced with the trustees but I wanted to size you up without you knowing who I was."

"So, have you come to any conclusions?"

"Well, just two so far. It's safe to say you pissed somebody off and you're going to need my services. So, how about you start filling me in."

For the next half-hour, I went over everything with Will that I thought the District Attorney might have. He listened intently without interrupting me. I explained how Dematteo was a CI and how I used him on previous cases while assigned to the Fifth.

"His specialty was stolen cars, chop shops—that sort of stuff," I explained to Will. "Things were different back then. There was a lot of graft going on. I'd be lying if I told you I was an angel. But the entire Department was different pre-Knapp. It may sound like I'm trying to justify my actions but I truly did hate the corruption. The thing is without the graft, we wouldn't have had the money to pay off these confidential informants or to grease guys on the streets for solid leads. I didn't get rich but I did play the game. I can't see the DA having any solid proof of what went on back then, nor do I think they want to dig too deep because the guys that are inspectors and chiefs today were the ones doing most of the organized corruption as sergeants and lieutenants back then. There was a time you weren't allowed to bring an arrest into a stationhouse without greasing the desk officer $3. It was an ugly time."

Will was in agreement that it wasn't about past history. This was all about Dematteo and the four infamous snow tires.

Will looked at me, and for the first time, I could sense he wasn't comfortable.

"Jim, I have one question for you before we proceed. Is there any possibility your fingerprints could be on the Intel Card for this wise guy that Dematteo was asking you to lookup?"

I understood the question and why it had to be asked, but it still was like a punch in my gut to have to plead my innocence. The Intel Card was relevant because that's where we kept the dossiers on people of interest, including the made-guy Dematteo wanted me to find out about. Having my prints on the card would be like catching a mouse in a trap. It would mean I divulged classified department files without authorization—a felony.

I looked Will in the eye and told him there was a zero chance my prints would be on the card. Without being asked, I added that if they checked my car, they wouldn't find the snow tires in question there either.

Will gave me a rundown on what to expect next.

"Once the indictment is handed down, the DA's office is going to want you to surrender yourself for the arraignment. The press loves getting pictures during the 'perp walk' of the department's fallen angels. I'm going to do my best to make certain that doesn't happen. Getting in front of this fiasco is the second smartest thing you could've done—next to hiring me of course," the seasoned attorney said with a reassuring grin. "I'll pull some strings and find out exactly when this 'ham sandwich' of an indictment is going to come down. I'll call you a day before it does. There's a good chance after I call you with such news that you might have chest pains and will have to call for an ambulance. Instruct the ambulance to take you directly to Sloan Kettering Hospital on the Upper East Side. Our mutual friend is a big benefactor up there. You wouldn't believe how some doctors might misdiagnose something like agita for a massive heart attack. My guess is you'll be in the hospital for at least a week for tests. Start making whatever arrangements you have to for your two boys."

I looked over at Will a bit surprised in him knowing about Francis and Dean.

"Jim, I didn't know who you were three hours ago, but I do my homework fast because the last thing I ever want is to be surprised. Now, you have your homework assignment. I'll be in touch. Oh, one last thing, I can keep your 'perp walk' off the six o'clock news, but the newspapers are still going to have a field day with you. Prepare yourself mentally for a lot of negative press. It will get ugly."

The next few days were torture. Waiting for the indictment to be handed down, waiting for Will's phone call, waiting to make the ambulance call, waiting, waiting, waiting.

Without any other options, I sent the boys to my sister Gwen's house in Bensonhurst. After Margaret passed, my Pollyanna sibling was always offering to help. But with five kids of her own, I previously didn't have the heart to take her up on her offer. Typical of my sister, she was thanking me when I dropped the boys off. I gave her a quick synopsis of what was going on and asked her to keep the television off and the newspapers out of the house when the story broke. I explained to her about my upcoming trip to Sloan Kettering—she was the last person I wanted worrying unnecessarily. I gave her a big hug, told her she was my angel, and headed back home to wait.

The next night, around midnight, my phone rang—it was Will.

"Jim, I wanted to let you know you should be taking better care of yourself. Your health is very important," and then he hung up.

At that very second, I really thought my heart was going to come out of my chest. Not since I was in Korea getting shot at on Pork Chop Hill was I this scared. That was the signal, no more waiting. It was time for me to call the ambulance.

When the paramedics arrived, they took my blood pressure—it was through the roof. I didn't need to act too much because they really thought I was having a coronary.

At the emergency room, I was met by Doctor Theodore Chesley. The burly, African-American physician was in his late-forties and looked like he could be the starting middle linebacker for the New York Giants. I had the impression my visit wasn't a surprise to the soft-spoken, southern doctor.

He told me not to worry about a thing and if I should need anything, all I had to do was ask.

Without any names being mentioned, I had a fairly good idea who my guardian angel was. I never asked and was never told, but I knew my former boss, the governor, and possibly more directly, his chief of staff Chuck Nagel, were pulling the strings on my behalf.

The next morning, Doctor Chesley checked on me. The cordial South Carolinian asked if my accommodations were satisfactory. With a beautiful view of the East River and Roosevelt Island in the backdrop, I told the good Doctor that it was the nicest hotel I ever stayed at. After a mutual chuckle, he again assured me that I was in good hands and that he'd be running more tests throughout the day.

I thought to myself, "More tests?" I'm a heavy sleeper but I'm pretty certain nobody came in during the night to take any tests. However, under the circumstances, I was more than happy to go along with the charade. I was well aware that at some point over the next few days, I would be arrested and that was a charade I wasn't looking forward to.

Later that afternoon, Will called me to tell me it was official; I was indicted. He gave little instruction except to tell me to take my time recovering. Although I was anxious to know what the next step would be after I was released from the hospital, I knew Will would spell things out for me when the time was right.

The next day, I had all the local newspapers brought up to my room. Fortunately, I wasn't on the front page of any of the papers, but page three or four wasn't exactly hidden from public view. The headlines served their purpose in smearing my reputation: "Hero Cop Disgraced"; "Medal of Honor Cop Caught Taking Bribes"; "Hero to Zero"; and my least favorite, compliments of the Daily News: "Fallen Hero."

I thought to myself they could've used the same headline if I was killed the day of the assassination attempt at the Plaza. For a moment, I allowed myself the self-pity of questioning whether or not I would've been better off if I had been killed. As quickly as the thought came into my head, I could hear Margaret's voice screaming, "Fight these bastards."

I was strategically released from the hospital a week later on a Saturday morning. According to Will, there'd be less media and brass around. Then my attorney arranged for me to turn myself in for the purpose of processing the arrest, with the arraignment to follow.

I knew the officer down at central booking from when I was there processing my own collars over the years. I could tell the old-timer wasn't comfortable with the assignment of having to print a fellow officer. I reassured him he was only doing his job and not to worry.

Will was spot on about the media. The story was nearly a week old and losing steam. Either nobody knew about the booking or the local news didn't want to waste a crew on a Saturday morning to catch a suspended detective doing a "perp walk".

At arraignment, the judge went through the motions of reading the charges and recording my plea: "Not guilty."

The assistant district attorney representing the state requested a $200,000 bond for my release. Before Will could say a word, the judge asked the ADA on what grounds he was making for such a steep bond.

It was clear that the first year ADA was nothing more than a puppet for the DA's office and only repeated what he was instructed to do by the puppet masters.

After an awkward thirty-second stuttering performance by the ADA, the judge finally cut him off and proceeded to give him an earful.

"Young man," the Honorable Jerome Friedman began, "I haven't a clue what you're trying to say or trying to accomplish. You just had a twice-convicted felon arraigned on armed robbery, criminal possession of a firearm, and assault with a deadly weapon and you requested I set bail at $50,000. Now, a highly-decorated officer stands in this courtroom with no priors, no violent acts, and from all accounts is a pillar in his community, but you feel compelled to ask for four times as much security to ensure his return to court. If I didn't know better, I'd think someone in the DA's office has an ax to grind with Detective Simpson. Counsel, your request is denied and Mr. Serrano save your breath, your client is ROR (released on his own recognizance)."

"Thank you, Your Honor," Will replied to the feisty Judge.

Will was pleased in the way the judge handled the situation. However, he was less than pleased that the DA's office wanted my testicles in a vice without any evidence.

"Somebody at One Police Plaza called in a lot of favors to the DA's office for that $200,000 stunt back there," the legal eagle barked as we walked down the stairs of the courthouse. "I love these cowards that hide behind a rookie ADA to do their dirty work. They won't have that luxury at trial—no hiding behind any curtains then."

The next step was going to be the "discovery period." To no surprise, the DA's office didn't introduce the Intel Card since it would've simply been a card without my fingerprints on it. However, they did produce copies of audio tapes that Dematteo made during our phone conversation, as well as the meeting at McSorley's. Turns out the bastard did have a wire on him that night.

Will agreed there was nothing in the phone conversation that was incriminating and the McSorley's audio was simply inaudible.

However, the State's "expert witness" put together a transcript of what he was able to decipher from the tape.

Will was incredulous after reading the transcript.

"This would be funny if not for the fact that this is your life we're talking about. I can't make out one word on the audio for two minutes but the State's expert witness has you thanking Dematteo for the tires and you telling him to put them in the trunk of your car. This is ridiculous. Someone has to answer for this crap."

I knew what was said that night, so nobody wanted those tapes to be more crystal clear than me. I didn't want to be at the mercy of some juror saying, "Yea, I can hear the cop thanking the guy for the tires—he's guilty."

The trial was set for April 24, 1973. It's funny how in life some dates repeat themselves. It was exactly the third anniversary of the assassination attempt at the Plaza. I was praying that it was a good omen. The other significance of the date was that it left me exactly a month shy of being eligible for retirement. However, my first hurdle prior to fighting for my pension, was fighting for my freedom.

Will told me he was going to make a motion to the judge to have the charges dismissed. He explained that in all likelihood it would be denied, since most judges rarely wanted to dismiss charges this far into the proceedings. It looked like the next step would be to select a jury.

At the beginning of the trial, Will made his motion for dismissal to the honorable Stephanie Nasser. The judge looked like my fifth-grade teacher from St. Anselm's, Sister Katherine. The Sister loved using the ruler on me. I truly believe she hated kids, or at least me. Now my fate lay in the hands of an equally mean-looking woman that resembled someone who just sucked on a lemon. I didn't like it. I prayed to Margaret to keep me strong in my time of need.

The judge glanced over at the District Attorney's table and asked the ADA if there was any evidence besides the audio tape that implicated the Defendant of said charges.

A more seasoned assistant district attorney than there was at the arraignment told the judge that the transcript by the State's expert witness made it clear exactly what had transpired between the Defendant and the State's witness: Dematteo.

Without looking down, Will scribbled the words, "This is good" on his legal pad and tilted it so I could see what he wrote. For the next few minutes, the judge questioned the ADA more about the inaudible tape. Will then wrote on the pad the words, *"Nolle prosequi."*

It had been a long time since I learned Latin in Sunday school, and now I wished I had paid more attention.

Will leaned over and whispered in my ear, "She's giving him the chance to voluntarily withdraw the charges before she does it herself. *Nolle prosequi*—be unwilling to pursue."

I would learn afterwards that the bench frowns upon having to dismiss charges, so they have little, subtle, and sometimes not so subtle signals to the prosecutor in order to get them to drop the charges before the court does. However, the DA's office had no intention of withdrawing the case under any circumstances. The judge went back and forth with the ADA in hope he'd do the right thing, but to no avail. Finally, she came down with the hammer, literally, as well as figuratively.

"I am honoring the request by the Defense to have all charges dismissed," said the Honorable Stephanie Nasser. "The Manhattan District Attorney's Office has lost sight of their responsibility to the public by bringing this suit into my courtroom. The evidence, or should I say, lack of evidence in this case is disturbing. Anyone who can call themselves an 'Audio Decipher Expert' after submitting a transcript that borders somewhere between fiction and criminally negligent, should have whatever license they might give these quacks revoked. As for you, Detective Simpson, I hope you can put back together whatever pieces that were torn apart from you by this affair. I'm not the one in this courtroom that owes you an apology, so you won't get one from me. You're free to go."

I repeated to myself her last set of words, "You're free to go." I don't think I ever heard a more powerful set of words in all my life. I wanted to run up to the bench and kiss the old-bag, but instead I hugged Will.

I couldn't help but notice Will was reserved in his reaction to the dismissal. His pensive demeanor had me wondering what I was missing, so I asked.

After closing his briefcase and removing his glasses, the legal eagle turned to me and said in a dejected voice, "I've seen a lot of nonsense in my day but this kind of thing shouldn't happen in a country that prides itself on rule of law. Jim, this should've never seen the inside of a courtroom."

For the moment, I was too elated to appreciate what Will was trying to say to me. It didn't take much for Will to shake me back to reality.

"It was never about getting a conviction for these scumbags. It was about settling a score. Do you think the press will run a story about this on page three tomorrow? All they wanted was two things: to humiliate you and go after your pension. We still have one more round to go with these bastards. Unfortunately for us, Jim, the next courtroom we'll be in will have kangaroos jumping around in it."

Will was referring to the NYPD's Department Trial down at One Police Plaza. In their courtroom, there'd be no principles of law and a complete disregard for true justice. It was a court filled with perversion, with the brass leading the way.

The five high-ranking Police Department officials that would hear my case at the trial would decide if I get to retire with a pension or be terminated, forfeiting all benefits. Will might be a legal eagle in criminal court, but this was completely different. The brass wanted my blood and now I was going into their den looking for justice. It was going to take a miracle.

Normally, after the charges are thrown out of the criminal trial, an officer would be giving the courtesy of being reinstated back to limited duty while awaiting the department trial. However, there'd be no courtesy, professional or otherwise, extended to this pawn.

Thanks to the white-hair pricks down at The Palace, I continued to remain suspended without pay until the department trial.

Soon after the criminal case was thrown out, I was given a date for the following month to report to One Police Plaza. In the notification, it read the charges and specifications I'd be facing. I realized Will was right, they were going after my pension—it was that simple.

The charges were the following:

1. official misconduct of an officer
2. unauthorized use of a department confidential informant
3. failure to properly notify the commanding officer of an ongoing investigation
4. insubordination

Charge number 1, Official Misconduct, was a "catch-all" that meant whatever the hell the brass wanted it to mean. Charges number 3 and number 4 weren't normally strong enough to warrant a dismissal. If I were found guilty on any of those three counts I'd be looking at a loss of vacation days—no big deal and my pension would be secured. The big charge that carried the pension death penalty was number 2—"Unauthorized use of a Department Confidential Informant."

After the French Connection case, the department came down with very strict guidelines regarding narcotics and Confidential Informants.

The French Connection was a famous case in the late '60s about a couple of NYPD detectives that stumbled upon a big heroin trafficking operation. The case, made famous by the 1971 movie by the same name starring Gene Hackman, exposed the department's lack of accountability when dealing with informants and evidence. In typical NYPD brass fashion, the department overreacted and now all procedures regarding CIs were to go through the chain of command. The brass was always good at making new policy after the fact, never before. The new policy covered the brass's ass but wasn't worth a nickel in the real, fast-paced world of intelligence gathering.

There was an ironic footnote to the French Connection case that hadn't been divulged in the movie. After the heroin was properly marked and held into evidence, it was secured at none other than One Police Plaza. After a year, The Palace had a major rodent infestation problem on their hands. It turned out the heroin was switched by somebody on the inside with flour. The rats were eating all the flour and the several million dollars of heroin had disappeared. My guess is the heroin was taken by a couple of rats but the kind that wore brass on their collar. Funny how that story never made it in the newspapers.

The instructions by Will were clear. "Don't antagonize these guys. They are going to say things to embarrass you and imply you're no better than a child molester. Don't take the bait—be cool. At the end of the day, if we're lucky, it's going to come down to a compromise. Remember, it's all about saving your pension. Jim, are we clear?"

I agreed. I knew I couldn't afford to lose my cool regardless of what was said. I understood the situation I put myself in and resided in the fact that things might go against me. Losing the pension and benefits that went along with it would be a big blow, but I couldn't allow the rest of my life to be defined by it. I felt somehow, someway, Margaret would guide me through the gauntlet.

On the day of the department trial, I was almost late. I couldn't sleep the night before and decided to take a couple of sleeping pills. Once I did fall asleep, I had a hell of a time waking up. Now I walked into One Police Plaza like a zombie. Will was in the lobby waiting for me and was concerned about my arrival time. I explained to him what had happened and he told me not to worry. He grabbed a pair of sunglasses from his assistant and instructed me not to take the glasses off until after the trial.

"We're going to use this to our advantage," Will told me. "Just remember my instructions—be cool."

We reported upstairs to the Trial Room. Unlike my Internal Affairs marathon, this time I was called in immediately.

I sat at the desk with Will across from the elevated panel. One of the chiefs opened the hearing by announcing the docket number to the Court Reporter. He then instructed Will to have his name and mine put into the record. After the departmental charges against me were read off, Will immediately requested they be dismissed. I wouldn't be so lucky this time.

One of the members of the panel immediately denied the request and then proceeded to do a character assassination on me.

"Your client is a disgrace to this department," the inspector said in an incredulous tone. "Your fancy lawyer tricks aren't going to work in this courtroom. By the way, are the lights too bright for your client?"

This gave Will the opportunity to explain to the panel that I was hospitalized due to the stress of the situation. He further explained how I was currently under heavy medication and the lights affected my eyes, hence the reason for the use of sunglasses.

The inspector was not sympathetic.

"Any stress your client is experiencing is because of actions that he brought upon himself. This department is in the process of weeding out corrupt cops and their wild west tactics. Your client is the lowest form of scum there is and I don't feel comfortable allowing him to be part of the greatest police department in the world."

It's interesting how some words can stoke one's emotions. For the entire time the inspector was talking, I wasn't paying much attention. I heard the charges and him referring to me as a disgrace but they were just words and I wasn't overly concerned with his rhetoric. After all, I knew I had to play things "cool." Unlike the criminal proceedings, I was now presumed guilty, not innocent, of the charges against me. The onus was on me to prove my innocence. Losing my temper would seal my fate. I had to eat shit and the brass pricks in front of me knew it. But being referred to as "scum" definitely grabbed my attention.

I looked up at the dais to see which one of these little pricks was using me as a piñata. I kept on looking at the guy. I knew I had seen him before but I couldn't place where. For two minutes, I stared at the inspector from behind my dark-tinted glasses asking myself how the hell I knew this guy. I hadn't realized it at first, but the members of the panel had name plates erected in front of them on the dais. As I looked closely, I noticed the name—Inspector Jonathon Anderson.

I couldn't believe the person calling me a "disgrace" and "scum" was none other than "Grease Me Up Johnny" from the bathhouse. It had been over fifteen years, and he was wearing more clothes, but that was definitely the scumbag.

I leaned forward in my chair and took off the sunglasses. Anderson was in mid-sentence when I interrupted him.

"I know you. Oh yeah, I know who you are. You're the greased-up scumbag that I pulled out of a bathhouse in the West Village back in the '50s."

I don't know who was more upset—Anderson or Will. Will was grabbing my arm to pull me back in my seat, while Anderson started yelling, "Stop the recording, stop the recording." One of the other brass members on the panel yelled to have the room cleared.

The next thing I knew, Will and I were in the hallway with him yelling at me, "Can you tell me what the hell that was all about?"

I calmly explained to Will that the guy referring to me as "scum" was someone I once discreetly escorted out of a gay bathhouse in the Village while I was assigned to Public Morals.

Will was furious with me. "You know you're finished," he said. "These guys aren't going to let you get away with that stunt. Goodbye pension!"

I explained to Will that my pension was gone the second I answered the phone call from Dematteo. The game was fixed and I was the mark. My attitude at that point was to let them do whatever it was they were going to do. But I wasn't about to sit there and be called "scum" from a pedophile that enjoyed having young boys rub oil up his ass.

While I was explaining things to Will, one of the clerks came out from the Trial Room and requested Will to come back in… alone.

As I sat on a bench outside the room, I prayed to Margaret. Although my actions were probably ill-advised, I think she got a laugh out of me turning things on the inspector. She wasn't much for authority figures. She'd tell me stories about how the occupying British soldiers would harass the locals in her hometown of Crossmaglen, in Northern Ireland. She didn't hide her dislike for the Crown and reveled in any embarrassment that came its way. She told me how her father would think of different ways to insult the soldiers to their face without them realizing it. Anytime he'd see a British soldier on a horse, he'd look back and forth at the horse and then the soldier until he had the soldier's attention. When asked what he was doing, he'd reply in his thick Irish brogue, "I can't determine who looks more handsome today, you or your horse." After a while, the soldiers caught on to young Frank's jokes and would serve him up some of their own humor in the shape of a billy club.

I was married to Margaret for sixteen years before God took her from me. I fell for the blue-eyed beauty the moment I laid eyes on her at the Emerald Society dance.

She wore red lipstick, the same fiery color as her hair, and a sky-blue dress that matched her sparkling eyes. I thought for sure I was looking at a movie star. I asked my friend Brendan who the looker was. He warned me to stay away from red heads. "Dangerous and fiery," he put it. It was too late. Like a moth to a flame, I walked over and introduced myself.

When the dance came to an end, I asked Margaret if she'd like to join me for a milkshake. She agreed and I took her to Tiffany's, a twenty-four-hour diner in Bay Ridge. We talked at the booth table for hours. I remember thinking to myself, "This girl is actually sitting here with me—how lucky am I?"

When we left the diner, it had to be about three in the morning. Not wanting the magical night to end, I asked if she'd like to go for a walk down by the water. She once again agreed to my request. It was there, along the Atlantic Ocean, I kissed Margaret for the first time. After that, I was hopelessly in love.

Regardless of what happened here today, I was going to walk out of this hellhole of a building a free man. It was only a few weeks ago I was in criminal court fighting for my freedom, now I'm only fighting for money. After putting things in perspective, I wasn't overly concerned regarding my fate in the NYPD.

Will walked out of the Trial Room and told me we needed to talk, fast. He explained to me that they had an offer on the table but it needed my approval. The offer was to plead guilty of all charges. The punishment are the following:

1. loss of all vacation time on the books
2. demoted to the rank of police officer
3. loss of all privileges due a Medal of Honor recipient.

The deal meant my pension was safe. It was the miracle Will and I were looking for. I would remain suspended until the following Monday, at which time I'd be processed out of the NYPD.

I told Will to get back in there before they changed their minds. As he went to walk back in, he turned and said to me, "Jim, I think your little outburst shook up the board and saved your pension. I get the feeling none of them want you back in there. I think they're afraid of what you might have on the rest of them."

After Will went back in to accept the deal, I started to laugh. The thing that had me laughing the hardest was the denial of privileges as a Medal of Honor recipient. The only privilege I had coming to me was an inspector's funeral.

Wow! They really didn't want me getting that funeral!

While sitting on the bench, I said a prayer to God and thanked him for his blessing. I then set my attention on Margaret.

I made the mistake of trying to forget about Margaret after she passed. The only time I'd think of her was when she popped into my head. It simply hurt too much. But I realized she was still with me and that I shouldn't fight it, but rather embrace it.

While sitting there on the hard-oak bench, I began to talk to Margaret as if she was right next to me.

"I miss you, my love. I'd give anything to hold you one more time. The boys are getting bigger. They pray to you every night before they go to sleep. Francis has a picture of you on his nightstand, while Dean keeps a small photo of the two of you in his little leather wallet.

"I wanted to thank you for guiding me through this ordeal. You've always been the best part of me and although you're not physically here with me anymore, my heart will always be with you."

CHAPTER 5

Summer Winds

Choose a job you love, and you will never
have to work a day in your life.

—Confucius

After the squad's dismissal from the Carnival, I decided to make a quick pit stop home. The dumpster had left a lingering, unpleasant scent on me. So prior to meeting up with the gang at the pub, I thought it might be a good idea to get cleaned-up.

When I arrived home, Dad was on the back porch having a beer with Father Gerald. The two men seemed quite content as they sat anchored in their chairs watching the traffic cross over the Verrazano. Despite neither one looking like they wanted to extricate themselves from their current position, I asked if the two would like to join me at Pipin's Pub for a cocktail. I wanted very much to tell them about my day and, at the same time, introduce them to my squad. However, I wanted to do so in the company of the guys and a pint of Guinness. To my surprise, they agreed but on one condition from Father Gerald—I took a bath first.

"You smell like the back end of a donkey's ass," the brutally honest priest barked.

I thanked him for his compliment and then left the two to get back to their reclining.

The elderly Father Gerald had been a good friend to the family over the years. The Pastor was from the same county as mother's family in Northern Ireland—Crossmaglen.

Dad and Father Gerald had always been close, but after my mom's passing they were virtually inseparable. As for me, my relationship with the pastor stemmed back to my grade school days when the man of the cloth handpicked me to be his alter boy. My biggest responsibilities were to make certain the cantor was always filled and to hold the oversized Bible steady during his sermon. He'd tell me if I could only handle one of the two tasks that it was a mere inconvenience if I couldn't keep the Bible from moving, but a sin if the cantor wasn't filled with wine.

In and out of the church, the pastor was known for having a sharp wit and a tongue that made even his fellow Irishmen blush. When Father Gerald drank, two things occurred: his cheeks became as bright as Rudolph's nose and his brogue became as thick as the early morning fog over Dundalk Road. However, there was one characteristic that never wavered when it came to Father Gerald—the dedication to his flock.

As far as I knew, Pipin's Pub was just another gin mill in a neighborhood filled with such places. There were so many watering holes in Bay Ridge that many referred to the small community as Bar Ridge.

When I arrived, I could see several of the guys were already there. I overheard the bartender telling Ryen he was just about to close due to most of his patrons being away for the holiday weekend. Ryen reassured the Santa Clause looking bar keep that more were on the way and would most definitely be thirsty.

Ryen spotted me and immediately waved me over. He introduced me to the bartender, his cousin Eamon. He told his cousin that I was the reason he was retiring.

"See here, Eamon, this young, innocent-looking kid is going to be chief of the department some day and I'll be damned if I have to salute his baby-wiped ass," Ryen said with a wry smile. "So, I'm getting out before he starts telling me what to do."

I assured the sergeant that it was highly unlikely I'd ever be in a position to tell him what to do, whether he stayed on or not.

I settled into a bar stool next to my boss and ordered a pint from the cheerful barkeep. Ryen slapped me on the back and told me how proud he was of me for my actions earlier. He then decided to give me some unsolicited advice.

"You're smart, Dean. I don't just mean book smart, I mean you have the instincts to do whatever you want on this job. You'll go up in rank but find the right details to do it in. Probably the greatest gift this job ever gave me was all the different and exciting assignments I was afforded. I worked undercover for three years in narcotics to get my gold shield. After making detective I went to the Eighteenth Squad, made a few friends, and from there went to the Anti-Terrorist Task Force. Working with the FBI boys taught me a lot about being a good investigator. When I made sergeant, the merry-go-round started all over again. Every three or four years, I was reinvigorating my career while still being a part of the NYPD. A smart guy like yourself can right your own ticket." Ryen paused for a bit, and then with a serious tone to his voice said, "If there are only two things you remember from your time here at the Third Division, let it be this: don't work for the job—let the job work for you. Whether it's picking a sweet detail to go to everyday or finishing school on the jobs time, use the job to your benefit. The second thing is to remember it's better to be tried by twelve then carried by six. Don't ever hesitate to pull that fucking trigger if you think you or your partner is in danger. I've gone to more police funerals than any individual should have to. I always wondered how many of those poor boys hesitated because of fear of an indictment hanging over their head. Take your chances with the twelve jurors because it's better than the alternative—six pallbearers."

I sensed Ryen wished he could bottle-up all his knowledge and experience and give it to me. It must've been frustrating for him not to be able to pass along all the wisdom he'd accumulated over the years. I hadn't thought about it much, but I now understood why he chose this detail to be his last—he wanted so desperately to pass on as much as he could to the next generation before he left.

I appreciated Ryen taking the time to talk with me and pass along the advice. However, I felt less comfortable about his words of praise toward me. I never was at ease about the deception regarding my first arrest and the help I received. I knew the processing of that arrest was why the bosses were so impressed with me. I further knew that I was a fraud. If not for Francis and Chris, I'd probably still be in the Arrest Processing Room trying to figure out all the paper work. I decided to come clean with Ryen.

"Boss, I have to confess something. The day I made my first arrest, I lied to you about doing everything myself. My brother and his partner did all the work. All I did was pay for lunch."

Ryen's reaction to my confession was not what I expected.

"No shit," he said, while breaking out into a hearty laugh to the point that I could barely understand him.

After regaining his composure, he told me of his confession. "I already knew you had help."

Ryen went on to explain that it would've been impossible for a seasoned veteran to process the arrest that quickly, not to mention a rookie.

"I knew something wasn't kosher, so after I finished with you I went back to the log to see who was in the stationhouse. I found out your brother and his partner happened to be in the command the same time you were. I put two and two together and came up with the missing link to your miracle. The only thing I couldn't figure out was why the perp went along with it. Afterwards, I came up with the idea to make you our Arrest Processing Officer, thinking you'd come clean—but you never did. I heard about your fingerprint expedition on the first day you were assigned to the office and the parade of Big Mac's that followed. We had a pool to see how long it would take for you to break. Marks thought you'd throw in the towel on day one, Gooden and Denny said one and two weeks respectively and I took the over. No one was happier than me to see you succeed—plus, I made thirty bucks."

"I bought him a hot dog," I told Ryen. "That's why he didn't tell you who actually printed him."

"Mystery solved. About tonight, Gooden is putting you in for a commendation. Congratulations!"

Before I could respond, I heard Eamon yell, "Everyone behave, the Church is in the house!"

I knew that could only mean one thing—Father Gerald had arrived with Dad.

"Eamon, get off your lard ass and start pouring me something non-lethal, you sinner you," Father Gerald said in a spirited voice.

It was apparent from the banter that Father Gerard was no stranger to the pub or the barkeep.

When Father Gerald and Dad approached, I stood up from my stool and introduced them to Ryen. One problem. I didn't know the sergeant's first name and hesitated on the intro. Ryen caught my hesitation and finished the introduction, "Gentlemen, I'm Bob, Bob Ryen."

"You would've been proud of your son tonight," my boss told Dad.

Ryen discussed the events of the evening and then had me take over the story from when the grandmother came out of her apartment.

"What did she say to you?" Ryen asked.

"Well, after she finished yelling at the kids on the rooftops, she turned her attention to me, asking if I was stupid brave or stupid crazy. When I started to laugh at the way the woman was talking to me, she concluded that I was simply just stupid."

When I finished, I expected Dad and Father Gerald to be laughing. Instead, they both had a worrisome look on their face. That's when I realized things could've gone far worse if not for the grace of God.

While I was telling my tale, I could see more guys from the squad arriving. I took Father Gerald with me to introduce him to some of my friends, leaving Ryen and Dad some time to talk "old school."

Father Gerald held court while the rest of us gathered around him. He blessed many of the officers' shields and told them his service was free of charge but he would accept donations in the form of "liquid currency."

The priest was never one lost for words or a good yarn. Tonight, he decided to tell the guys of my days as an altar boy.

"Nice boy, but couldn't keep the Book steady to save his ass," the animated priest began. "Dean, do you remember the time you filled in for me during confessionals?"

Of course, that never happened but who was I to let the facts get in the way of a good story, so I just grinned and remained silent.

"Oh, what an embarrassing day that was for me," the devilish priest quipped. "I was a bit under the weather after a night of refreshments, if you could imagine, and I was the only priest available to listen to confessions that day. After a grueling morning of listening to one sinner after another, as you could imagine, my bladder could hold no more. So, I called over this young whippersnapper (as he pointed in my direction) and had Mr. Simpson fill in for a few minutes. I told Dean they'd never see his face and to just mumble his voice a bit. I showed the young lad on my side of the confessional booth the list of sins and the proper penance to be doled out for each. If the person confessed to using the Lords name in vain, all Dean had to do was look at the list and it would instruct him how many Hail Mary's and Our Father's the sinner would have to pray in order to receive absolution. All the garden variety sins were listed to help the boy. Without me realizing it at the time, the next person in the confessional line was Lucy Gustello. If I knew the troubled young lady was next, I would've never let the little tyro take over. See, Lucy was a fine Catholic girl, but she had trouble keeping her legs crossed—if you could imagine. So, Lucy goes into the confessional and my poor blessed, virgin ear altar boy listens to things no good, ten-year-old Catholic boy should ever have to listen to. She speaks of fornication, lust, and words the simpleminded boy just couldn't understand. She then told him about her biggest sin; her enjoyment in performing oral sex. Dean looked up at the board to see what he was to give out for such a sin, but nothing was found. In a complete state of panic, the poor lad opened the confessional door to see if there was anyone near he could seek help from. To Dean's relief, another altar boy named Johnny came walking by. Dean grabbed the seasoned altar boy by his vestment and asked him what Father Gerald usually gave out for oral sex. The less discreet Johnny responded back, 'He usually gave me milk and cookies.' Could you imagine? I never should've left little Dino in that predicament, and as for Johnny, I'd be damned if I ever gave that blabber mouth milk and cookies again."

The guys let out a roar of laughter. Then Father Gerald inquired why he had an empty glass in his hand.

"Dean," he said, "You didn't tell me I'd be drinking amongst Protestants tonight—such deep pockets and such short arms."

His not so subtle hint for someone to buy him a drink didn't go on deaf ears. Everyone wanted to buy the priest a cocktail and listen to more of his anecdotes.

The day had been bizarre to say the least. Several hours prior, I had been watching half-naked women dancing in the West Indian Day parade, then I jumped into a dumpster in order to dodge bullets, and now I'm in a bar with my coworkers, my priest, and my dad. I know it's difficult to predict the events of any given day. However, it's safe to say when I woke up this morning, none of "these things" were on my radar.

At one moment during the night, I stepped back and took in the positive energy of the Pub. I knew this was a special evening. I gave praise to the Lord for letting me be a part of it and finished the prayer by thanking Him for looking over me earlier. It was at that moment and in this place, everything was seemingly perfect.

While I glanced over the watering hole, a song I never heard of before came over the juke box. As I listened to the lyrics, I was put into a trance like state. I walked over to see which artist was singing these heavenly words. It was the crooner Frank Sinatra, and the song was "Summer Winds." I felt goose bumps as I stood there listening.

> The summer wind came blowin' in from across the sea
> It lingered there, to touch your hair and walk with me

> All summer long we sang a song and then we
> strolled that golden sand
> Two sweethearts and the summer wind
> Like painted kites, those days and nights they
> went flyin' by
> The world was new beneath a blue umbrella sky…

Without realizing it, I fell in love that summer. My sweetheart was the job and the "golden sand we strolled" was Times Square. And, "like those painted kites," it had become clear to me that time was indeed "flyin' by."

As I listened to the song and looked around the bar at Dad, Father Gerald, Eddie, Mike, Ryen, and the rest of the gang, I sensed this was a special moment with special people. If there was ever a moment I could freeze in time, this was it.

No sooner had the song finished did the mood drastically change. Gooden came walking in the door and proceeded to give me hug. He told me the good news first. He was putting me in for a Commendation Medal. Then he told me why he was late. He'd gone back to the command to start the paperwork requesting the immediate dismissal of Sharlene. The sergeant's ecstatic mood didn't match with what he had just told me, so I asked him to repeat what he just said. With even more joy and enthusiasm, he reiterated that he put in the formal request to have Sharlene terminated.

Being that Sharlene was still in her probation period, like the rest of us rookies, virtually any reasonable grounds for dismissal by a supervisory official would be granted. The fact that she put herself, Gooden and me in harm's way left little doubt regarding her fate.

I went from such a euphoric feeling a moment earlier to feeling as though I was just punched in the stomach.

From what Ryen previously told me, I already knew there was a good chance Sharlene wasn't going to make it into the division. However, since I was directly involved in the incident that was used as the catalyst for her dismissal, I was troubled greatly by the news. Equally disturbing to me was the joy Gooden was now displaying over it.

Over the past several months, Sharlene and I worked countless times together, whether it was in the squad car, parades, or on the deuce. I'll never forget the first day we worked together. She helped me write my first summons and I helped her get her first collar.

I understood that it was within Gooden's scope of duty to request Sharlene to be fired, but I couldn't help but wonder if things would've been different if she was considered part of the group. Instead, the bosses waited, and when the time was right, acted on a decision that had been made long before this evening's incident. Maybe it wasn't the sergeants' job to instill self-esteem and confidence, but no one, including me, went out of their way to help Sharlene.

The morning Mike lost his gun and shield, I heard all the sergeants drove out to Long Island to assist him in scouring the expressway for his lost bag. I respected the bosses efforts because they were trying to help one of their own. The same couldn't be said when it came to Sharlene.

No longer in a festive mood, I discreetly pulled Dad to the side and informed him I was leaving. The roller coaster day was officially over.

Newbies

It was now mid-October, and with the latest Academy class graduating the day before, everyone in the squad was anxiously awaiting the arrival of the new rookies.

The group of twenty fresh officers started to arrive one-by-one for their orientation. Like sheep, they followed the signs directing them to the room where I reported three months earlier. I noticed there were more females in the group this time—eight out of the twenty. I figured Sergeant Marks would be happy with those numbers.

At muster, away from the newbie's, Ryen instructed the group to lend a helping hand to the recent additions to our squad. That seemed to be the purpose of the new, overlapping policy regarding the classes. Ordinarily, when a class graduated, they would replace the members in the division, allowing them to move onto their permanent assignments. Instead, with the new policy in place, the green rookies would be assigned with officers that now had a few months experience under their belts. In a way, Sharlene indirectly started the program three months earlier when she was held back, giving me the opportunity to ask her for assistance on my second day on the street.

The following day, having finished their orientation, the rookies were now officially part of our squad. At muster, Sergeant Denny reemphasized what Ryen told us regarding the importance in helping one another. Denny further explained Eddie's and my position in case someone needed extra assistance regarding an arrest or vouchering of property. The sergeant finished by giving out our assignments and dismissing the squad.

I was assigned to the Deuce with one of the newbies, Officer Anthony Dwyer. The barrel-chested officer stood six-foot-two and weighed somewhere north of two hundred pounds. At first glance, the newbie was an intimidating figure with his size an obvious strength, but once he smiled, it was easy to see the baby-faced rookie was nothing more than a gentle giant.

As the two of us made our way to our foot post, I heard someone behind us say, "If you really want to learn something today, that's the guy to watch."

Intended for me to hear, the kind words were coming from Eddie. He was talking with one of the new officers, Sheldon Kastor. When I turned, I told Eddie I was surprised to see him, since normally one of us would be back at the stationhouse. He explained that because of all the new rookies, the bosses wanted everyone paired off.

I could tell the new guy I was assigned with couldn't wait to get started. Like a hound dog on a scent, Anthony smelt someone smoking marijuana and wanted to investigate where the source was coming from. That's when I shared my first lesson with the recently graduated officer.

"Making drug collars takes us away from our main purpose on the Deuce which is to be visible. The bosses would rather we stayed out on the street and let the Narcotics Division or Quality of Life Officers make those types of arrests."

Anthony then asked a questioned I wasn't prepared for.

"Is it true someone in the squad was fired?"

Eddie, realizing I didn't have any desire to discuss the matter, explained to Anthony that the girl was fired because of her poor Monthly Activity Reports. This only sparked more questions from the rookie.

"What do you have to do to prevent something like that from happening?"

Finding that question a lot easier to handle, I told him, "Do your job, write summonses, don't do anything stupid and you'll be fine."

Anthony, in a squeaky high-pitched voice, began impersonating Inspector Moretti.

"If you don't write summonses—you're fired, if you don't make any arrests—you're fired? If you call me a guinea bastard, you're fired… and I'll kick your ass while I'm firing you."

It was apparent from the spot-on impersonation by Anthony that the inspector must've given the same "fire and brimstone" speech at his orientation as he did at Eddie's and mine. I could tell by his quick wit that the newbie was going to fit right in with the squad.

To the frustration of Anthony, the tour went by without much action. I sensed the young man from Elmont seemed eager to rid Gotham of crime overnight. I explained to him that he'd see plenty of action over the next six months and not to worry about the anomaly.

During our downtime, we talked about each other's families and got to know one another a little better. He shared with me how he played Santa Claus for his local church, Saint Vincent DePaul Parish. I could picture the jolly giant giving out candy canes to the children while he listened to what they wanted for Christmas. Something told me the big-hearted officer made a seamless transition when it came to playing his role as Kris Kringle.

During the shift, I was able to spend a little time with Eddie. Similar to Anthony, the polished officer lived out on Long Island in the town of Massapequa. His father was retired from the NYPD and a Korean War veteran, just like my dad. I always felt we had a lot in common, especially when it came to our desire to wear the blue uniform. I respected Eddie because he had a quiet strength about him. He was by far the most accomplished officer in the unit, leading the squad in felony arrests, but he was never one to toot his own horn. We discussed our future plans once we finished at the Third Division. The two of us agreed that the North (Midtown North Precinct) would be our first choice on our wish list.

The Holiday Assignment

One morning prior to muster, Sergeant Denny informed Eddie and me to report to the lieutenant's office asap. As Eddie and I walked up the stairs, he playfully said that he didn't do anything wrong, so it must've been me. I retorted jokingly that he was probably right because between the two of us, I was the only one doing any actual police work.

We were both loose until we arrived at the commander's office. As we stood outside the door, I asked Eddie, "All kidding aside, do you have any idea what this could be about?" Eddie shrugged his shoulders and then knocked on the door.

The Vietnam veteran, Lieutenant Higgins, instructed us to enter. Eddie and I saluted the lieutenant and advised him we were reporting as ordered.

"I wanted to personally thank the two of you for a job well done," the lieutenant told us. "My Sergeants have praised you both and appreciate the little bullshit things you've done the past several months in order to free them up. Next month, January, you're off to your new commands. As a thank you, you've been selected for special assignment. Around this time of year, we put a team together to work plain clothes. The undercover detail is for robberies, purse snatches, larcenies, and things like that—no drug collars. Sergeant Ryen and I pick the team, and that would be you two. Go report to him and he'll go over the particulars—dismissed."

Eddie and I thanked the lieutenant and then quickly departed his office to find Ryen. We didn't have far to go. Our boss was sitting at his desk with his feet up and already dressed for the assignment—jeans, a parker, and an Irish, tweed cap.

With a big grin, Ryen said, "Ready, gentlemen? Or maybe you'd like to get out of those uniforms and change into something a little more appropriate for our new assignment?"

I couldn't believe for the next couple of weeks we'd be working plain clothes. The idea of walking around Midtown with nobody knowing we were cops was going to be awesome.

Ryen had one more pleasant surprise for Eddie and me. He explained how he was allowed to pick three rookies, at his discretion, for the detail. Still needing one more, he wanted to leave the last choice for Eddie and me. Without hesitation, Eddie and I both asked for Dwyer to be our third. I could see Ryen was a bit surprised. Maybe it was because Anthony had less time than some of the other guys in our squad and thought we would've chosen one of them. We explained to the sergeant that Anthony was a smart guy with a terrific attitude, plus he was as strong as an ox. Ryen gave the okay and told us to 10-2 him back to the command, and for all three of us to be back in his office in twenty minutes.

The unexpected news gave me a bolt of positive energy. I couldn't wait to change out of my uniform and get started.

Eddie called on the radio for Anthony to report back to the command. While getting changed, Eddie suggested playing a little prank on the rookie and asked if I had any ideas.

I told him about my Academy classmate from Long Island who was mistakenly sent to Staten Island when the assignments came down—a nearly two-hour commute for him. Eddie loved the premise but added we'd tell him that all three of us were transferred, effective immediately.

When Anthony arrived, Eddie told him to get changed and report upstairs to Ryen. When he asked what was going on, Eddie said that the Thirty-Sixth Division in Staten Island was shorthanded and that all three of us were immediately transferred to the "garbage dump." To Eddie's credit he kept a straight face the whole time. Anthony started getting nervous and wondered how he was going to manage the long commute from Long Island to Staten Island. "Maybe we could commute together?" he asked Eddie. Eddie told him to hurry up because Ryen was waiting to give us our orders.

A few minutes later, the three of us reported upstairs. When we entered the office, Ryen told us to have a seat. He looked over at Anthony and asked him if he knew how fortunate he was to be chosen. Anthony, thinking the sergeant was being sarcastic, responded with a somber, "Absolutely, Sarge."

Ryen then began going over our new assignment. "All right guys, listen up. This isn't going to be a walk in the park. The department is going to expect major activity out of us."

Anthony, looking completely baffled, asked the sergeant if he was coming with us. "Of course," Ryen replied.

Eddie was trying to get my attention, but I didn't dare look over at him for fear that I'd start laughing.

Ryen continued with his instructions. "Now, the priority is going to be catching these guys in the act. We're going to concentrate by the tree (referring to the Rockefeller Center Christmas tree). There's always somebody up to no good around the tree. Besides the purse-snatches, the other thing I want you guys looking out for are the whackers." Ryen could see from the expressions on our faces that we hadn't a clue what a "whacker" was. He continued, "Whackers are deviant men dressed in long trench coats that masturbate under their coat and then open it in order to ejaculate on some unsuspecting female's backside. It's very crowded and most of the time the women go unaware they'd been the victim of a sex crime until sometime afterwards. If by chance you catch one of these disgusting perverts, I will expect that you'll use the necessary force to affect the arrest—if you catch my meaning."

The Sarge didn't have to spell it out for us—he wanted the guy roughed-up. Not a problem as far as I was concerned.

Before Ryen continued, Anthony raised his hand to ask a question. "Sarge, I don't understand. We're being transferred to Staten Island to catch guys masturbating around trees?"

Completely dumbfounded by the question, Ryen asked, "What the hell are you talking about?"

Eddie was able to maintain a straight face but as for me—no way. I started laughing to the point that I thought the back of my head was going to split open.

Anthony was completely lost. Ryen had to explain our new assignment to Anthony before he realized he wasn't being transferred to Staten Island. Anthony was so happy that he didn't mind being the victim of an awfully mean practical joke by Eddie and me. Even Ryen started to chuckle when he repeated what Anthony said. "We're being transferred to Staten Island to catch guys masturbating around trees… Holy Mother of Mary," the sergeant said in disbelief.

After clarifying our true objective, Ryen then finished going over the assignment with us. The four of us would work as a team. We were assigned one unmarked car, but Ryen advised us that we'd be on foot most of the time. He wanted us to set a trap for the bad guys. If a foot pursuit ensued, the other guys would be in position on each side of the street to snag the perp. We had radios but Ryen went over some simple hand signals in order to avoid using them. If one of us spotted someone acting suspicious, we would signal to the other guys and then as a team would follow the suspect. With our instructions done, we were off to Rockefeller Center.

Ryen was like hawk. We'd no sooner arrived when he gave the signal he'd spotted a possible perp. The individual on our radar was a white male teen in front of Saks Fifth Avenue. Once he was pointed out to us, it was easy to see why the teen garnered the boss's attention—the suspected perp's eyes were bouncing back and forth casing the holiday shoppers' bags. Finally, one of the unsuspecting tourists put down their bag, and in the blink of an eye, the perp was sprinting down Fifth Avenue with bag in hand. The punk never had a chance. Anthony was positioned perfectly. He put his arm straight out to his side like a middle linebacker and clothesline tackled the perp. For a second, I thought Anthony might've decapitated the teen because all I saw was the perp's feet fly into the air, while his head disappeared.

It didn't take long to establish that Eddie and I would be the sprinters, while Anthony and Ryen would be the enforcers. Simply put, we were fast and they were strong.

Anthony took the collar to the stationhouse while the three of us went back on the hunt. With our cover blown due to all the commotion, Ryen decided to move our location to Radio City Music

Hall. There was a subway station adjacent to the landmark building which the boss felt was a good place to find some bad guys.

We no sooner arrived when some guy walked up to Eddie and asked him if he wanted to buy a brand new $1,500 video camera for only $200. Ryen and I kept our distance so we could observe the situation.

The guy should've been a salesman. He was telling Eddie about all the features—how it could zoom in so close that, as he put it, "count the pimples on someone's ass."

There was one little problem that most unsuspecting civilians weren't aware of: there wasn't any camera in the box. However, there was a beautifully packaged red brick inside. The charge for this little devious, but clever act was Fraudulent Accosting. Instead of Eddie taking out $200 from his back pocket, he took out his handcuffs.

While Eddie and Anthony were busy back at the stationhouse processing their collars, Ryen decided it was time to grab some lunch. He took me to a restaurant on Fifty-Fifth Street called the China Pavilion. The entrance to the restaurant was nothing special but the inside was quite a spectacle of Chinese fountains, art work, and plants. Ryen introduced me to the owner, Kerry Ming. I could barely understand a word the gauntly, middle-aged owner was saying. It was quite apparent the restaurateur was well-intoxicated and it wasn't even noon yet.

Shortly after being seated, a lovely, young Asian waitress came over with two bottles of Budweiser, two frosted tall glasses, a full bottle of chilled Finlandia Vodka, and three shot glasses. I didn't need a detective shield in order to figure out that this was going to be a liquid lunch.

Kerry sat down and starting pouring the vodka. I wasn't much of a vodka drinker and I certainly wasn't looking forward to doing shots of it. I thought it might be a good idea to just sit and observe.

It was apparent by Kerry's nervous energy that he was excited to have Ryen at his restaurant. I could tell the two men knew each other for some time. Kerry started to ask Ryen all the questions one would expect from a cop buff: had he shot anyone recently, were there any big cases he was working on, and if so, was he allowed to discuss them or were they top secret.

Kerry hung on every word Ryen had to say. Although the Asian owner had a difficult time speaking without slurring his words, he showed nothing but the utmost respect toward the highly-decorated Sergeant.

Ryen poured his beer into the chilled glass and I followed. He then started drinking and I didn't. I was still on probation and any minor infraction could boot me off the job. Kerry then poured the Finlandia in all three shot glasses. He raised his glass and toasted, "To New York's Finest." I raised my glass but didn't drink the vodka. Kerry had been so preoccupied with the sergeant he hadn't noticed. I didn't want to be disrespectful but the last thing I wanted was to drink on duty with my boss.

When Kerry excused himself to greet other customers, Ryen sarcastically asked me how my beer was. I told him the truth, which was that I was afraid to drink while on duty.

"I guess you haven't reached that part in the Patrol Guide yet?" Ryen inquired, knowing that I had been studying for the sergeant's exam during some downtime in the office. "You're allowed to drink on duty as long as you're not in uniform and you remain 'fit for duty.' As for the shots of vodka, simulate drinking it and then discreetly pour the contents into the plant behind you. There are thirty shots in that bottle. That's ten shots each. There's no way I could do ten shots and still be able to walk out of here—as for the beer, cheers."

After listening to the sergeant's instructions on how to handle the situation, I was more at ease and decided to enjoy a cold beer with my boss. Halfway through our beer, the young, attractive waitress came back with a tray filled with food. Ryen organized the dishes and we began to eat. I never tasted Chinese food this good before. One dish had peels of tangerine and hot peppers, it was called Tangerine Beef. The beef was so tender that I could break it apart with just my fork. The other dish had colossal-sized shrimp mixed in a lobster sauce that was unbelievably good. I thanked Ryen for the culinary treat and for sharing the place with me.

"When you get a radio call for a dispute or theft of service at one of these restaurants, don't just take the report and leave," Ryen explained. "Ask to see the owner. Show him you care and are concerned about the safety of his restaurant and patrons. Make suggestions. The first time he invites you for dinner, and he will, turn him down. Tell him you appreciate it but maybe another time. You don't want to come across like a pig. Then after a few drive-by visits, you finally accept. Buon appetito! Lastly, always leave a good gratuity for the service and don't share your good fortune with greedy, big mouth cops."

I amusingly thought to myself how the instructors at the Academy skipped over this part in their lesson planner. However, I understood the not so subtle message by my sergeant; the meal was not to be mentioned to anyone else.

Before we left, Kerry came over to finish the last of the Finlandia. He thanked us for coming and pleaded for us to stop back before Christmas.

Amazingly, he was the one thanking us, while Ryen and I enjoyed a delectable meal on the arm—my first!

Ryen took out a five-dollar bill and put it on the table and I followed. "A fin a piece is always fair," he explained.

After we left the China Pavilion, Ryen wanted to stop by the Diamond District located on Forty-Seventh Street between Fifth and Sixth Avenues. He hadn't bought his wife a gift yet for Christmas and decided it might be a good idea to at least do some window shopping. The several-block walk helped me digest my lunch, while the cool air cleared whatever fuzziness was left over from the two Budweiser's. While we were walking I could see Ryen was still searching the streets for prospective perps, but none seem to garner his attention.

When we arrived at the Diamond District, there was a crowd of people gathered together. Apparently, something was going on but due to the large crowd, I was unable to see exactly what it was. I asked Ryen if he had any idea and that's when he explained about the "Three Card Monte" con game.

"It's similar to guessing the nut under the shell," he explained. "There are three cards, one of which is the queen of hearts. The dealer starts off by showing the mark where the queen is. The dealer then begins to move the three cards sporadically around. If the mark picks correctly, he wins the bet. However, the game is fixed. The dealer has his cronies in on it. The shill wins huge amounts of money and brags about how easy it is to win. Finally, someone always takes the bait. It's usually some stupid white guy who thinks they're smarter than the less formally educated black, street person. The fact is the black guy has a PHD in being on the streets, while the white guy from New Canaan has a PHD in being a schmuck. The greedy white guy loses every time."

Ryen saw my curiosity, so he moved us into position to get a closer look. He whispered in my ear not to make a move on the dealer no matter what happened. "This is for visual tutorial purposes only," the sergeant instructed me. Ryen then pointed out the dealer's spotters. If the cops were near, they'd give a signal and in Olympic Trial speed, the makeshift cardboard box table would disappear along with the dealer and his gang.

While Ryen and I stood watching the action, there was a heavy-set, well-dressed black man winning a boat load of money. His laugh was reminiscent of the 1970s 7UP pitchman, Caribbean native, Geoffrey Holder. The unsuspecting coconspirator was so amusing that I caught myself laughing along with him. The crowd was in a frenzy, cheering each time the shill won. The dealer finally told the man he was too good and that he couldn't afford to allow him to continue. "Is there anybody else that wants to try their luck?" the con man shouted to the anxious crowd. Like sheep to the slaughterhouse, all the stupid white guys jockeyed for position to be the first in line to win their fortune.

The first guy up to the cardboard box whipped out a bankroll of hundreds. I whispered to Ryen, "Is he in on it?" Ryen shook his head that he wasn't. Within two minutes, the mark lost all his money. The irate participant and his girlfriend demanded their money back. On cue, the spotters gave the signal and the dealer was off to the races. Just in case I had the notion of running after him, Ryen was holding onto my coat. He explained that this was not of our concern. I could tell by his actions he hadn't much sympathy for the victim.

A squad car was now on the scene, as the once large crowd dwindled down to a few. The victim and his hysterical girlfriend were telling the responding officers that they were robbed by a black man.

The boyfriend explained that they were at the Diamond District to pick-out an engagement ring for Christmas.

"We brought along $2,000 in cash for the ring and when I took the money out of my pocket, the black man grabbed it out of my hand and ran toward Times Square."

Ryen, having heard enough from the selective memory complainant, walked over toward the officers and interrupted the interview. "Excuse me, officers." The officers recognized the sergeant out of uniform but instinctively knew not to address him as a member of the service. "Is it a crime to be a participant in a Three Card Monty game or to make false statements to a police officer?"

The one officer responded that both were considered unlawful acts. The officer realizing where Ryen was going with his questions asked the victim if he was certain the man actually grabbed the money out of his hand. With that, both the victim and his irate girlfriend started changing their story and quickly decided not to pursue the matter any further.

When I asked Ryen if there was any recourse in regards to the victims loss, he decided to give me an earful.

"Victims? There were no victims, just a greedy couple looking to make a score. When things didn't go their way, it was time to call the police and have us clean up their mess. I'm tired of people coming into our city and blaming everyone else for their mistakes. Some pimpled-faced teen from Upper Montclair drives over the George Washington Bridge to buy drugs and the deal goes bad—what does he want? He wants the police to get his money back, of course. A guy solicits a prostitute and she clips his wallet while performing her professional services on him—is he embarrassed or ashamed for his conduct? No! He demands that she be arrested and his money returned to him, including the thirty bucks he paid her for the blowjob. And what's today's little tragedy? A greedy couple got hustled by some street punks. What to do? Make up a story to the police and then demand justice. If these hypocritical idiots wouldn't put themselves in such predicaments, the crime rate statistically wouldn't look so bad. Instead, everybody thinks this city isn't safe, when in fact, it actually is. They want to play with Satan in his backyard, but if things don't go their way, they call us to fix it. Bullshit! If you don't want to get burned, stay the hell out of Satan's kitchen."

I wasn't sure how to fill about Ryen's rant. Yes, what he said was true, but that didn't make what happened to the couple right. They lost all their money and there wouldn't be a ring to show each other's families come Christmas. I guess some lessons in life come with a costly price tag. For this couple, their lesson would cost them exactly $2,000 dollars. Maybe in time I'd feel differently but for now, I felt bad for the couple Ryen referred to as "victimless."

Over the next several weeks, the newly formed detail, nick-named "The Untouchables," produced dozens of top-quality col-lars. The combination of Ryen's guidance and being out of the bag (no uniform), gave us a major tactical advantage over the bad guys. Before too long, each of us started spotting things before even the sergeant himself did. I think it was Anthony that summed it up best. "I love this shit. I absolutely love this shit!" Perhaps not the Queens English, but the sentiment was clearly shared by the rest of us.

For the record, it was Sergeant Marks who made the conde-scending "Untouchables" reference at one of the squad's musters. It was obvious the remark was not meant to be endearing by the uptight Marks but that's exactly how Ryen chose to take it. In fact, after the sergeant heard the comparison to Kevin Costner's character and his handpicked "untouchables," he loved it so much that he insisted we adopt the name.

Meanwhile, Marks wasn't the only individual in the squad giv-ing us an attitude. Evidently, some of our fellow officers weren't warm to the idea that Eddie, Anthony and I were selected for the brief, but awesome detail. One of the female officers, Sue Smith, seemed to be the most vocal regarding our assignment. Earlier that summer, Sue graduated number one in our Academy class out of 1,100 cadets. As impressive as that was, we were no longer being judged by written exams but rather actual police work. Both Sue and Beth were dead last in arrests. At least Beth kept her mouth shut, but as for Sue, she felt entitled and didn't like being skipped over for the assignment.

The brazen rookie decided to question Ryen at muster as to why there weren't any females in his group. Ryen wasn't pleased with the book smart rookie's inquiry but he kept his cool. He chose to take the opportunity to not only address her but the entire squad. Eddie, Anthony, and I had been standing off to the side waiting to go out when Sue asked her loaded question. Ryen called the three of us to the front of the muster and then addressed the squad.

"Officer Smith poses a question that I will assume many of you were wondering but only one had the courage to ask."

I could see the masculine female rookie was pleased with the sergeant's words, but I knew Ryen was only setting her up.

"I'm even more impressed, considering this individual's lack of activity, that she feels comfortable enough to put herself in the spotlight. Most inept officers that haven't made any quality arrests would hide in the shadows. But not this officer."

The egotistical grin by my peer had all but vanished by this point. Then Ryen went in for the kill.

"I don't have to explain my actions to you piss ants, but for the reputation of these three individuals, I will. In my nineteen plus years of service to this department, I have never had the privilege of working with a better team than the one I've assembled right here. These "Untouchables" have made more felony arrests in the past few weeks than most of you will have in your entire careers. I understand when permanent assignments are given out next month that several of you will be transferred to One Police Plaza or the Police Academy. I'm also aware that in those details you will do nothing more than sit on your brains and study for the next promotional exam; all the while having never made a quality arrest. Allow me to amplify my response to Officer Smith's question. I don't care what sexual organ an officer has. I don't care if the individual is hung like a porn star or needs to squat in order to take a piss. I judge people by the content of their character, and in my opinion, there is no better representation of that in this room than these three individuals standing here before you.

Does anyone else feel the need or urge to ask their Superior Officer any other questions?"

There was silence.

After Ryen stormed out of the Muster Room, he went upstairs to his office. I wasn't sure what to do. Anthony thought we should follow, but I thought it might be a good idea to give our boss a little time to cool off. After a few minutes, I decided to go upstairs to see what was going on. Before I entered the office, I could hear Ryen and Marks in a heated argument. Ryen was telling the junior sergeant that because he was sleeping with the spoiled brat, she felt empowered to question him in front of the squad. Marks told Ryen to go fuck himself. The next thing I heard was bodies and furniture being tossed around. I was truly afraid someone was going to get killed. I ran into the room and found the two men in the middle of a fist fight. I pulled Ryen off of Marks and separated the two.

As Marks wiped the blood from his lip he said, "At least my bitch gives head, what's your bitch do?"

Marks was referring to me being Ryen's "bitch." I knew I wasn't Mark's favorite, but the unprofessional comment left me disgusted. I let go of Ryen and walked out of the office. If not for worrying about my mentor throwing away his career, I would've liked to have seen Ryen beat the crap out of the smug bastard.

I knew Marks was acting like a petulant child by using words to get under Ryen's skin. He was a self-absorbed, narcissistic sociopath that didn't care about anyone or anything but himself. He was jealous of Ryen for many reasons, but most of all for the plain clothes detail. Marks would've loved picking his own harem to walk around the city with. There's little doubt he was the one fanning the smoke for Sue's inflammatory question. I knew it, and so did Ryen. Marks was a manipulator with rank. He used his position to get girls that were his subordinates nearly half his age.

My time in the Third Division had been the best several months of my life. However, the confrontation between Ryen and Marks left a black cloud over the unit right up till the last day.

The Last Day

Tuesday, January 12, 1988

The holiday assignment had been finished for over two weeks. I was glad to be back in the bag (in uniform). The plain clothes detail was awesome but there was something about putting on my NYPD uniform that made me feel special.

I hadn't expected the past six months to go by so fast. The truth is I enjoyed my time so much I wish I didn't have to go, but that wasn't an option. The next day, I was to report to my new command, which meant starting all over again; new bosses, new locker room, new squad members. There was a lot I wasn't sure about prior to the transfer, but there were two things that were a certainty: I'd be low man on the totem pole and first in line for the worst assignments. Before worrying about all that, I still had one day left at the Third Division and I was looking forward to spending it with the squad.

At our final muster, we were told by Sergeant Denny that there was a three-alarm fire the previous evening resulting in several fatalities. While the fire was being investigated, the entire squad would be responsible for securing the East Fiftieth Street building. We loaded up the police vans and made our way over to the ten-story residential apartment building. Upon arrival, Denny assigned each of us a partner and the floor we would be securing.

During the fire, many doors were broken down in order for the Fire Department to ensure no one was trapped inside. It would be our responsibility that no unauthorized personnel enter the apartments until they were secured and the Fire Marshall gave the "all clear" order.

I was assigned the top floor with Beth. Several months had passed since the two of us spent the night together and in that time, we both did a good job in avoiding one another. However, because of the current geographical proximity of our assignment, it was going to be a little difficult to continue playing dodge.

As I entered the building, I was immediately struck by the overwhelming smell of charred remains. The walls in the lobby were blackened from the smoke and fire, and water was still dripping down from the upper floors where the firemen doused the flames the previous evening. The limited emergency lighting made the already dreary scene look even bleaker.

I wasn't completely aware of the magnitude of the tragedy until I reached the top floor. The exit doors to the roof had slide-bolt locks, making it difficult to unlock in a dark, smoky environment. I could see next to the roof door broken-off fingernails embedded in the wall. It was here at this location that two of the fatalities occurred.

Between the six months in the Academy and the six months at the Third Division, I learned a lot about being a New York City Police Officer. However, until today, there was one lesson still missing from my training: death.

At twenty, I was about as naive as one could be regarding the subject. Besides my mother's funeral when I was younger, I hadn't the experience or the understanding to know what death was and the impact it left behind.

Today was not going to be a day of joy and laughter. It wasn't going to end with the raising of a pint and a quick quip. Today was about people I never met before and the horrific way they met their end.

Sergeant Gooden made his way up to my floor. He noticed Beth and I were as far apart as could be. He jokingly asked me if she hadn't taken a shower. Ignoring the comment, I asked the sergeant if he knew any details regarding the fire. He told me he heard there were some difficulties trying to gain access to the roof. That's when I took him over and showed him the broken fingernails in the wall next to the roof door.

Gooden then explained that for there to be a tragedy like this, several things had to go perfectly wrong.

"For instance," he started, "the stairway doors were left open. This was a violation that the owner of the building had been previously cited for. Because of the doors being open, the smoke had a path to travel up to this floor. The ones that were killed in their apartments had metal doors but the doors were useless because of the half-inch space at the bottom of them. People had smoke detectors but most were without batteries. The origin of the fire was in a doctor's office on the first floor but he didn't have a smoke detector installed. And here's the kicker: most of these buildings were built pre-World War Two; meaning they're exempt from most of the city's fire codes. These buildings are tragedies just waiting to happen. For instance, if the roof door was equipped with the proper hardware, two of the fatalities don't occur. If the doctor's office was hard-wired with a smoke detector that was equipped to notify the NYFD directly, in all likelihood we're not looking at any fatalities. This building, just like most of them in Midtown, lack the minimum fire protection equipment; no alarm system, no illuminated exit signs, no emergency egress lighting, and no panic hardware on doors. A perfect tragedy."

After explaining the details to me, Gooden could see I was troubled by the event and asked if I was all right. I explained to him that the image of fingernails in the wall was going to stay with me awhile.

"Hey, don't take this shit home with you," he said. "This is just another day on patrol."

Maybe that could be the case for him, but not for me. Except for Sharlene, he didn't seem to let anything bother him. I just don't know how something like this couldn't affect the sergeant—or anyone else for that matter.

Gooden began to walk down the stairs, when he turned to me, pointed down the hall at Beth and in a low voice said, "Don't think you were the only one she played during the past six months."

"I'm glad to know I wasn't the only schmuck," I politely responded.

I didn't ask but was curious how he knew about Beth and me. I figured the sergeant either had good instincts or he was the other schmuck.

About halfway through the shift, Gooden came back to tell me he needed me to drive down to the Medical Examiner's office. One of the victims that perished in the fire had been severely burned and hadn't been identified yet. It was suspected that the girl was Veronica Washington, a twenty-four-year-old resident of the building. In order to properly release the body, a positive identification had to be conducted with the next of kin. The parents of the victim were going to be arriving at the examiner's office at noon to see if they could identify their daughter. Gooden explained that if the parents could make the identification, I'd be finished relatively quickly with the process. However, if they couldn't, then I needed to complete a Missing Person's Report.

As gruesome and joyless as my current surroundings were, there was one place that was worse; the ME's office.

The depressing building is located at East Thirtieth Street and First Avenue. The last time I was there was when my Academy class went to observe an autopsy, something every recruit must attend. Our instructor explained to the class that the reasoning behind the dreary field trip was to familiarize the recruits with the building, the process, and being around a corpse. Many of the recruits, me included, hadn't much experience when it came to dealing with dead bodies. As officers, we would be first responders to many life and death situations. The department thought it best for the recruits to adapt to some of these gruesome sights in a controlled environment.

The day my class visited the "death dungeon," there were several corpses laying on gurneys in the Examiner's Room. One was a baby with the umbilical cord still attached, and the other was a young, teenage, white girl. The sight of the lifeless bodies left me feeling mournful. I'd seen enough and the autopsy had yet to start.

A man walked into the room wearing a surgical gown, gloves, and a mask that was pulled down below his mouth. The individual was Dr. Elliot Gross, the chief medical examiner.

If there was ever a person that looked like someone that dealt with dead people, it was Dr. Gross. He had huge bags hanging underneath his beady eyes, and his skin had an unhealthy ashen color to it. His round face and bald head made him a lookalike for Uncle Fester. There seemed to be an uneasy way about him. I didn't think he seemed comfortable with us, the cadets, in his work space.

In a low whispering voice, the doctor introduced himself to the class. He pointed to the other side of the room where an elderly-looking deceased man was laying on one of the gurneys and instructed the class to gather around the corpse.

Doctor Gross began the procedure by explaining why he was performing an autopsy in the first place.

"This individual wasn't under a doctor's care. He was a street person and although foul play wasn't suspected, a full examination was required by law."

The coroner started by noting the deceased's height, weight, age, sex, and any distinguishing body marks, such as tattoos and scars. He explained that fingerprints had been previously taken in the hope of identifying the body but proved unsuccessful. He examined the outside of the corpse and noted that there weren't any signs of trauma. As the coroner spoke of the deceased, it seemed to bring back some color to the doctor's anemic face. He picked up the scalpel and began the "Y" incision. With great enthusiasm, he explained how the incision was made from each shoulder across the chest and then down to the pubic bone. At that point, he spread open the skin and began to split the ribcage. He examined the heart and lungs, and took a blood sample. After examining each organ in the chest cavity, he repeated the procedure for the organs in the lower body. He noted that it was important to check the eyes for ruptured blood vessels. He explained that this could be a sign of strangulation or choking. The once aloof doctor was now starting to find his groove. He then took out the mini electric saw and proceeded to make a cut from ear to ear on the lower back of the head. At this point, two of the cadets excused themselves from the room—in all likelihood to get sick. After the incision, the coroner pulled back the layer of skin from the head exposing the skull. After another whip of the saw on the skull, he was able to remove the brain to weigh it. The entire autopsy procedure from beginning to end took less than fifteen minutes; but for me, the visualization would last a lifetime.

When finished, the class walked out of the examining room. That's where I saw a couple in the waiting area sitting on a bench. The husband had a blank stare of disbelief in his eyes while he held his inconsolable wife. They were both in obvious emotional pain. I couldn't be sure but my best guess was they were the parents of either the baby or the teenage girl. I wanted to walk over and tell them how sorry I was for their loss, but I lacked the courage.

A strange thing happened to me when I saw those bodies on the gurney: I felt sorrow for people I never met before. I didn't have the same, deep-seeded emotional attachment as a parent, but I still felt for those people that no longer were amongst the living. Like a child, I searched for an understanding for something that I simply couldn't understand—death.

I arrived at the Medical Examiner's office just before noon and was informed by the attendant that the parents hadn't arrived yet. I looked over the paper work that was available and saw that the victim was an unidentified black woman, approximately in her mid-twenties. I asked the attendant if I could view the body prior to the parent's arrival. He took me to a refrigerated room where her body laid covered. I pulled back the white linen sheet enough to view the decease's partially charred face. The frozen image clearly showed the painful last moments of the deceased's life.

Although she suffered significant burns, I thought the parents could still be able to identify their daughter, if it was indeed her. I asked the attendant for a Polaroid camera and took a picture of the deceased's face. I put the photo in my pocket and waited for the parents to arrive.

A few minutes past when a middle-aged black couple came walking in the main entrance of the building. I was nervous and reminded myself I needed to be as compassionate as possible. There wasn't going to be anything pleasant about what I had to do, but for the first time, I was glad it was me, and not some insensitive bureaucrat handling the situation.

The African-American couple introduced themselves as Mr. and Mrs. Washington from Queensbury, New York. I told them there was more than one way to do the identification—we could go to the viewing room or I could show them a photo. The stocky Mr. Washington asked in a somber voice for my opinion.

Before I could answer, Mrs. Washington abruptly interjected and said, "I already know it's my baby. We didn't come all the way from Upstate to look at a photo. Please, officer, take me to my daughter."

As we walked down the widen-hallway toward the viewing room, I thought of how torturous this had to be for the couple.

The room was a cold, sterile place. Everything was white except for the metal gurney that carried the sheet-covered body. I had barely pulled back the white sheet when the mother exclaimed that it was indeed her "baby." I looked over at her husband to confirm and he gave me a simple nod of the head, indicating the deceased was their daughter.

After the positive identification, I offered the grieving parents to take as much time as they needed. The mother explained to me that her daughter was no longer there, only her body. She then pulled out a Bible from her purse and asked if there was somewhere her and her husband could go to pray. I told them there was and began to escort them to a private room.

While I walked the couple to the grieving room, the thought of the parents I hadn't consoled several months earlier came to my mind. Not wanting to make the same mistake, I expressed my heart-felt sorrow to Mr. and Mrs. Washington. I told them how sorry I was for the loss of their daughter, Veronica, and confessed to them my ignorance to why such things occur. Mrs. Washington grabbed my hand and asked me if I would like to pray with them. Her compassion and kindness under such difficult circumstances was something I never witnessed before. I accepted, and for the next hour listened to the Washington's read scriptures from the Bible and tell stories of happier times, all the while professing their love and trust in the Lord.

Mr. Washington asked if I had ever visited Lake George in Upstate New York. I explained that my vast experience of travel had come via the New York City Transit system. "If the subway didn't go there, neither did I," I lightly remarked.

He spoke of a beautiful, historic lake near his home that was surrounded by vast mountains along the Adirondack Range. He said he wasn't sure what heaven looked like but was fairly certain it had to have lakes and mountains just as beautiful. He told me that every Sunday during the summer, the three would hike Black Mountain together after mass.

"My little girl loved that mountain," he told me. "We will spread her ashes over the summit so she can be with nature once again. I know the subway doesn't go Upstate but Amtrak does. Maybe someday you'll visit and see for yourself."

I gave Mr. Washington my word that one day I would make the trek and visit the place he said "is like heaven on earth."

Before the day started, I didn't know Mr. and Mrs. Washington. I didn't know of their daughter or a place called Black Mountain. These people touched me, prayed with me, and enlightened me. They will walk out of this building to a city of strangers with no one knowing or caring of their pain except for one other person: me.

A few hours earlier, I was cursing being the officer assigned to this task. Now, as I was getting ready to leave, I was thanking the Lord for the privilege He bestowed upon me.

The three of us walked out of the bleak Medical Examiner's office together and said our goodbyes. They gave me something I so desperately wanted to give those grieving parent's months earlier, a hug.

I began walking down First Avenue when I turned to take one last look at the couple. While unsuspecting strangers passed by, the two were locked in an embrace. Forever imprinted in my memory is that image of the couple from Queensbury, New York. An image I would always remember as being filled with love, heartache, and faith.

On my walk back to the command, I thought of Dad and the times he'd come home from work. It was then he'd share stories like these to mother while I hid in my secret fort listening. He'd always finish the story with the final line from Jules Dassin's enigmatic police procedural, "The Naked City." So, to describe the occurrences of my last day at the Third Division, I will borrow the words of Mr. Dassin:

> "There are eight million stories in the naked city—this has been one of them."

The next day I would be reporting to my new command. On this, my last day as a rookie, I was given "death" as my final lesson.

Unfortunately, the lesson would be continuous, for over the course of the next several years, I would be dealing with death on a scale I never would've imagined. In fact, in less than a month, I would be attending my first police funeral.

Over time, I would come to appreciate the words Sergeant Ryen told me that night at Pipin's Pub: "I've gone to more police funerals then any individual should have to."

I just never expected out of a police department of over 35,000 members that the first funeral I'd be attending would be for someone so young, so full of life, and so close to me.

CHAPTER 6

RMP 1041

The dead cannot cry out for justice. It is a
duty of the living to do so for them.
                                    —Lois McMaster Bujold

By the time I arrived back at the precinct, everyone from the squad had already left. Being the last day together as a group, it would've been nice to say goodbye and find out everyone's new assignment. I was particularly interested to know if Eddie's father came through with his hook and if he'd be going to the North with me.

The next morning, I reported to the Midtown North Precinct for orientation. When I arrived at the stationhouse, I saw Mike and Beth along with a few other familiar faces from the Third Division. There were only six of us in total—Eddie wasn't one of them.

The orientation was much different than the previous one I attended. There wasn't any inspector's threatening to kick our ass or speeches about the do's and don'ts. The purpose of the day was primarily to fill out paperwork and pray to find an available locker.

The West Fifty-Fourth Street Command was a four-story building that housed over two-hundred-and-fifty officers. Although, most of my time was spent in Midtown South, I was familiar with the North and the impressive landmarks within the confines of the precinct. Whereas the South was known for being the "busiest in the world," the North was dubbed "the most prestigious." With landmarks that included Rockefeller Center, Saint Patrick's Cathedral, Trump Tower, Radio City Music Hall, The Waldorf Astoria and The Plaza Hotel, there was no wonder why the midtown command was the most sought after.

In my limited experiences in both commands, the one glaring difference to me wasn't the landmarks or structures but rather the personnel. The officers assigned to the South never seemed to mind that we rookies were sharing their command with them. However, on the rare occasions one of us went to the North, the officers there didn't seem too pleased with our presence. To put it simply, I thought the officers in the North were a bit snobbish, whereas, the officers in the South seemed down to earth and more willing to lend a helping hand. Now that the North was my permanent assignment, I was hoping things would be different.

Out of a possible nine different squads I could've been assigned to at the North, I ended up in my brother's. I never asked but simply assumed my dad wanted it that way—big brother looking after little brother. There were some advantages to this nepotism-induced arrangement. I knew Francis would help me get acclimated to my new squad members and in case I did need some assistance, who better to ask than my big bro?

However, there was a downside. Now that Francis and I would be working the same schedule, I knew it would be just a matter of time before he'd rope me into being his personal chauffer. I wouldn't have had an issue helping Francis with a ride to and from work but it was the reason behind it that disturbed me. Francis's girlfriend, Mary, was constantly borrowing his car. One day, she complained to him that she was afraid of taking the subway, not because of the crime or cat-sized rats, but because she feared the trains would collide as they passed one another. Francis bought the bull and handed Mary the keys to his '78 Firebird.

Francis had been living with the hedonist Mary in Bensonhurst for the past year. Dad wasn't pleased with the cohabitation, but he knew there wasn't much he could do about it. Personally, I didn't care for Francis's girlfriend, but then again, I wasn't the one living with her. She was loud, chewed gum like a cow, and dressed like a cheap Eighth Avenue hooker. The first time I met her, she was wearing leopard-spotted, skintight pants with matching leopard stiletto shoes, and a top that would've been too small for my three-year-old niece—we were going to a Mets game.

I knew the type of girl Mary was—a narcissist that treated my brother like crap. What I couldn't comprehend was why Francis wanted to be with her.

Growing up, Francis, with his all-American good looks and bad boy image, caught the attention of many female admirers. While I was still in grade-school, I would listen to the girls talk about the "cutie" that lived in the big brown house across the street. I knew the girls were referring to my house and yes, my brother. So, as my classmates and I stood in the schoolyard getting ready to start the day, Francis would be leaving the house to go to high school, and that's when all the girls acted like Elvis was leaving the building. I never did tell Francis of his admirers but now that he was with Miss Queen "B" I wish I had. Maybe than he'd have more confidence and not settle for such an unpleasant person.

On my second day at the North, I was given the lowly assignment of watching over a corpse. I'd be assigned to the DOA until the Medical Examiner's office arrived to retrieve the body.

After muster, Francis and his partner, Chris, gave me a ride over to the Hell's Kitchen apartment house. On the way over, Chris asked me if this was my first DOA. After telling him it was, he took out a cigar and tossed it to me in the back seat. I thanked Chris but told him I didn't smoke. When I went to give it back to him, he told me to keep it because I might find it useful. Chris and Francis could tell I didn't understand the purpose of the cigar and began to laugh at my ignorance.

When I entered the lobby of the West Fifty-Second Street walkup, I started to smell something very unpleasant. As I ascended the stairs, the pungent smell only worsened. The source of the incredible odor was clear once I reached the DOA's apartment.

Lying on the floor of the three–hundred square foot studio apartment was the deceased. Nearly every inch of the cramped studio unit was filled with garbage and old newspapers. The sink was overloaded with dirty dishes and crawling roaches. I didn't know what was worse—to live like this or to die like this?

I'd never been a fan of any form of smoking products but probably despised the smell of cigars the most. The heavy smoke seemed to grab onto everything and linger in the air. However, given my present circumstances, the masking of cigar smoke seemed pretty good to me, which I now realize was the purpose when the veteran Chris gave me the stogie.

After waiting the better part of my eight-and-a-half-hour shift, the men from the ME's office finally arrived. When the two orderlies lifted the deceased's body to place it in the body bag, a gushing flow of fluids came spewing out from the corpse's rectum. The overwhelming, indescribable stench was no match for my cigar. I ran down the hallway desperately trying to escape from the penetrating odor. After holding my breath for over a minute, while getting as far down the hallway as possible, I finally allowed myself to take a breath of air.

I knew the odor had to be exceptionally worse than usual since the orderlies reacted in the same way I did. The three of us were standing at the end of the long hallway while the body lay where the two men left it in the room. One of them looked over at me and said, "That sucked." Trying to conserve my oxygen intake, I nodded my head in agreement and thought to myself—that sure did!

Later that first week, I was assigned to guard an EDP (emotionally disturbed person) at Bellevue Hospital's Psychiatric Ward. The Department's policy was if the NYPD brought the individual in for psychiatric treatment, then we were responsible for guarding them until he or she was admitted. Because of the number of patients and lack of doctors, the process took hours.

On this particular day, my assignment was to guard a patient that tried to jump off the Manhattan Bridge. The apparent schizophrenic individual was hearing voices in his head telling him to fly across the East River. Emergency Service personnel were able to corale the individual prior to any fatal Superman impersonations.

For the next twelve hours, I sat in a room surrounded by dozens of mentally ill people that were waiting their turn to be evaluated by the attending psychiatrist. Some of them were restrained like my patient, while others walked freely around the ward.

After spending the better part of an entire day with these individuals, a sense of sadness had come over me. From what I witnessed, these people were in a living hell. Tragically, and all too often, if not treated properly, their hell can become our hell in one violent, schizophrenic episode.

Toward the end of the shift, I thought it might be me that was going to be admitted into the ward. An entire day of listening and observing irrational yelling, chanting, and bizarre behavior was nerve-racking. One of the individuals in the room had an imaginary piece of rope that he tried making a hangman's noose with. For the entire time I was there, he simulated making a noose with the rope and just before putting it around his neck he'd yell, "Oh shit, that's not right," and then he'd start the entire process all over again.

I had many long days as a rookie, but that day at Bellevue was by far the longest twelve hours of my life.

To say the first several weeks in my new command sucked would've be an understatement. My day started by having to get up extra early so I could pick up Francis—who was never ready. Then I had to deal with the construction traffic on the BQE (Brooklyn Queens Expressway) heading into Manhattan, and when I finally did make it to work, I was given the worst of the worst assignments—usually a smelly DOA or a trip to the hospital to guard an injured prisoner or my favorite, babysitting an EDP at Bellevue. It didn't take long for me to start missing the Third Division and Sergeant Ryen.

After weeks of such assignments, I was finally given a reprieve in the form of a foot post on Restaurant Row. The one block assignment was situated just west of Times Square on Forty-Sixth Street between Eighth and Ninth Avenues. When I arrived at my post, I started the shift by taking notes of the addresses and the array of different businesses on the block. There were a couple of parking lots, several gift shops, and of course, lots and lots of restaurants.

I spoke with numerous proprietors while making my rounds up and down my post. Some informed me that there had been several purse snatches and robberies in the area recently. Everyone seemed genuinely pleased with the extra police presence on the block.

Around lunch time, I noticed a line forming just off Eighth avenue. I went over to investigate and noticed a group of men congregating in front of a small Lutheran Church. I was informed by the people waiting in line that St. Luke's offered a hot meal to anyone seeking one on Tuesday and Thursday afternoon's.

While I stood there watching the street people orderly file into the side door of the church, I heard someone in a pleasant, deep voice greet me as Officer Simpson. At first, I didn't recognize the individual dressed as a maintenance worker but then soon realized it was my first collar, James Love. I hadn't seen James since the arrest. I asked him how things were going and he told me he was doing a lot better than the last time we'd seen each other.

"I'm working here now as a handyman," the able-bodied James told me. "Everybody here treats me good."

James went on to explain that on the days the soup kitchen was open, he'd stay outside to keep things in order. I told him that with his size, they had the right guy in charge. I asked him how things were in his personal life. He explained to me that he made some necessary changes and felt that he was heading in the right direction. For his sake, I truly hoped that was the case.

I asked James if the pastor was nearby, in the hope of introducing myself to him. He immediately took me inside to seek out the reverend. After walking down the basement stairs, James shouted from across the makeshift cafeteria, "Reverend Gray, Reverend Gray." Having been startled by James, the slender, silver-haired pastor quickly walked over toward us.

With a concerned tone, the reverend asked, "Is everything all right, officer?"

I told him everything was fine and that I simply wanted to introduce myself and to see if there was anything I could be of assistance with. The pastor went onto explain that over the years, there had been several incidents that required a police response. He requested for an officer to be assigned to the block and finally it was granted.

"Unfortunately, every time something occurs, I can't seem to find one of you guys," the pastor said with disappointment in his eyes.

I promised Reverend Gray that I would make my presence known throughout the shift.

Over the next several weeks, I was sporadically assigned to the Restaurant Row foot post. I made every effort to get to know all the proprietors along the touristy block and made it a priority to visit with James, Reverend Gray and their soup kitchen on a regular basis.

One afternoon, the pastor asked if I liked being assigned to the block, to which I responded, "Absolutely." He told me there was a community board meeting coming up and that he was going to ask my captain if I could be permanently assigned to the post. I was thankful Reverend Gray felt confident enough in my abilities to make such a request on my behalf. However, I didn't get my hopes up due to the fact that I was still low man on the totem pole.

In the first several weeks in my new command I had been so caught up with my own adjustment period that I hadn't given much thought to anyone else. As February was coming to a close, I wanted to get in touch with Eddie and wish him a happy birthday. I was curious how he was doing and to see if he was getting stuck with all the crappy assignments the way I'd been. Through the department mail, I sent a note to his precinct, the 103 in Queens. It read: "Hey, Eddie, I hope your hook is still trying to get you to the North. Happy B-Day! DS."

Tragically, the transfer would never occur.

On February 26, 1988, at approximately three-thirty in the morning, five days after his twenty-second birthday, Eddie was assassinated by a couple of street thugs.

That morning, while driving into the city with Francis for our day shift, I listened to a 1010 WINS news report that an officer had been shot and killed while protecting a witness's house in Jamaica, Queens. Francis and I made the sign of the cross and then shook our heads in disgust, knowing that one of our brethren had fallen. The report hadn't mentioned the officer by name—in all likelihood, the department was still going through the next-of-kin notification process. I asked Francis what precinct covered that part of the city and he informed me that he thought it was the 103. My head immediately sank. Francis asked what was wrong and I told him I knew someone that worked there. Francis stressed that he wasn't certain regarding the command and to not worry since the chances were remote that out of 35,000 cops it would be the officer I knew.

I knew my brother made sense, but I simply couldn't get the uneasy feeling out of my stomach. Being assigned to guard a witness's house on an overnight shift was exactly the kind of crappy assignment a rookie like Eddie would've been given. It didn't take long for that uneasy feeling to only get worse.

As Francis and I approached the steps of the North stationhouse, Mike Burke, who was finishing the overnight shift, came up to me and said, "It was Eddie." Those three words were like three cannon balls hitting my midsection. My former Third Division coworker kept talking but I didn't hear anything he said after that. I went upstairs to change, still trying to figure out what just happened.

As I sat in front of my locker, I thought of Eddie. I still couldn't comprehend that the young man, so full of life and promise, was no longer. I thought of the hell his family and girlfriend were about to go through. I wondered why in a world filled with so many bad guys did God have to take one of the good ones. It simply wasn't fair.

The funeral was on Monday, February 29. I was scheduled to work, so I put in a request to take the day off. Since I was low man in the squad, my request was denied by Clerical. When I was informed of the denial, I went to their office to see if there was any discretion that could be used. I spoke with a civilian worker by the name of Mrs. Jones. I could see as I was explaining my reason behind the request to the bureaucratic individual, she wasn't interested. When I finished, the insensitive paper pusher said there was nothing she could do because, as she stated, "The maximum amount of personnel with higher seniority already have the day off—only two per squad, per day."

While standing there in front of Mrs. Jones, I thought how sad it was that this woman, who'd been working in clerical for so long, had forgotten the numbers she was referring to were actual people. I wasn't looking to take off Fourth of July or Christmas. I was looking to take off in order to pay my respect to a friend that gave the ultimate sacrifice.

I walked out of the office and recalled Sergeant Ryen telling me if I ever needed something vitally important to go directly to the captain. "At the end of the day he's the say all and do all," he stressed.

I went to the captain's office with my denied 28 (the form used for taking time off) and explained to the captain the reason behind my request. Without saying a word, the captain signed off on the form—overriding the denial. I went back to the ornery Mrs. Jones with my approved 28 in hand. Apparently, she didn't like having officer's go over her head. Personally, I didn't care. She glared at the 28 and then quipped, "I hope you don't expect to do this too often." To which I replied, "Well, let's pray I won't be going to anymore police funerals."

The funeral was held at St. James Catholic Church in Seaford, Long Island. I arrived early and watched the sea of blue under a gray sky swell to over ten thousand officers. We lined up outside according to our precincts. The formation was nearly a half-mile long and six deep of officers. Early on, while the officers were gathering, I noticed something I found to be odd. It seemed to be more like a high school reunion than a funeral. From listening to the men and women in blue around me, I sensed many hadn't seen each other in quite some time. At first, I thought their laughing, hugging, and reminiscing to be disrespectful, but I quickly learned that this was part of the grieving process. These more seasoned men and women knew at what point in the proceedings they could enjoy a laugh with old friends and when it was time to pay one's respects. That time came when the Pipes and Drums of the Emerald Society started playing, as the black hearse pulled-up to the front of the church. Immediately, the laughs and good cheer were replaced by tears and sobbing.

As the Ceremonial Unit Officers removed the coffin from the hearse, I could see the green, white and blue NYPD flag draped over it. I still couldn't comprehend that Eddie was inside the coffin and that his life was now over. How could this have happened?

While I struggled to make sense of the inexplicable, I thought how horrific this had to be for Eddie's parents.

I don't remember much about the days immediately following my mother's death. All I knew was everybody was quiet, and the mood was one of sadness. One day, shortly after the funeral, Grandpa Frank came by the house to visit Dad. While playing in my fort, preparing GI Joe for battle, I could hear the two men conversing but wasn't paying much attention to what they were saying. It wasn't until I heard what I thought was my grandfather crying that I took notice. In a voice filled with sorrow, he said to my dad, "I don't understand. Parents aren't supposed to bury their children."

It's strange but I hadn't thought about that day or those words since they were spoken by my grandfather years earlier. That is, until I saw Eddie's parents, Ann and Matt.

Outside the church, I watched Ann rest her head on Matt's shoulder. I'd seen this same love-filled embrace a month earlier in front of the Medical Examiner's office when the Washington's were grieving over the loss of their child.

In many ways, Eddie's father was similar to my dad. Physically, both men were tall, strong and distinguished looking. Both served in the Korean War, marrying their sweethearts upon their return. Soon thereafter, both men embarked on their police careers. These men are family men. They're men of honor, character, and integrity. These are the types of men that don't loosen their necktie or remove their suit jacket at social events. They're the epitome of old school. They're family men that have made numerous sacrifices along the way to assure a better life for their loved ones.

As Eddie's mom stood there in her husband's arms, I sensed a quiet, reserved strength about her. The image had me thinking of a woman with similar traits that went through a tragedy of her own.

I wasn't born yet when President Kennedy was killed, but I did see the old news footage of the assassination and funeral. In a time of unspeakable grief, the First Lady carried the burden for her children and her country.

On that cold, gray day in February, Mrs. Byrne took on a similar burden. She too had to be strong for her family, and her extended family in the NYPD. In what must've been the worst day of her life, she endured the unthinkable. The strength and courage her and her husband showed that day could've only come from two things: love and faith.

All officers understand there's an inherit risk that's taken when one puts on the blue uniform. We understand it's a dangerous profession and know sometimes luck plays a vital role. Training, preparation and learning the tactics that go along with being a police officer are absolutely paramount in helping improve the odds for survival. But the truth is all the training in the world is no match for dumb luck. An officer can do everything right, and it can still end up badly. Conversely, an officer can do everything tactically wrong and go unscathed. For Eddie and his assassination, it was a perfect storm of bad luck.

During the interrogation of one of the perp's involved, it was discovered that they were going to assassinate a different officer but changed their mind on two separate occasions. Apparently, on the first occasion, the officer was a female and on the second, the officer was a male black. For a reason that was never fully explained, these factors influenced the killers to wait. How scary for those officers to now realize how close they came to suffering the same fate as Eddie. It wasn't superior training that saved their lives, it was dumb luck.

When I first heard of the details of Eddie's death, I began to think of all the "what ifs." What if Eddie was transferred with me to the North? What if Eddie stayed a Transit Cop instead of transferring over to the NYPD? What if he took off that night? And the most selfish one of all, what if it was me that was transferred to the 103rd Precinct instead of Eddie? After all the "what ifs," I came to one glaring conclusion—it didn't matter. Eddie was now dead and none of the "what ifs" was going to bring him back.

If there was one positive that came from Eddie's tragic death, it was that he didn't die in vain.

Throughout the eighties, countless unnamed victims of rampant crack use lined the streets of the inner city without garnering much national attention. But after the cowardly act of Eddie's assassination, the crack epidemic now had a martyr and his name was Police Officer Edward R. Byrne, Shield number 14072.

Eddie was killed while protecting the life of a witness and his family. Because the courageous civilian cooperated with the police on the war on drugs, the witness had his house firebombed on several occasions by drug dealers. Eddie was killed upholding the belief that the good should be protected from evil and that justice should prevail over tyranny.

The four killers responsible for Eddie's murder were eventually apprehended, convicted and sentenced to twenty-five years to life. Whether justice was served or not, I don't know. What I did know was nothing was going to bring back Eddie or ease the pain left behind from the wake of evil by those four cowards. I believe Eddie's dad described the perps best when he referred to the four as "scum."

The end of the funeral was much different than the beginning. There were no laughs but certainly lots of hugs and heartfelt wishes amongst the sea of blue.

While walking back to my car, I recognized a familiar face. Across the street, getting into his Jeep was Sergeant Ryen. As much as I missed my mentor, I was simply to emotionally drained to walk over and say hello to my former Third Division boss. I figured there'd be other days, better days, to catch up with the sergeant. Unfortunately, that day would never come.

The sergeant retired that spring and moved to Lake Hopatcong, New Jersey. He was an avid freshwater fisherman and loved the thought of being able to enjoy his pastime all year round. The following winter, during one of his ice fishing expeditions, he saw a young boy on a snowmobile go through the ice. Always the first responder, Ryen jumped into action. Without regard to his own safety, he plunged into the freezing water in an attempt to rescue the boy. The State Police found the boy's body the following day. As for my mentor, the strong current took him under the thick ice. His body wasn't recovered until later that spring.

Throughout my life, I would relive the lesson taught to me on the day of my first police funeral. That being the things that haunted me the most in life were related to my inactions rather than my actions. How I wish now I went over to say hello to my sergeant that day.

Half of "The Untouchables" was no longer. I sometimes think back about the four of us working the holiday detail and wonder if it was real or simply a dream. Is any of this real? How can it be that Eddie and Ryen are gone? I don't think I'll ever understand the cruelty of death.

The next day, I was back at work. In retrospect, I probably could've used a few days off after the funeral to clear my head, but I think the clerical-minded Mrs. Jones would've had a nervous breakdown.

Thanks to Reverend Gray, I'd been approved to the Restaurant Row foot post on a permanent basis. Being that we were still in the middle of a frigid winter, none of my senior coworkers raised any eyebrows with my new assignment.

That afternoon, while the soup kitchen line was forming, I was conversing with James and a few of his buddies. All of a sudden, I heard a woman scream and a man running with a purse down Forty-Sixth Street. I immediately called for backup on my radio and started a foot pursuit. I began to gain on the perp when all of a sudden, in one motion, he stopped, turned, and punched me in my left eye. I was stunned but still standing. As I wobbled back a few feet, I noticed James and half the guys from the soup line run past me and jump on the perp. I was no longer worried about the perp being a threat but rather that the guys—my guys—were going to kill this bastard. I started yelling for them to stop when the first of several squad cars pulled up. They had their batons out and were ready to hit anything that was moving and black. I had to explain to them that the black guys were helping me, and the perp was the white guy lying on the ground clutching the purse. Thankfully, James and the rest of the guys were uninjured, but the perp took a pretty good beating.

I knew James had been boxer while he was in the service in Vietnam and I'm guessing he was able to get a few good punches in before I was able to restore order. I thanked the guys, especially James, for their help. Then James said something that touched me deeply. "You're my brother, and nobody messes with my brother."

During the commotion, I observed three Hassidic Jewish men talking with the captain that was now on the scene. The three men, dressed in their traditional black overcoats, black pants, and black wide-brim hats, were visibly upset over the incident. At first, I thought their anger was toward James and the guys for aggressively taking down the perp, but I soon realized that wasn't the case. The three men were telling the captain how the guy with the purse assaulted me.

Their words were a relief since the perp was still lying on the ground in obvious pain. His head was split open and blood started making a puddle on the pavement.

The Duty Captain, now wanting to get my side of the story, asked me how he suffered the injuries, to which I responded, "After the man assaulted me, he went to take off again, slipped, fell, and suffered the injuries in question."

I did emphasize that I wasn't clear on all the facts since I just suffered a head injury myself.

Overhearing what I told the captain, the group of black and Jewish men started agreeing with one another.

"Yep, that's what happened."

"The guy just slipped and fell after assaulting the officer."

"Yep, clumsy dumbass should've watched where he was going."

The Duty Captain instructed one of the officers in the squad car to transport both the perp and me to the hospital.

Maybe it was the adrenalin pumping through me, but I hadn't noticed that I couldn't see out of my left eye. When I looked in the reflection of the RMP window, I noticed the punch left me with a grapefruit-sized, swollen black eye.

After getting into the back seat of the squad car with the bandaged perp, the officer took off for Roosevelt Hospital. A few blocks from the hospital, the officer pulled the RMP over and then turned to me and said, "Go ahead."

I had no clue what the hell the guy was talking about. "Go ahead and what?" I asked him.

He told me that the guy needed a beating for what he'd done to me. I looked at the perp with the bloodied, bandaged wrap around his head and told the officer that I thought he'd been given enough street justice for one day. The aggressive cop wasn't satisfied with my answer.

In a voice filled with anger, the insistent officer responded, "If you don't take care of this piece of shit, I will. If you let the perp get away with assaulting a police officer, what's to stop him from doing it again?"

I explained to the officer that the fight was over—the guy was cuffed—and I wasn't about to assault a cuffed prisoner. The officer's response showed great intelligence, wit, and sophistication on his part. "You're a pussy," he exclaimed.

Without incident, we finally arrived at Roosevelt Hospital. As I walked the prisoner into the emergency room, he thanked me for not hitting him in the car. I grabbed the slimy little drug addict by the chest and told him we weren't buddies and not to thank me for a fucking thing. I further told him if he made a move in the hospital, I'd shoot him in the nuts.

The adrenalin was wearing off and the sting of this prick's punch was starting to make me a bit cantankerous. The one silver lining was that I found out nurses like men in uniform, especially ones with a big, swollen black eye.

The doting nurses at Roosevelt Hospital attended to my injury with lots of tender loving care. One of the nurses insisted on holding the ice pack over my eye, even after I told her I was more than capable of doing it myself. Another nurse, while rubbing my hand, asked me how I suffered the injury. In my best James Cagney impersonation, I told the attractive brunette, "See, I guess I should've been bobbing instead of weaving—oh, that dirty rat got me good."

After graduating from the academy, my dad told me there'd be lots of perks working in Midtown. I guess being pampered by pretty nurses was part of what he was talking about. Once again, thanks, Dad!

The following week I was assigned to the "barrier detail." The one day, six-man assignment was a sweet way to spend a spring afternoon out-of-the-bag. The sanctioned overtime was offered by the department to MOS on their day off. The detail consisted of either picking up or dropping off barriers used for parades and special events throughout the city.

The Saint Patrick's Day parade was coming up and members were needed to drop off barriers along the Fifth Avenue parade route. The experienced driver of the barrier truck planned our final stop to be at the Cathedral in order to coincide with our lunch break. Besides Central Park, there was probably no better place in the city to take in some sun and be surrounded by beautiful women.

Across the street from the Cathedral was Rockefeller Center. The Christmas tree had long been gone and the ice rink covered over with tables for the seasonal, outdoor restaurant. While sitting on the steps I thought about Eddie and "The Untouchables." Diagonally across the street from where I was sitting was where we had our first foot pursuit. While sitting there daydreaming, I could envision Ryen giving the hand signals, Eddie taking off like a bat out of hell, and then Anthony using a straight arm to take down the perp.

While still musing, I spotted a young teen pick up someone's Sak's Fifth Avenue bag and start walking in my direction. The kid was smooth and for a moment, the unsuspecting victim had yet to realize her bag was gone. I got up, took my police shield out from under my shirt and stopped the teen. I thanked him for finding the lady's missing bag and told him it would be a good idea to return it to the rightful owner. The young punk thought he was going to be able to bullshit his way out of the larceny by telling me it was his bag.

Knowing the barrier detail wasn't exactly to be used as an Anti-Crime Task Force, I had no intention of arresting the individual but did want to get the bag back to its rightful owner.

I gave the teen a choice. We'd give the lady back the bag or I'd be taking him to jail. After realizing he was out of options, the teen decided to walk back with me to make the return.

"Excuse me, ma'am, is this your bag?" I asked, as the teen handed it back to her.

"Oh, thank you, I don't know how I misplaced it," the confused tourist declared as she was waiting to cross the street.

She then insisted on giving the teen a reward, to which I told her wouldn't be necessary. Before letting the young petty thief go, I told him that it was his lucky day and to think about a new career path.

When I returned to the Cathedral steps, the other guys in the barrier detail hadn't noticed what transpired. However, there was one person that did.

As I sat back down, I heard a female voice behind me say, "I suppose New York's Finest are taking a holiday from locking up bad guys."

The comment was spoken in the direction of the female's companion but it was obviously meant for me to hear. I turned to see who was making the facetious remark and saw a mid-twenty-year-old female smiling at me. She had on a white button-down blouse, a black and white checkered skirt that went just below her knees, white silk stockings and black stiletto shoes. The confidently-dressed young lady had a full figure and knew how to dress to compliment her assets.

I politely interjected and told the attractive brunette that I was sorry if she felt her tax dollars weren't being properly allocated.

With a playful smile, she replied, "Well, if you were to let all the bad guys go, I'd be out of a job."

"I must say you dress very nice for a defense attorney."

"No, I'm on the much more sinister side of the law. I'm an ADA (assistant district attorney)."

"In that case, counselor, I apologize for letting one get away."

The young woman introduced herself as Kim Mulholland. The beauteous barrister told me she worked for the Manhattan DA's office and was in one of the nearby Fifth Avenue office buildings taking a deposition. She decided, like half of midtown on any nice spring day, that the steps of the cathedral would be a pleasant spot to take a seat, people watch, and have lunch.

Kim told me she lived out on Staten Island. When I asked her how she made the commute, she explained how the Staten Island Ferry dropped her off close to the courts in lower Manhattan. I told her I was on the ferry once when my parents took me to the Staten Island Zoo after receiving my first communion.

"Did you like it?" she asked.

"The zoo was great, but the ferry not so much. I was probably the only passenger to ever get seasick going across the harbor."

While watching Kim laugh at my comment, I noticed how her head perched back and forth, bouncing her shiny, long brown hair. The attraction was instantaneous.

The female that was sitting next to Kim reminded her that it was time to get back to the office.

"Well, Officer Simpson, it was nice talking with you. Feel free to bring some business my way, that is, if you stop letting the bad guys go."

Desperate to want to see her again, I blurted out the first thing that came to mind. "If I remember correctly, they have pretty good ice cream cones on the Staten Island Ferry. Maybe I can treat you to one sometime?"

As she looked at me with her warm brown eyes, she said with a smile, "Oh, I wouldn't want you getting sick again but thanks for the offer."

She, along with her companion, proceeded to walk down the steps of the Cathedral. I watched her for as long as I could until she disappeared into the sea of pedestrians along Fifth Avenue—hypnotized with every step she took in her tightly fitted skirt.

Although Kim hadn't accepted my offer, I didn't take it as a complete rejection. I knew where she worked and if she wasn't interested, she would've never parted with that kind of information.

After lunch, the driver informed us that we had to stop by the Chelsea Pier to pick up some barriers. The partially enclosed pier was located along the West Side Highway and jetted-out into the Hudson River.

When we arrived, the driver proceeded to drive the truck onto the pier. There were a few barriers lying off to the side near the front of the entrance, but otherwise, the decrepit structure was virtually empty. Maybe in its day it was something special, but not anymore. The pier was about the length of three football fields and about a third as wide. The structure that encompassed the pier resembled an airport hangar. The pigeons loved the open-air building and showed their appreciation by crapping all over the place. Both the pier and structure were in serious need of repairs. The city had been using the priceless piece of real estate to store things like the barriers and confiscated vehicles that were waiting to be transported to the impound.

Thus far, the early spring day had been beautiful. The weather was perfect and meeting Kim only added to the positive energy. With a few minutes to kill before we had to move on, I decided to walk to the other end of the pier. I was hoping to find a way outside and take in some sun along the Hudson River.

When I started walking I noticed an RMP parked at the west end of the pier. Although the vehicle was a couple of hundred yards away, I sensed something wasn't quite right about the squad car being where it was. As I moved closer, I could see on the panel door the lettering "103 PCT" and on the back-quarter panel the RMP's number—1041. I knew it had to be Eddie's car. My heart was beating out of my chest. The closer I approached, the more I could see of the vehicle.

RMP 1041 told a gruesome story of evil, brutality and death. The driver's window was blown out. Small chards of glass were scattered throughout the front seat. I could see where Eddie's dried blood ran down the dashboard. It was clear from looking at the inside of the vehicle that Eddie never had a chance.

While standing there in front of RMP 1041, I said a prayer to Eddie. I described to him the beauty and love I witnessed within the sea of blue the day of his funeral. How it not only brought over ten thousand men and women to tears along Hicksville Road, but how an entire nation had now rallied in support of ridding evil in his name.

I never made it outside. Somehow, the beautiful spring afternoon I was enjoying didn't seem so nice anymore.

When I returned back to the barrier truck, one of the guys asked me what I was doing. I told him I was saying goodbye to a friend. I let the guys know there was a squad car at the end of the pier that told a gruesome story of how a fellow officer was killed. With that, the rest of the guys walked down the pier to pay their final respect to Eddie and his RMP 1041.

"*Lest We Forget.*"

CHAPTER 7

Satan's World

Death is always around the corner, but often
our society gives it inordinate help.

—Carter Burwell

My assignment to the Restaurant Row foot post had been working out nicely. The community-style policing allowed me to get to know everyone on the block and protected me from other, less desirable assignments.

One of the true characters along the block was Dario, the General Manager of Barbetta's Restaurant. The wiry restaurateur used so much olive oil in his hair and mustache that he appeared to glisten in the sunlight. In case that didn't make him stand out enough, which was the entire purpose to Dario's antics, he wore a bright red, wool sports coat.

One day while making my rounds, I saw Dario writing the specials down on the board outside the restaurant.

"Ciao, Officer Simpson," the gracious migrant greeted me in his heavy, Northern Italian accent.

"Ciao, Dario."

"You *mangiare oggi, oggi.*"

I thanked Dario for inviting me to eat but respectfully declined. While talking with him, I heard someone behind me asking, "How's the food here?" When I turned around, the mayor, along with Police

Commissioner Ward, was standing in front of me. I wished both men a good afternoon and saluted the commissioner.

It had been the mayor, Ed Koch, doing the inquiring about the food, but from the way Dario acted toward the two men, greeting them as regular patrons, I presumed it wasn't the first time the mayor and commissioner were dining at the eatery.

I could've taken the rhetorical question by the mayor as a wry comment, but I chose to enjoy a little spontaneous banter with the city's highest-ranking official. Without thinking of filtering my words, I said, "I'm sorry, Mr. Mayor, but I haven't had the pleasure of eating at Barbetta's on only a cop's salary."

The mayor chuckled as he entered the restaurant, while the commissioner looked at me as if he wanted to take my head off.

With Ward's no-nonsense reputation on the job, I should've known he wasn't going to be amused by my off-cuff remark. I made a mental note after that to leave the comedy act at home when dealing with the upper brass.

My dad knew Ward from when they both entered the department in the early 1950s together. He'd tell Francis and me that anything was possible if we worked hard enough—referencing the PC's parabolic rise from street cop to top cop.

However, according to Dad, Ward's path wasn't an easy one. Being the only black officer in an all-white precinct, Ward dealt with racism on a daily basis. Things were so bad for the future police commissioner that he was forced to change in his car due to the other officers not allowing him the use of the precinct locker room.

Unfortunately, the ignorant sentiment that existed three decades earlier was still present in some pockets throughout the department. On more than one occasion, I would hear a few disgruntled officers refer to the commissioner as a "nigger." This hate speech came from cowards and was spoken with a whisper in corners of the stationhouse. But the fact that it was being uttered at all showed how ignorant many still were. As for me, I thought any individual that achieved as much as the commissioner should not only be respected, but looked upon as an example for what every patrolman should want to achieve.

I waited outside the restaurant while the mayor and commissioner had lunch. After about an hour, the two gentlemen quickly exited the front door to an awaiting Town Car. The men were moving with such a purpose that the commissioner failed to see my salute. As the car began to pull away, it suddenly stopped. The rear tinted window lowered, and in a deep voice, I heard the police commissioner say, "Be safe, officer." Before I could acknowledge the commissioner, the Town Car sped off. It was only a quick quip, but after thinking I made a complete ass of myself earlier, I appreciated the PC's kind words.

Crack and Aids

During the 1980s, there were two new epidemics police were dealing with on a daily basis: crack cocaine and aids. One was a highly addictive drug, the other a deadly transmittable disease. By the time the decade was over, this one-two combination would leave a wake of devastation and death.

Crack was the perfect street drug—a homemade, inexpensive narcotic that was easily manufactured and could produce extreme euphoric highs. Initially, a user could get high for as little as ten dollars. However, the problem for these users was the desire to sustain the euphoric feeling. What started out at as being relatively inexpensive quickly grew into a several-hundred-dollar-a-day addiction.

In the first few years I was on the job, I saw firsthand the devastation linked to this horrific drug. Most of the arrests I made as a rookie were linked to the narcotic. Sergeant Ryen coined the phrase "crack and effect" due to all the residual consequences attributed to the drug. People that normally wouldn't commit such acts were now so desperate that they'd do "anything" for their next fix. With scores of citizens falling into addiction of the drug every day, Satan had a new conduit to spread his unrelenting evil.

The money earned by successful drug dealers helped pave the way to entice corruptible cops in providing the much-needed protection these scumbags needed to stay in business.

During this time period, Brooklyn's Seventy-Seventh and the Seventy-Fifth Precinct became poster children for this new wave of police corruption.

One of the ring leaders at the Seventy-Seventh Precinct was a police officer by the name of Henry Winter. The dirty cop was caught on video surveillance shaking down local drug dealers while on duty and in uniform. After getting pinched, the disgraced officer, now looking to save his own hide and limit his prison time, was more than willing to cooperate with authorities as an informant. With Winter's help the district attorney's office was able to get indictments on thirteen other officers in the precinct—all guys that once considered Winter their friend.

In 1988, Mike McAlary authored an eye-opening account of the organized corruption of Officer Winter and his cohorts in the Seventy-Seventh Precinct. The book was ironically titled "Buddy Boys."

In the book, Winter tells McAlary, "I should have started every tour by putting handcuffs on myself."

Too bad the dirty cop didn't.

In 1995, with a broken marriage, a disgraced police career, and an addiction to the same drug he brazenly stole from drug dealers (crack), Winter put a bullet in his head and killed himself. Another lost soul paid in full to Satan.

Dad witnessed firsthand the organized, systemic corruption and feared that one of his sons would be tempted by such greed. He further knew how many of these disgraced officers dealt with such things once they were caught. This was the selling of the soul he was referencing the day I graduated from the Academy. As Dad explained, "Once you go down that path, there's no coming back."

Winter wasn't the only cop in Brooklyn using his gun and shield to rob drug dealers. Just a few miles away in Bedford Stuyvesant, within the confines of the Seventy-Seventh Precinct, there was another officer taking hubris to a whole new level. The officer's name was Michael Dowd. Just like Winter, Dowd was in business to profit from the lucrative drug trafficking by offering dealers police protection. Those that didn't pay him were either robbed, arrested, or both.

Dowd's initial success afforded him fancy sports cars, luxurious trips, and on occasion, he would have a limousine waiting in front of the stationhouse to take him on a three-hour trek down the New Jersey Turnpike for a gambling rendezvous in Atlantic City.

The NYPD had several corruption complaints on Officer Dowd, but for whatever the reason, the brass hadn't pursued him. It took another police agency on Long Island to bring down the dirty cop. The Suffolk County Police Department had Dowd on a wire-tap organizing a cocaine deal with a known drug dealer. The embarrassing incident for the NYPD had many wondering why it took another police agency to bring down one of their own. It was as if a teacher from another school called out a student for cheating, while the students entire faculty was standing right there in the classroom watching and doing nothing.

The revelation not only brought down Dowd and some of his cohorts in the Seventy-Fifth, but it also made the brass in the NYPD look like a bunch of incompetent imbeciles. Like any inept bureaucracy in crisis mode, the city put a commission together to figure out what went wrong.

The 1992 Mollen Commission—named after the retired judge who headed the panel, Milton Mollen—looked into how police corruption was investigated within the department. In the commission's findings, it showed that it was the upper brass that created "a willful effort to impede" when it came to investigating the serious charges of police corruption in the Seventy-Fifth Precinct and Officer Dowd.

It was as if the brass put their heads in the sand and hoped nobody would notice the explosion in police corruption. However, once the scandal broke, Mayor Dinkins was quick to act. Aside from the mayor putting together the commission, he promised more supervision over the officers in the NYPD.

Dinkins was coming across like Claude Rains's character, Captain Louis Renault, in *Casablanca*. When the charismatic Renault is forced to shut down Rick's night club, he exclaims, "I'm shocked, shocked to find that gambling is going on in here!" as the roulette dealer hands the corruptible captain his winnings.

I'm not suggesting the mayor was profiting from the police corruption that was going on in places like the Seventy-Fifth and Seventy-Seventh. However, many in the city and throughout the department were left wondering why it took a scandal in order for the mayor to finally look into organized police corruption. Did he not think that maybe out of 35,000 cops there might've been a few to succumb to the temptation provided by the avalanche of money now being generated due to the explosion in the crack cocaine boom?

I thought Dad's insight regarding the corruption scandals had merit: "The Mayor didn't want to have an issue with police corruption on his watch, so he simply pretended it didn't exist."

Scumbags like Winter and Dowd were no different to me then the drug dealers they preyed upon. Making things worse was the fact that they did all this while hiding behind their badge. These wolves in sheep's clothing had blood on their hands for what happened to Eddie. As for the politicians that weren't brave enough to weed out the corruption because they wanted to pretend all was well in the NYPD, shame on them as well. These spineless, hypocritical bureaucrats were more worried about perception than reality. And what was that reality? The fact that good cops were getting killed, while corrupt scumbags and inept politicians went on with business as usual.

The police locker rooms could be used as an unofficial barometer for morale throughout the department. By nature, most cops like to bitch and moan to let off some steam. While getting dressed, I would listen to fellow officers complain about everything from our measly one percent pay increase offer from the city to resolve our contract dispute, to being forced to write a minimum number of summonses each month. I noticed that the guys that complained the most did the least. The complaining didn't bother me. On some occasions, it was comical, and on others, perhaps even warranted.

However, it wasn't until the noise of discontent was absent from the locker room that I realized how low morale had become. I took the silence as a sign that the guys I worked with no longer cared. It seemed wherever we turned, someone was pointing a finger at the men and women in blue proclaiming us as a collective group of no good, corrupt cops. All that negativity was starting to take a toll.

The media didn't do anything to help quash the sentiment. Once things were seemingly quieting down, the press would run stories to help stoke the flames. If they couldn't find a new story about police corruption, they'd find one in the form of police abuses. They loved taking pictures of police squad cars parked adjacent to a fire hydrant or in bus stops with captions that read: "Above the Law" and "Thanks for the Spot, Suckers."

Of course, there wasn't any explanation given that the officers might've been responding to an emergency and parked the vehicle in the most convenient location at the time. The truth was that because of a few bad apples, the entire rank and file was now an easy piñata for everyone to take a swipe at.

By autumn, I didn't think the morale on the NYPD could get much worse, but it did.

On October 18, 1988, within three hours of each other, two of New York's finest were gunned down in separate incidents in Manhattan.

Officer Christopher Hoban, twenty-six, and Officer Michael Buczek, twenty-four, were the latest victims in the war on drugs. Hoban was from my neighborhood in Bay Ridge and worked out of the Manhattan North Narcotics Division. Buczek, worked out of the drug-infested Thirty-Fourth Precinct in Washington Heights.

Both men were part of the tragic, and all too often story of young officers being violently executed by street thugs throughout the inner cities. Eddie was a victim to these senseless acts of violence, and now Christopher and Michael were as well.

It was the first time in the department's history that two officers were killed on the same day in separate incidents. Another first would be conducting a funeral for both officers simultaneously.

The funeral for the slain officers was held a mile from my home in Brooklyn at Our Lady of Perpetual Help. Nearly fifteen thousand officers comprised the sea of blue along Fifth Avenue on that late autumn morning.

During Eddie's funeral, I'd become overwhelmed with sadness when the Emerald Society started playing the bagpipes. I knew Eddie and thought my emotions were because of the personal relationship I had with him. But on this day, as I stood there saluting the draped covered coffins and listening to the wind instruments playing Amazing Grace, I realized my emotional bond with them was just as strong. They were my brethren, my coworkers, and two of over 35,000 men and women I called family. Holding back the tears was no longer an option for me—or anyone else for that matter.

In a written statement, the family of Officer Michael Buczek wrote, "Michael gave up his life to fight the war on drugs. All we ask is that our nation's local and Federal governments support the death penalty and provide the funding necessary to win the war on drugs."

Police Commissioner Ward carried on the cry to rid the drug epidemic from our communities. While addressing the families of the slain officers at the funeral, he said, "I know what drugs are doing to the world and this city, and I know the anger wells up in me. All of us will never give up. The police officers of this city will never give up."

After hearing the commissioner's words, I said a prayer. I prayed that before the next street dedication ceremony or little league park, or a five-kilometer race was dedicated in the name of another slain officer, that somehow true change would occur. After all, I'd much rather have these places named after dead presidents than dead cops.

The second part of the one-two combination of the '80s nightmare was a new and mostly unknown disease called AIDS.

HIV and AIDS were simply acronyms that I didn't know or care much about. Being that I wasn't gay or a drug user, I believed I was immune to the disease. All that changed on Thanksgiving Day 1988.

My foot post was like a ghost town that early holiday morning. Mostly everyone in Manhattan was a few blocks east getting ready for the Macy's Thanksgiving Day parade. While walking my post, I noticed a street person lying inside one of the apartment house vestibules. I took out my nightstick and tapped the disheveled man on the foot to wake him up. At first, the individual was nonresponsive, but after a few more nudges with my stick, I was finally able to render him from his stupor. While the individual was turning his head to see who was disturbing his rest, he spat in my face. What started out as a routine move along was now anything but.

I learned from my dad if I was ever going to tune-up a perp, not to hit him in the face but rather the legs. According to him, the face left too many visual marks and bled like a son-of-a-bitch.

I proceeded to use what I considered the "necessary force" under the circumstances to affect the arrest. The individual could now add difficulty walking to his issue with saliva control.

After placing the unhygienic perp in handcuffs, I put on my latex gloves and asked the question all officers normally ask prior to searching an individual in police custody. "Do you have any weapons, drugs or anything sharp in your pockets—like a needle?"

The uncooperative perp wasn't responding, so I began my search. During the pat-down I felt something hard inside his crusty coat pocket. I thought it might've been a knife, so I reached inside to remove the item and "it" happened. The item was not a knife but a hypodermic needle. The bee sting type feeling I was experiencing was the needle pricking the skin of my right index finger.

If getting spat in my face pissed me off, then getting pricked by a needle sent me into a rage. I had a rule about not hitting cuffed prisoners, and thankfully for both our sakes, I honored that rule. I think if the scumbag wasn't cuffed, I would've seriously hurt the guy. I started yelling at the perp in frustration, but I knew it was me that I was upset with. I used poor police tactics and should've been more careful. Now my concern shifted to whether or not this individual had the dreaded HIV.

I called for a squad car to take the perp and me to the hospital. I wasn't about to take the perp's word that he wasn't HIV positive, so I was going to get him tested.

The squad car dropped me off at St. Claire's Hospital on West Fifty-Eighth Street. I explained to the administrator in the emergency room that I wanted the prisoner tested for HIV. The impervious female worker acted as if I wasn't there and then proceeded to advise the perp that he wasn't under any obligation to submit to a blood test. I felt like I was in a bad dream—one of those dreams where everything goes wrong and I couldn't wake up. However, this wasn't a dream, it was my life. Now I had some "save the world, tree-hugging" bureaucrat explaining to the patient his rights—just what I needed.

Before I allowed the perp to say anything, I pulled the administrator to the side. It was apparent that she knew the removal of blood from an individual was protected under the Fourth Amendment's right of reasonable searches and seizures. However, there was an exception to this law. If an individual was involved in an accident that involved death(s) or serious injuries that could result in death, and was suspected of being under the influence, then the hospital could forcibly obtain a blood sample without the individual's consent.

With a look of disinterest on her face, the administrator looked on as I tried explaining how this case was no different. Instead of the car being the instrument of lethal consequences, it was a needle. And because of this person's actions, I now could be at risk of dying.

Realizing I wasn't going to be able to persuade her otherwise, I decided it was time to go and try my luck at a different hospital.

I radioed the squad car and asked for them to return to Saint Claire's. After picking us up, I had them take me a few blocks over to Roosevelt Hospital. I then turned my attention to the perp. I explained to him when we arrived at the hospital, he was going to voluntarily submit his blood for analysis. I wasn't about to live with a black cloud hanging over my head, waiting to see if one day I'd test positive for the virus.

The squad car radioed the dispatcher that he was transferring the prisoner and me to Roosevelt Hospital. The call must've raised a flag because when we arrived at the hospital, the Duty Captain was waiting there for us. He immediately demanded an explanation as to why I was hospital shopping.

I explained to the captain in great detail the circumstances leading up to the arrest and the lack of cooperation I was receiving from the personnel at the previous hospital. The poker-faced Captain walked over to the squad car where the perp was sitting in the back seat and asked if he'd submit to a blood test. The perp, sensing the captain was on his side, proceeded to refuse.

The unapologetic captain turned to me and said, "The prisoner has rights and they need to be respected."

Just when I thought my nightmare was over, it started back up again. I couldn't believe what I was hearing and decided it was time for me to push back.

"Hey, Cap, what about respecting my rights?"

With complete disregard, the brass prick told me to get back to the stationhouse with my prisoner and process the arrest before he suspended me for insubordination. I saluted the captain and wished him and his family a Happy Thanksgiving—my way of telling him to go to hell.

For the first time in my career, I knew what it felt like to be a pawn. Dad used the expression "blue pawn" whenever explaining stories to mother about how the brass treated the bottom half of the rank and file. This was his description of what it meant:

> "Just like the lowest pieces on a chessboard, the men in blue are treated like pawns. Without regard or respect, the more powerful chessmen allow the pawn to exist at his discretion—to do with as he pleases. The insignificant blue pawns are merely expendable foot soldiers that should be content to exist at the pleasure of the brass."

The captain could care less whether or not I contracted a lethal disease. After all, I was merely a pawn. So, as a good foot soldier, I followed my orders and proceeded back to the precinct to process the arrest.

After a restless night of sleep, I arrived back at the command the next morning seeking to speak with the only openly gay person I knew, Officer Charlie Hill.

Charlie was assigned with me to the North and a member of the NYPD's GOAL society (Gay Officers Action League).

I didn't know Charlie that well, but from seeing him around I could sense he was different than the other cops in the precinct. For starters, he was polite, soft-spoken and was always smiling. He dressed differently, too. Most of us didn't care what we wore to work because we knew we'd be changing into our uniform. So, instead of wearing jeans and sneakers like the rest of us, Charlie wore slacks with penny loafers, usually with a Polo shirt and a pink sweater tied around his neck. He looked more like he was heading to a country club than a foot post.

I approached Charlie after muster to explain my unfortunate mishap with the hypodermic needle. His first piece of advice was simple: "Get tested." He recommended getting tested several times over the next few months, because as he explained, "The virus could lay dormant and go undetected for several months." His second piece of advice was more for my mental health. Charlie told me not to worry. "Chances are everything will be fine," he said with a reassuring smile.

He must've realized I was stressed and offered up those words to comfort me. Then Charlie caught me off-guard with a question of his own. He asked me why I came to him for advice. Although surprised, I didn't hesitate with my answer.

I told him that his nickname around the command was Mr. Britannica (after the encyclopedia). But besides being considered the smartest individual in the North, I also let him know that he was the only gay person I knew and thought he might have a better insight than most when it came to understanding the disease.

I sensed my candid answer resonated with the conscientious officer because he went on to discuss the matter with me in great detail. During our conversation, Charlie pointed out an alarming uptick in suicides amongst gay men. He explained that being diagnosed with AIDS was a double whammy—a leprosy type stigma that went along with a horrific death. I could sense Charlie was not only trying to educate me about the virus but also trying to enlighten me in regards to the disproportionate impact HIV was having throughout the gay community.

With a sadness in his voice that could only come from one's true life experiences, Charlie said, "Besides the apparent death sentence, there were those in mainstream society that felt the disease was a godsend. His way to rid society of the "abomination" of homosexuality. Those that are diagnosed feel abandoned by everyone. Feeling completely overwhelmed, outcasts, and fearing the loss of their dignity, many simply decide to give up. Some choose pills, while others decide to jump off a bridge or in front of a train. The method is merely a means to an end. I would think it's the last bit of control one feels they still have. I can only hope it doesn't take a person being afflicted themselves to show compassion for people with such a tremendous burden."

Prior to talking to Charlie, I felt indifferent toward the gay community. In no way did I show prejudice toward them, but I didn't exactly have compassion or an understanding for what was transpiring. It wasn't until my little mishap with the hypodermic needle that made me want to know more. Now that I was, I realize my stance on being indifferent wasn't good enough.

I thanked Charlie for his time and his courage. I knew it couldn't have been easy for him to be an openly gay cop amongst a testosterone-filled precinct of homophobes.

I took Charlie's advice and had my blood tested several more times for HIV. Thank the Lord, each test came back negative.

The Unthinkable

The holidays were always a special time of year in my neighborhood. Home owners, stores, bars, and even my church, Saint Patrick's, would try to outdo each other with their decorative lights and Christmas decorations. In many ways, the year had been difficult, but at least for the final week of 1988, I could share in the holiday spirit with those I loved and cared about most—Dad, Francis, and Father Gerald.

My Academy Instructor, Sergeant Vella, explained how not everyone shared in the holiday cheer.

"Because of the time of year, people have the tendency to be more susceptible to depression," he told Class 87–18. "There are numerous reasons for the holiday blues—loneliness, the missing of a love one, and financial woes, to name a few. Whatever the case might be, it becomes amplified this time of year. Suicide rates spike in the weeks leading up to Christmas. So, look for the signs. Listen to what people say. Don't let a comment regarding suicide just go by without questioning it. Most people that kill themselves give hints in desperation for help. Give them your time. Sometimes it can be as simple as keeping your mouth shut and your ears open. Be suspicious of uncharacteristic behavior. If need be, seek counseling on their behalf. Don't put yourself in a position of regretting not doing something before a tragedy occurs."

The sergeant stressed that besides the rise in suicide rates around the holidays, homicides, armed robberies and other violent crimes spiked as well. He instructed the class not to fall into Norman Rockwell's holiday trap.

"Cadets, be aware and keep both eyes open. Let the mothers and children be without worries. For us, it's our job."

Sergeant Vella went on to tell the class of a personal experience he had as a rookie one Christmas Eve.

"There was a liquor store on the corner of the Queens Boulevard foot post I was assigned to. I noticed the store was busy throughout the evening; lots of folks getting their last-minute hooch before Santa arrived. At around ten, I saw the lights to the store were still on and the security gate pulled halfway down. When I walked over to investigate, I could see through the front window the owner lying on the floor behind the counter in a puddle of blood. The merchant had been robbed and now he was dead. Later, when the detectives apprehended the two perps they were asked why they did it. They responded, 'Because we needed money for presents.'"

Sergeant Vella asked the class what mistakes he made that evening. He pressed us for comments, but no one seemed eager to put any of the blame on him. One cadet stated, "You can't be everywhere and prevent everything?" Another cadet suggested that if he was in front of the store at the time of the robbery that perhaps he could've been the one killed. When the instructor asked for my opinion, I thought of Dad and his view on how misfortune plays a role in such tragedies, so I replied, "Maybe it was bad luck."

Sergeant Villa's face turned to sadness. In a low voice he said, "No, it wasn't bad luck… it was sloppy police work on my part. I should've known the store was going to have a lot of cash on hand. I should've been more diligent to find out what time the store closed since that's when most robberies occur. In all likelihood, my presence in front of the store prior to closing would've deterred the crime from ever happening. During my shift, I should've made inquiries to find out whether or not the merchant was going to deposit the money at an all-night bank drop or take it home with him. I could've made plans to be there at closing time to walk him to his car or the bank. I could've been more aware about my responsibilities instead of watching the pretty snowflakes fall along Queens Boulevard. I could've not had my head so far up my ass that I allowed a homicide to occur on my foot post on Christmas Eve. Mr. Paul Castronova (the liquor store owner) could've celebrated Christmas with his wife and five children, but instead he was now going to spend it at the Medical Examiner's office. As for his family, they were going to receive a phone call that would change their world forever. So, be aware. Be alert. Talk to people. Ask questions. In less than a month, you're going to be walking the beat and people are going to look to you for leadership. They're going to look for you to solve all their problems, cure all their ills. And although you won't be able to solve everything, at least don't have your head up your ass. Prepare yourselves, ask questions and open your eyes."

As I listened to the sergeant, I could sense the pain of that night had scarred him for life. Norman Rockwell's scene of children ice skating in the park was no longer the eidetic image he envisioned when it came to the holidays. The sergeant's view of Christmas had been jaded. It was now one of death, regret and guilt.

While sitting there listening to our instructor talk about things I hadn't any firsthand experiences with, I realized just how young and naive I truly was.

By the sergeant sharing his story, it helped me begin to appreciate the responsibilities I'd soon have. I knew after listening to him I wanted to do all I could to prevent such a tragedy from ever happening on my watch.

On Christmas Eve, I went to church with Dad. I hadn't a choice since Father Gerald would've excommunicated both of us if we were to ever miss one of his Christmas midnight masses. Francis met us there without his girlfriend, Mary. Dad was kind enough to ask if she was feeling all right, where I was just happy she was a no-show. Francis's uneasy response to the innocuous question, explaining to us that she had a headache, had me thinking the two had yet another quarrel.

After mass, Francis told me he was meeting up with some of the guys from our old squad in Manhattan. They were scheduled to work the midnight shift and Francis was going to meet them for a holiday drink at McHale's in Times Square.

I told him I wasn't up to taking the ride into the city but would rather go down the block with Dad and Father Gerald to Pipin's for a nightcap. I invited him but he scoffed at the idea.

In many ways, Francis was an enigma to me. I know Dad wished he and I were closer, but certain things couldn't be forced. There was a time when we were kids that my older brother looked after me. He'd protect me from the neighborhood bullies and made certain I didn't stray with the wrong crowd. The day Francis helped me with my first collar brought back memories of how things use to be between us—big brother looking out after little brother.

As a youngster, he was the one who taught me how to throw a football and use my body to knock down ground balls. He showed me how to throw a punch and equally important, how to take one. I missed having Francis as my big bro. I'm not sure when things changed between us, but I knew his excessive drinking and choice of companions didn't help with our relationship.

The last memorable time we spent together as siblings was my eighteenth birthday. Dad made reservations for the three of us at Peter Luger Steakhouse in Williamsburg, Brooklyn. I'd never been to the famed eatery before and was very much looking forward to a good steak and my first legal beer.

At the last moment, Dad called the house and explained to Francis he was stuck at his new security job and wouldn't be able to take us to dinner. Francis, knowing how much I was looking forward to the evening, decided he'd take it upon himself to keep our plans.

When we arrived at the unassuming brick corner building, I remember thinking how the place looked more like a rundown apartment house than the legendary steakhouse I heard so much about.

Entering the restaurant didn't help change my opinion on the dilapidated establishment. With saw dust on the floor and plain block slabs being used for dining tables, I thought there must've been a mistake. I asked Francis if we were at the right Peter Luger's to which he responded, "There's only one."

Francis ordered two beers at the bar without asking me which kind I wanted. When he handed me my first beer as a legal adult, I asked him what it was. He told me it was Beck's on tap, and before I could ask why, he volunteered that it was the only beer they served.

After a forty-five-minute wait—with a reservation mind you—we finally were seated.

The crotchety, gray-haired, German waiter approached the table, and without saying a word, took the order from Francis: "T-Bone for two medium-rare with potatoes and cream spinach."

That was my last straw. I asked Francis what kind of place this was. There was zero ambiance, one type of beer, rude service and no menus. I wanted to leave.

Francis began to laugh and told me I was right on all accounts but one.

"They do have menus but only a pretentious yuppie or a novice would ever ask for one," he explained. "As for leaving, it's your birthday and I'll do whatever you want, but at least try the steak first. If you don't like it, then we'll go."

A short time later, a bountiful, picturesque-looking T-bone steak was delivered to our table. The sizzling piece of meat was precut into pieces of about one inch by two inches along the bone and laid on a plate filled with the meat's juices. The stone-faced waiter served each of us two pieces and some of the sides. Francis then put some of their homemade steak sauce on the strips and I followed. The next thing that happened could only be described as a culinary orgasm. I took one bite of the steak and all the rest made sense.

I wasn't there for good service or a beautifully decorated restaurant with fancy linens and glasses. I was there to have a great steak and that's precisely what I received.

After my first mouthful, Francis, seeing I was in food heaven, asked if I'd prefer to leave. I was too busy enjoying my steak to answering such a ridiculous question. He then told me to try the spinach and potatoes with the steak sauce. Not wanting to use my mouth for anything but chewing, I simply nodded my head and scooped-up some of the sides.

After ten minutes of nonstop, pure succulent decadence, I finally pushed my plate away and uttered, "No mas."

Francis made my eighteenth birthday a memorable one. We ate and drank like men might've done back at King Arthur's court. We told stories to one another and laughed throughout the evening. For the first time in my young life, I felt I was on an even keel with my older brother—I felt like a man.

But instead of having more of those special nights together, things seemed to worsen over time. Going out with Francis became a night of woes. There were the barroom fights and the arguments over unpaid tabs. My goal wasn't to have fun when we went out, but to get him home without having a police report being filed against him.

After turning down Francis's invitation, Dad encouraged me to reconsider. I explained to both of them that I was tired and wished to make it an early evening. I again invited Francis to join us, knowing he wouldn't pull off any of his antics in front of Dad and Father Gerald, but he was adamant about going into Manhattan to see the guys. Then Francis did something uncharacteristic—he asked me to go with him a second time.

Francis wasn't one to ask anyone for anything, but if he had, he certainly would never ask twice. I knew something was up, but I chose to ignore that little voice that was telling me to go with him. So, I made the decision I'd rather be home waiting for Santa to arrive then babysit my older brother.

After telling Francis for the second time that I'd pass, we hugged, wished each other a Merry Christmas, and then he walked down the steps of the church toward his car. While watching him walk away, the little voice inside me was now joined by an uneasy feeling in my stomach. Not knowing it at the time, choosing to ignore both would have major consequences.

Dad, picking up that something was troubling Francis, asked me if I knew if everything was all right between him and Mary. I told him that I wasn't aware of any issues, but in my opinion, he'd be better served by moving on from the drama queen.

After finishing our pints at the pub, Dad and I walked Father Gerald back to the Rectory. It was now after two in the morning, and the thought of sleeping in the next day was a warm welcome. I hadn't been sleeping long when the phone rang. The clock next to my bed read 4:44 a.m. I hesitated to answer, somehow knowing it had to do with the little voice that was nagging me earlier.

As the phone continued to ring, I started wondering if Francis had been in a fight or a car accident. I knew before I ever picked up the receiver I was going to regret my choice of not having gone with him earlier. It was time to find out what happened.

In a nervous, hesitant voice, the caller asked me, "Is this Dean?" After acknowledging that it was, he said, "Dean, this is John, John Young. I don't know if you remember me from the second squad, but ah… ah… I don't know how to tell you this…"

Before John uttered another word, I knew my brother was no longer a part of this world. John continued to tell me what I already knew. "He's dead."

I asked John what happened and he told me that Francis shot himself.

There are some phone calls in life one never forgets. I'm certain the call the liquor store owner's wife received the night her husband was gunned down stayed with her for the rest of hers. I could live to be a hundred and have lost all my marbles, but unfortunately, I'll always remember that call.

I sat at the edge of my bed for what seemed like an eternity, but it was only a few minutes. I thought of my brother and the life that was now gone. I thought about that uneasy feeling I had when Francis walked to his car. I thought about how I should've gone with him and then I thought about the unthinkable—telling my father that his twenty-six-year-old son was now dead.

I lived upstairs from my dad in the apartment of the two-family house I grew up in. Although there were a set of interior doors that separated the two units, the two of us always left them open. The unspoken, symbolic gesture was a way to let the other know they were always welcome. Many of my friends had already moved out from their parents', but I enjoyed the closeness of staying home near my dad. Every morning that I wasn't working, I'd get the newspaper and the two of us would sit at the dining room table and have breakfast together. Dad would read the paper to me, highlighting those articles that showed how evil was running rampant throughout our society. He truly believed we were living in the "last days." As far as he was concerned, Judgment Day couldn't come soon enough. He believed the world was in the grasp of Satan with all his deception and would be until Jesus's return.

Before descending down the stairs, I said a prayer to God, asking him for the strength to do what I now needed to do.

As I entered the downstairs apartment, I still didn't know how I was going to tell my dad what happened. It was now five in the morning, and by the sound of his coffee cup clicking the saucer, I knew he was awake. When I entered the kitchen, I could see him sitting by the window watching the traffic go over the Verrazano Narrows Bridge.

Growing up in Bay Ridge, everyone had a sense of pride when it came to the bridge. One could see it from almost anywhere in the neighborhood. Every store owner in the community hijacked the name for their business. There was The Verrazano cleaners, deli, laundromat, car service, fish market, candy store, and the list went on. The only merchants in the neighborhood that didn't want to be associated with the bridge's namesake were the countless Irish Pubs. According to Father Gerald, there was no way the Irish were going to name their bar after a wop.

But as for Dad, his admiration for the bridge went well-beyond local pride. He loved the spinning hunk of steel as if it were part of the family. He knew every detail there was to know about it. He watched it being built and took some 8mm movies in the hope of making his own documentary one day. Since the bridge's opening in 1964, he'd admire the traffic flow over the span the way one might appreciate the serenity of watching a sunrise. He knew how many bolts (one million) and rivets (three million) were used in construction of the bridge. "Did you know that the Verrazano is so long that the engineers had to take the curvature of the earth's surface into account when designing the bridge," he'd rhetorically ask out loud on occasion. He'd love repeating "the curvature of the earth."

As I walked into the kitchen, my dad sat there with his back to me looking out at the bridge. I said good morning to him, forgetting for a moment it was Christmas. He didn't turn but kept looking at his bridge.

"Dean, did you know because of thermal expansion of the steel cables, the roadway in the middle of the bridge drops twelve feet in the summer?" I told him I wasn't aware and then he continued. "It's truly amazing what man can engineer when they put their minds to it. But every great accomplishment comes at a cost, doesn't it son? Did you know while building this magnificent bridge, three men were killed?" As I stood there with tears rolling down my cheeks, I told him I wasn't aware of that fact either.

Of all the history Dad ever spoke regarding the bridge, he never once in all those years mentioned anyone perishing. It was then I realized that he already knew his oldest son was gone.

"The youngest was nineteen, a boy by the name of Gerald Mckee," he went on to say. "Do you think his parents still feel the pain of that day when they were notified of their son's death? Or do you think time has eased it any? Besides his parents and a few quacks like me, do you think anyone else will remember Gerald's name?" Then he paused, turning in his chair to see my tears, and then finished by saying, "Or Francis'?"

Dad explained to me that shortly before I came downstairs, several members of the department came to the house to make the notification and offer their support. Never a big fan of the brass, Dad acknowledged the notification and then closed the front door behind them.

I can't imagine the heartache a parent feels when the unthinkable happens. My dad was a strong man, but no man should have to endure such pain.

In his moment of sorrow, he stood up from his chair, walked over to where I was standing and consoled me with a hug. I had grown physically bigger than my hero, but at that moment, I felt like a child in his arms. It was an embrace I wished never had to end.

The year would finish the same way it began—with a tragic, senseless loss of a young life and a funeral.

One question lingered for me. Why? Why did Francis end his life? What was so bad that he felt ending his life was his only way out?

The wake was at McLaughlin's. The last time I set foot in the funeral home was when my mom died sixteen years earlier. I don't know if it was the overwhelming smell of flowers or the same dreary look on the undertaker's face, but I immediately flashed back to her death. I hated being there. I hated the perfume scent of the floral arrangements, the gaudy décor of the room, and most of all, the closed casket just like Mom had. For me, the place screamed of only one thing—death.

While at the wake, I talked with several of the officers that were with Francis just prior to the shooting. I knew the booze was simply a catalyst behind Francis's actions. What I didn't know and needed to find out was what the trigger had been. For most cops that make such a tragic choice, it came down to one of two things: the job or the girl.

It didn't take long for me to discover which of the two it was—it was the girl.

John Young, the officer that called me, filled me in on the missing pieces. He explained to me that Francis arrived at McHael's Tavern to have a holiday drink with the guys. Then Francis began to drink heavily, doing shots of Jack Daniels, while chasing them down with pints of beer. In Francis's stupor, he began to confide in John that Mary was leaving him for someone else.

I knew Mary was a handful. She loved the drama and attention she'd create by her promiscuous ways, going as far as to provoke Francis into arguments or worse, getting him involved in fights with guys that she'd flirt with while they were out. She was a shallow person that personified narcissism. Her idea of love was judged by how much someone would spend on her at Tiffany's.

Why the Bensonhurst bitch had to dump Francis on Christmas Eve, I'll never know. However, as much as I couldn't stand Mary, I didn't blame her for what Francis had done. Ultimately, he was the one responsible for this nightmare.

"Dean, if I thought for a second he was going to do something like that, I would've taken his gun," John said. "We were all sitting around the back booths having a few beers. I could tell he wasn't his jovial self, so I asked him what was up and that's when he told me about Mary. He said he was glad that it was over and that he was ready to move on. When we all got up to go back on patrol, Francis told me he was going to finish his beer and take a cab home. Next thing I know, we're getting a radio call. 'Shots fired at McHael's.' I don't understand what happened. I truly am sorry."

I told John he had nothing to feel guilty about. I explained to him that I should've been with Francis that night. Now I had to live with that decision for the rest of my life.

Dad never did show his pain which made it more difficult for me to try and discuss the matter with him. Just like mother's death, this was not going to be open for discussion.

Several weeks after the funeral, I sought Father Gerald's counsel. While the Priest and I sat together in the back pew of the empty church, he explained to me that I needed to be patient with my dad and to simply just be there for him. He then directed his attention toward me, asking how I was. I told him I was confused and felt responsible for what had happened. He immediately debunked the idea.

"Dean, it wasn't you that made that choice," Father Gerald said. "That's why I get so mad at people that commit such a selfish sin. They're gone while the rest of us have to pick up their pieces. God gives us the grace of life and this is His reward."

The priest's words didn't go over well with me. I told him that I thought it to be odd that he believed God to be the victim in this situation. Trying to regain my composure, I stood up from the pew and walked a few feet away. But my anger, along with my frustration in trying to comprehend why Francis committed suicide, had taken over my emotions. I began to blame God in God's house in front of my friend, mentor and priest.

"Grace… God's grace," I exclaimed. "Where was God's grace when it came to Eddie, Michael, and Christopher? God gave them the grace of life only to be taken away in their prime. But the drug dealers, sodomites, and murders get to live on. This is God's grace? Why is this the way it is? Why? This sounds like a bad deal to me. When is the ransom paid in full, Father? How much longer do we live with Satan pulling the strings? Maybe Francis committed a sin or maybe he was a victim of a world engulfed in sin. I'm not going to judge him, Mom, or anyone else that is tired of living in this world. If it's a sin, then so be it. If God is so disappointed, then maybe he should do something about it. Instead, we have more evil, more wars, more diseases, and more people electing to die than live. Forgive me, Father, but I'm failing to see God's grace from where I'm standing."

In a calm, compassionate voice, Father Gerald quoted the scripture of Titus:

"Which he shed on us abundantly through Jesus Christ our Savior; that being justified by his grace, we should be made heirs according to the hope of eternal life… Dean, don't you see that without His grace and our faith, we have no salvation from our sins? But you're not alone when it comes to the struggles of faith. No apostle struggled more with his initial faith than Paul. 'But by the grace of God I am what I am: and his grace which was bestowed upon me was not in vain.'"

As my priest spoke, I looked up at the cross above the altar. I thought to myself how in my entire life I never questioned God's word or His motives, but at this moment I had nothing but questions and little faith to understand the explanation Father Gerald was desperately trying to convey.

I came to the church seeking something, anything that would help me understand why Francis and mother would rather be dead than alive. I left with more questions than answers.

However, prior to leaving, Father Gerald told me he loved me.

I knew my words had to trouble, possibly even anger my pastor, but in the most difficult of moments, he gave me love.

I told Father Gerald that I knew he loved me, but my lack of faith in God left me questioning his.

CHAPTER 8

Good Cop, Bad Cop... Ill-Fated Cop

No one can confidently say that he will still be living tomorrow.
—Euripides

The New Year brought some unexpected changes at work. A senior patrolman of the North named John Buchannan asked if I'd be his partner. His previous partner of three years had been transferred to the Robbery Unit—an elite detail that provided a path to the much sought-after detective shield.

I knew the only way to move up to these types of elite details was by producing solid activity, which could only come via the squad car. So, as much as I enjoyed my foot post on West Forty-Sixth Street, when the opportunity came knocking to be John's partner, I took it.

On my final day on Restaurant Row, I informed Reverend Gray that I was being reassigned within the command. The Reverend thanked me for my service and wished me well. I reassured him I'd still be around, and if he needed anything, not to hesitate to call me.

My next goodbye wasn't going to be as easy.

Before leaving, I sought James out to tell him the news. An unlikely friendship between the two of us—a cop and his first ever collar—had been established over the past year. During that time, I was able to get to know James on a personal level. I knew he very much loved his children and wanted nothing more than to have them in his life. Each week, James and I would have lunch together and discuss life and all the wonderful, difficult things that went along with it. In many ways, I was James's mentor, and now that I was leaving, I was afraid he'd take my departure as an abandonment of our friendship.

I found my friend in the basement mopping the floor. As I approached James, he looked up and saw it was me. Smiling as though he'd just won the lottery, he said in his deep, good-natured voice, "Top of the day to you, Officer Simpson." It was at that moment I realized just how difficult the task at hand was going to be. The words I needed to express to James had escaped me.

Sensing I wasn't myself, he asked if everything was all right.

I continued looking at James, desperately searching my mind for the right set of words. The impromptu pause had lingered way beyond the awkward stage. What was to be a simple, light-hearted conveying of news, had now become a graceless display of social incompetence. With each attempt at speaking, I reversed course and floundered like a bumbling idiot. However, James, sensing I had something important to tell him, threw me a lifeline.

He resumed with his mopping, focusing on the floor as he began to speak.

"You know nothing lasts forever," he said. "Sometimes that's a good thing. For one, I couldn't wait to get the hell out of Nam. But then there are things you wish would never end, like that first beautiful day in spring after a long, cold winter. I know they'll be other nice days, but it would be nice if that day lasted a bit longer." Looking up from his mop, James then said, "Don't be a stranger."

The veteran with PTSD and a broken education was keen enough to know my time on Restaurant Row had come to an end. I gave the man I once feared I'd have to wrestle in a welfare hotel a hug, along with a promise that I'd be anything but a stranger.

When my new assignment started in the squad car, it didn't take long to figure out who was going to be in charge. Whether it was which jobs we were going to respond to or where he wanted me to patrol, John called all the shots. In between the jobs we'd accept from the dispatcher, the cantankerous, potbellied veteran with the permanent five-o'clock shadow would have me drive him around to take care of his own personal errands. Whether it was picking up his laundry, stopping by the bank, or deciding which deli he'd go to for a free lunch, it seemed as though police work always took a back seat. I understood I was the junior officer and should be thankful for the opportunity, but I couldn't help but think that in John's eyes I was nothing more than the backend of a donkey costume.

A few weeks had gone by with me keeping my mouth shut and doing as I was told. However, one day while on patrol, we received a radio run that would change all that.

The job was an aided case at the Plaza Hotel. An aided could be any type of medical issue from a slip and fall to an assault. Without any other details available from the dispatcher, I started heading over to the hotel to investigate. That's when John told me to stop at the Flame Diner—he wanted to get breakfast prior to handling the job. I told John that I thought we should answer the call first and then go to the diner.

John, not pleased with me having voiced my opinion, said, "Listen kid, I'm hungry, the job can wait. After all, I'm sure it's going to be a 10-90 (unfounded) or some bullshit slip and fall."

As I approached the diner, I deliberately drove passed it and proceeded straight to the hotel. That's when my partner went nuts.

"Stop the car, stop the fucking car," he screamed. "I told you to go to the Flame Diner. What the fuck do you think you're doing? Would you rather be back on your fucking foot post freezing your nuts off?"

It was at that point I realized John didn't want a partner but rather someone he could bully around.

I decided to confront John's anger with a little wit and calmness. "John, you know the Plaza has the best breakfast in town and are super friendly to cops?" I didn't know this to be true but my white lie accomplished two things: it defused John's anger for the moment and provided him with a new prospective establishment to mooch off of.

With my temporary success in averting a civil war, I continued en route to the Plaza Hotel.

While entering the five-star hotel, I pointed out to John where my father, years earlier, thwarted an assassination attempt. More interested in eating than going down memory lane, John asked where the breakfast was served. I directed him down the corridor to the indoor courtyard. Before walking away, he asked me if I was certain the meal was going to be "on the arm." I told him, "Absolutely," and then went on my way to investigate the call.

The aided case was a bit more serious than John's "slip and fall" scenario. A couple visiting from Charlotte, North Carolina, with their six-year-old son and eight-year-old daughter, had an unfortunate accident in their hotel room. While the children were playing, the boy, not knowing his sister had her finger between the door and door jam, closed the oversize oak door, severing the young girl's thumb clean off.

When I arrived at the room I could see the family was in a state of shock. The girl was hysterically crying, while her mother desperately tried comforting her. I immediately noticed a blood-soaked towel around the young girl's hand. I asked where the digit was and the father pointed to the vestibule table. I immediately grabbed the ice bucket and told the housekeeper to fill it. Then I radioed the dispatcher to get an "ETA" on the bus (police jargon for ambulance). Dispatch informed me that the bus was in an accident and another had to be dispatched. I told the dispatcher there wasn't enough time and that I was going to have to do the transport myself.

I quickly escorted the family to the squad car and then proceeded to go lights and siren all the way to the Bellevue Hospital. About half way to the hospital, I had a feeling come over me that I was forgetting something. I asked the father who was sitting in the back seat with his wife and daughter, if he had the ice bucket with the digit, to which he responded that he had. I still felt like I was forgetting something when I looked over at the young boy sitting in the passenger seat and realized my partner was still at the Plaza Hotel having breakfast.

When we arrived at Bellevue, the medical staff was in position to take over. Besides the Aided Case Report that I needed to fill out, my job was done. I drove back to the hotel where I noticed John talking to one of the doormen by the front entrance. He got into the car without a word being exchanged between us. After about a minute, he uttered, "You owe me $32 for my fucking breakfast." I didn't acknowledge his comment but inside I was quite happy the one-way scumbag had been on the hook for a $32 breakfast—one which I had no intention of paying for. However, I would've gladly paid twice as much to see the look on John's face when the waiter handed him the check for his lavish meal. That would've been priceless.

Besides police work, we didn't say a word to each other for the rest of the shift.

The following day after muster, John and I returned to patrolling Sector Henry. Fortunately, there weren't any lingering signs of the previous day's incident. In fact, John seemed to be in a rare, good mood. The often dispassionate, hag-bag was to my surprise initiating conversations that weren't related to his errand's list. I wasn't sure what to make of the mood swing, but for the moment, I was happy with the armistice.

However, this didn't mean there was a complete stoppage of John's "to-do list."

Today's first errand was to stop by OTB (Off Track Betting) so John could lay money on some "sure winners." When he came back from placing his bets, he handed me a newspaper opened to page three. There was a picture of the eight-year-old girl from the previous day surrounded by her parents, brother, and the medical staff that helped reattach her thumb. The procedure was, "Thumbs-Up," according to the New York Post.

The article in the paper gave me a real sense of pride for having played a small role in the happy outcome. John was quick to try and put a damper on the good news by pointing out that I wasn't mentioned in the article by name, but only that the family received a police escort to the hospital. I laughed as I told him I should've waited around long enough for the press to arrive instead of going back to retrieve my partner. Not to my surprise, John wasn't amused at my comment.

As much as I didn't like working with John, the new sector assignment was perfect for what I needed to accomplish. The disgruntled hag-bag hated everything about being a police officer; doing paper work, making arrests, helping people, and driving the squad car to name a few. Thanks to John's laziness, I was now doubling my monthly activity, which was essential to moving up the ladder.

There was another benefit to the bustling activity, as well. While assigned to my often-idle foot post, I had too much time to think about Francis—time to think of all my regrets and the wave of guilt that always followed. By staying busy, I afforded myself the distraction of not having to deal with the harsh reality that Francis had inexplicably killed himself. However, no distraction in the world could prevent the inevitability of something occurring that would spring me back to Francis and 4:44 on Christmas morning.

Later in the shift, John and I handled an apparent suicide in an apartment on the west side. Unlike Francis, the man left a suicide note. It read:

February 3, 1989

> I don't wish to wait for death to arrive at my doorstep. In my younger years, I lived with ridicule and shame because of my sexual preference. Now, that I've finally found my voice, God has chosen to silence it by inflicting me with a disease that has no cure. I choose instead to exit stage left and gracefully bow out. To those lives I've had the privilege of intersecting with while on this planet, I thank you for your patience and love. To the individual(s) that discover my body, I'm very, very sorry.
>
> Au Revoir,
> Chip

The thirty-two-year-old male performer had been part of the toughest, most unforgiving fraternity in NYC—he was an actor. In an industry known for its brutal coldness, there was never a shortage of those willing to come and subject themselves to the inevitable rejection and ridicule that went along with their profession. Having listened to friends in the acting business tell me of their horror stories, I always wondered why anyone would subject themselves to such affliction. To wait on a "cattle call" for hours only to have someone with less talent, but better connections, tell you you're too big, too small, too thin or too fat. Then there's the narcissistic casting director who feels it's his personal responsibility to crush the dreams of aspiring actors, so he takes the criticism barrage to another level by telling the trusting sheep that they're simply talentless and should find another line of work.

As for Chip, it wasn't his profession that drove him to kill himself, but rather the contracting of HIV. As Charlie explained to me months earlier, many of these individuals would rather kill themselves than go through the social and medical hell that would undoubtedly await them.

So, the out-of-work actor came home after his shift from waiting tables at Wolf's Delicatessen, wrote his suicide note, went into the kitchen of his studio apartment, opened the oven door, blew out the pilot light, put his head in the oven, and began to inhale the gas fumes. Chip consumed the natural gas until he was unconscious—and then he died.

The entire time I was at the scene, I thought of Francis. I felt angry. I was mad for what Francis had done, and worse yet, I failed to understand why he would commit such a selfish act. Francis didn't have a terminal disease. He wasn't an invalid. He was young, strong and full of life. Why then did he throw it all away? Why?

While looking at the bloated corpse lying on the kitchen floor, I realized at that moment I had more understanding and compassion for this stranger, Chip, than I had for my own brother.

One day while standing at muster, I noticed a sign behind the sergeant in front of the room. The sign was about 3' × 2' and had the NYPD logo in the middle of it. Above the logo was the radio call-sign for a police officer in need of immediate assistance: 10-13. However, the numbers on the sign were not meant to bring attention to the radio call, but to show the awful irony that ten of the thirteen officers killed the previous year were done by their own hand—Francis had been number ten.

On the bottom of the sign was a number to the department's medical office in Lefrak City, Queens. The sign urged any officers needing help to reach out and make the call. What the sign failed to mention was that the city's first order of business if an officer did seek help was to have that officer's firearms taken away. Since an officer without a gun is useless, the city's second act would be to reassign the officer to the "rubber gun squad (desk duty)." The next step for the city was to determine whether or not they should terminate the officer.

The city's policy was less about the welfare of the officer and more about covering its own ass. So, faced with these directives, it was no wonder why hardly anybody on the job reached out for help.

For many officers, they chose booze to deal with the stress of the job. Instead of a shrink's office with a couch, it was a bar with a stool. Taking turns, the therapist role was played by fellow officers listening to each other's woes, while the bartender doled out our medication in the form of alcohol.

The hypocrisy of the city's 10-13 poster was to give the perception that the department cared. In reality, as long as the department went along with the same antiquated policy, more blue pawns would handle things the same tragic way.

I don't put all the blame on the department for what happened to Francis. I knew my brother had a drinking problem and a self-destructive personality. However, I do think if there had been a better program in place for cops coping with stress, maybe a few of the "ten" could've been saved—maybe one. Maybe even Francis.

Having gone most of my life without the presence of death, I noticed the dark reality to life becoming a more frequent, unwelcomed guest.

While on the job, death usually came in threes.

As anticipated, the second death came two days later and was yet another suicide. This time, the method of choice was a pirouette off the twenty-ninth floor of the Marriot Marquis. Sadly, it wasn't the first time someone looking to end their life checked into the Times

Square hotel, rented a room on one of the higher floors, and then used gravity to complete their objective.

In this particular case, soon after checking into the hotel, the jumper ordered room service—a bottle of Dom Perignon. After finishing its contents, the troubled young man walked out of his room toward the side railing of the atrium and proceeded to finish his stay by hurling himself over the side—falling nearly three hundred feet to his death.

The mess, as well as the psychological imprint left behind for the hotel staff and guests, was horrific. The sight was as gruesome as any horror flick with the difference being that this was real. On the way down, several body parts were severed off as the individual collided with the metal railings. There was an arm recovered on the twentieth floor, part of a leg on the sixteenth and the torso laid splattered on the lobby's eighth floor. Each time my partner and I heard a scream, we knew another body part had been found.

John and I were able to identify the young man from a wallet that was found near the body—or should I say what was left of the body.

The eighteen-year-old was Timothy Hutchins from Bayonne, New Jersey. There wasn't any suicide note found in the room or on him, but after notifying his parents, the answer to why the young man took his life became much clearer.

Timothy had been addicted to heroin and used hypodermic needles to administer the drug. His mother explained that he recently was diagnosed with the HIV virus and believed her son contracted it by sharing dirty needles with other addicts.

Within three days, John and I handled two suicides related to HIV. I couldn't help but wonder if this was an anomaly or soon to be the norm.

The third death came on the last tour of the week.

John and I received a radio call from the dispatcher: "…aided case… elderly man needs medical assistance."

Upon arriving at the rundown Hell's Kitchen apartment, the two of us were met by the homecare assistant—a young, female Haitian. As the nervous aide escorted John and me into the apartment, she began to explain to us in her thick Creole accent that her client had been sick all morning. While following the aide into the bedroom, I noticed John stayed behind. I knew John to be apathetic when it came to any sort of police work, so I wasn't surprised with his lack of gumption. However, it didn't take long to become aware of John's true motivation for staying in the other room.

Moments before receiving the radio call, John was complaining about being famished and was trying to decide on where to eat. Without anything ever being said, I felt that the Plaza breakfast fiasco set a new precedent in the squad car. I knew I was still John's whipping boy, but at least now radio runs took precedent over deli stops.

While I waited for the paramedics to arrive, I asked the female assistant what issues the gentlemen was experiencing. She explained that the elderly man had been violently vomiting all morning, and she was concerned that it could be something serious. After asking her if he had eaten breakfast, the nurse responded, "Just some coffee and a piece of coconut custard pie."

I took the rest of the pertinent information down and proceeded to fill out an Aided Case Report. The paramedics were now on the scene and took over.

When I walked out of the bedroom, I saw John at the kitchen counter filling his mouth with pie—coconut custard pie.

"What's going on in there?" the hag-bag asked while remnants of the pie went flying from his mouth.

"The paramedics are looking into it. The poor guy has been vomiting all morning."

"Dean, you've got to try this pie. I don't know if it's the best pie I've ever eaten or I'm just starving. This is my second piece."

I couldn't believe the lack of professionalism John was displaying. Here he was in someone's home on police business, and the idiot is acting like he was at an all you can eat Golden Corral. I waited until he had another mouthful of the pie before I broke the news.

"The paramedics think its food poisoning. Funny, I guess."

"What's so funny about that?" he questioned, as more crumbs spewed into the air.

"The only thing the guy ate all day was a piece of that coconut custard pie."

The not so amused officer ran to the kitchen sink spitting out the rest of the pie and then washing his mouth out with water. I couldn't help but take some pleasure in his displeasure.

John, noticing my amusement of the situation, barked at me, "You think this is funny?"

I remained quiet while John continued to wash his mouth out.

The paramedics were getting ready to leave with the aided and his assistant when a man approached me and introduced himself as Geoff.

"Officer, I'm sorry to disturb you, but I think I may have a problem on the fifth floor," the polite custodian of the building informed me.

"What kind of problem?" I asked.

"I smell something foul coming from an apartment and the older woman is not responding to my knocking on the door."

After confirming he had a key to the unit, the three of us preceded up the stairs to investigate.

As I approached the fifth-floor landing, there was no doubt from the smell what we had—a DOA.

The smell is unmistakable, as well as indescribable. Once someone has smelt a decaying human corpse, there's no confusing it with anything else.

I had the custodian unlock the door and wait in the hallway while John and I investigated. Being that most of the residents in the building were over eighty, we were fairly certain we had a straight forward DOA. However, anytime there's a death involved, it's always best to treat it as a crime scene until proven otherwise by the detectives.

John and I entered the foul-smelling bedroom and could see the decaying corpse of an elderly woman lying peacefully in the bed. Nothing in the room looked disturbed or suspicious. The dresser drawers were closed while the jewelry box on top was full and untouched. Not wanting to disturb anything in case my initial assessment of a non-suspicious death was wrong, I walked out into the hallway and started the standard operating procedures regarding a DOA. I notified the dispatcher to send a bus and a supervisor to the scene.

After I finished with the dispatcher, I realized John had stayed in the apartment. When I went back in to see what was going on, he was walking out of the bedroom. I asked him if everything was all right and he simply ignored me.

An uneasy feeling came over me. My instincts were telling me John was up to no good, but I was praying I was wrong. When I went back into the bedroom, my suspicions were confirmed. The jewelry box on the dresser that was filled moments earlier was now empty.

I always prided myself in keeping my cool. I saw cops let the adrenalin of a foot pursuit or car chase turn them into raving lunatics—cursing and screaming at the top of their lungs, but not me. I always tried to remain professional, regardless of how hairy the situation. However, the actions by my partner pissed me off more than when I was pricked by the needle.

I walked out into the hallway where John was talking with the custodian and grabbed him by the back of his jacket and pulled him into the apartment. I slammed the door behind us and held John by the collar. I then let loose.

"You fucking scumbag. If you think I'm going to risk my career or go to jail for a piece of shit like you, you're crazy. The sergeant will be here in two minutes and that's how much time you have to put the shit back or else."

"I don't know what the fuck you're talking about," the defiant, dirty cop pleaded.

I let go of his collar and reminded the scumbag he had two minutes or I'd be putting the cuffs on him myself.

I waited for the sergeant in the hallway while John stayed in the apartment alone. When the boss arrived, we entered the unit together where I saw John sitting on the couch looking like he hadn't a care in the world. He waved to the boss, while the two of us made our way to the bedroom. I already made the decision if the jewelry wasn't back in the box, I was going to lock the scumbag up.

As soon as I entered the room, I looked over at the jewelry box and noticed that some of the jewelry had been returned. I knew there was more than what was currently in the box, but the truth was I couldn't swear to it. I wasn't about to take my gun out on a fellow officer only to find out he didn't have any stolen jewelry on him. I decided it was best to let the matter go.

The sergeant looked over the room and informed me that I had some vouchering and paper work to do.

I was in no mood to stay and play nice with John, so my response to the sergeant was cold and short, "Not me, Sarge. I'm taking lost-time."

"Well, I don't care who does what but somebody has to do some paperwork," the sergeant mildly responded.

Before walking out of the apartment, I glared at the scumbag as he sat there on the couch like a common thief pretending I didn't exist.

Upon returning to the command, I went directly to the lieutenant's office. I asked the Administrative Lieutenant to immediately take me out of the squad car. I knew my request would raise some eye brows, but I didn't care.

"Officer, what seems to be the problem?" the senior desk jockey asked.

"Sir, I'll go back to a foot post, guarding prisoners in a hospital or sitting on DOA's again, but I no longer wish to continue my current assignment, sir."

The perceptive supervisor went right to the heart of the matter. "Son, if there's something going on that I or Internal Affairs should know about, this is the time to say something. You may not be aware of it, but Officer Buchannan is under investigation for several corruption allegations."

I wasn't certain what pissed me off more: being called "son" by someone other than my dad or priest, or finding out that my partner was allowed to be on patrol while under investigation.

"Boss, I'm the one that has to work in this precinct with these guys. I have to dress in the same locker room and when need be, call them for backup. If I get labeled a rat, my life turns into a living hell. If you know you have a bad apple, why would you keep him in the barrel? It makes no sense to me. It's the department's job to rid these scumbags, not mine."

I went onto explain to the lieutenant that I had a three-day swing coming up and wouldn't be back to work 'til the following week. He told me he'd see what he could do but made no promises.

The following day, I decided to visit Father Gerald. I hadn't seen much of my mentor as of late, only during his regularly scheduled Saturday evening mass. I walked over to the Rectory, and as I had done for years as a youngster delivering groceries, rang the back-door bell. I could've used the front entrance but then I risked not seeing Mrs. Strahan.

The always upbeat matriarch greeted me with a big smile and hug, and then proceeded to scold me for being too thin.

"Young man, when's the last time you had a homecooked meal?" the nurturing lady of the house asked in a chastising tone.

"Well..."

"Well, nothing! Get in here and let me fix you something to eat."

I enjoyed the kindness and attention Mrs. Strahan bestowed upon me. My friends all had mothers that doted on them. I had Dad. Don't get me wrong, Dad was my best friend, but he simply wasn't wired for doting.

As we walked together up the back staircase, I couldn't help but notice an attractive woman peeling potatoes in front of the kitchen sink. The bronze-skinned beauty was in her early twenties, and despite the hideous, full-length, flowered-apron she was wearing, it was still quite apparent that the Latin knockout had a perfect hourglass figure.

"Mrs. S, don't tell me these cheapo's finally broke down to get you some help around here?" I facetiously asked.

"Dean, this is Diana my new assistant. She's from Bogota, Colombia."

I told the shy assistant that it was my pleasure to make her acquaintance. With little eye contact and a smile, the South American looker acknowledged my comment and then went right back to feverishly peeling the potatoes.

After eating a dish of Mrs. Strahan's beef stew and catching up on the news of the congregation, I asked her if I could see Father Gerald. When she went to retrieve the pastor, I made an attempt at small talk with Diana. Not knowing what to talk about, I looked around the kitchen to come up with something and saw a bowl on the counter filled with oranges. *Perfect*, I thought.

"Diana, how do you say oranges in Spanish?"

She glanced over in my direction with her innocent, dark brown eyes and said, "Naranja."

In a feeble attempt to repeat what I just heard, I stammered with the pronunciation by saying, "Na-ringa… ni-ranga… ninja."

The butchering of her native language made the serious, but attractive assistant chuckle. While the two of us were sharing a laugh, Father Gerald walked into the kitchen. Diana immediately composed herself and went right back to peeling potatoes.

I greeted my pastor as I always had by kissing him on both cheeks, but this time after I finished, I held both his arms and told him I was sorry. It had been several weeks since our one-on-one conversation in the back of the church, and I wanted him to know that I was sincerely sorry for my attitude on that day.

"Sorry? Sorry the good Lord didn't make you as pretty as me?" the priest said in an attempt to make light of the situation.

"No, Father. I was wrong to talk to you the way I did."

"Boy, you can do no wrong in my eyes, so enough of that malarkey nonsense. By the way, have you met Diana? Bonita, eh?"

I asked the pastor what he meant by *bonita* and he responded, "Beautiful, you dumbass."

While looking at Diana, I replied with the only other Spanish word I knew. "Sí!"

"You may want to brush up on your Spanish if you plan on dancing the salsa, young man. So, how's New York's Finest doing these days?" he asked, as the two of us proceeded across the hallway to the dining room table.

After taking our seats, I replied, "Well, funny you should ask."

I went on to explain the incident with my partner and the missing jewelry. I further told him about my decision to leave the squad car.

"Sounds like you've made your peace with the situation, so what's the bugger?"

"My Lieutenant wants me to make an official complaint with Internal Affairs."

Always one to help in guiding a person to find their own answers, Father Gerald asked, "What do you think?"

"I'm okay leaving things the way they are. If he didn't put the stuff back, I wouldn't have had a problem putting the cuffs on him. But he did, or at least some of it, and now I don't think John Buchannan should become my responsibility to police."

"Dean, if you caught a common crook in the apartment stealing the women's jewelry, would you have arrested him?"

I didn't give an answer to what I understood the pastor's implication to be—why should wearing a police uniform make a difference?

"When I was a young priest in Dublin, I heard whispers of wrongdoings amongst my fellow brethren in the priesthood. These wolves in sheep's clothing hid behind white collars, similar to how your friend is hiding behind his silver shield. At the time, I made the cowardly decision to ignore those whispers. I had my reasons, all of which were self-serving. But by protecting my place in the clergy, and sidestepping the ridicule, I would've undoubtedly endured by being a whistleblower, I dishonored my Lord. I never saw anything but I didn't look too hard either. If I did, maybe some young boys would've had a better childhood and I wouldn't be ridden with such guilt. Doing what's right and doing what's easy are sometimes worlds apart."

After talking with my mentor, and listening to his words of wisdom, I knew whatever decision I made was going to have consequences.

Before leaving, I thanked Mrs. Strahan for the hot meal, and in turn she reminded me not to be a stranger. I then walked over to where Diana was and whispered, "Ni-ing-ga-ga." Once again, my poor attempt at trying to say orange in Spanish brought a burst of laughter from the bonita, Bogota girl.

Prior to the start of my next schedule work day, I came in a few minutes early to speak with the lieutenant. I decided to make a formal complaint on John. When I arrived, the lieutenant told me to close the door behind me and have a seat. Before I could begin, he advised me that Officer Buchannan had been transferred to the Peddler Unit—a detail designed to weed out knockoff goods such as Gucci handbags and Rolex watches. The Lieutenant further informed me I'd be given a temporary partner until I had time to choose one.

With his head buried in a file to avoid eye contact, the lieutenant said, "As far as I'm concerned, the issue is closed. I don't want to hear any more about it. The apple is in somebody else's barrel now, understood?"

After acknowledging the news from the lieutenant, he abruptly dismissed me from his office, never as much glancing in my direction.

At muster, everyone in the squad had already heard about John's transfer. Apparently, John put in for the detail over a year ago but hadn't heard anything.

"What a sweet detail for John," I overheard one of the cops in the room say. "Plain clothes, lots of collars, plenty of overtime—what a sweet gig indeed!"

However, the gig, along with the graft, was a little too sweet for John.

About a year after his transfer to the peddler detail, I was reading an article in the New York Post. The two-paragraph story was about the arrest of a New York City Police Officer, John Buchannan. In the article, it mentioned that the disgraced cop was assigned to the Peddler Unit and was allegedly shaking down peddlers for protection. The majority of these peddlers were scared migrants from Senegal—easy targets for a rogue cop like John. It wasn't mentioned in the article, but I would later learn that the informant was one of the peddlers that grew tired of John's demand for more protection money. In the end, John was fired from the department and copped a plea to the criminal charges. Through the grapevine, I heard he moved out to New Jersey and was selling used cars in a Chrysler dealership in Dover. The scumbag finally found his calling.

After muster, I was introduced to my new, temporary partner, Chris Channing.

Chris was new to the squad, coming over from the steady midnight shift. The six-year veteran had more time on the job than me, but because I was assigned to the sector first, it was left to my discretion as to whom I'd choose as a partner. That explained why so many guys that never said as much "hello" to me were now acting like my best buddy. As it turned out, I had something they sought—an open seat in a squad car.

My first impression of Chris was that he reminded me of a combination of Anthony and Eddie. He had Anthony's herculean size and Eddie's quiet demeanor. He sported a tight, military-style haircut along with a well-trimmed mustache. His shoes were brightly buffed and his shirts perfectly creased. His professional appearance exemplified a discipline not found in many of the other officers within the confines of the North.

Eight and a half hours can be a long time to spend in a squad car with someone. With my previous partner, my patience was often tested. However, with Chris, things just seemed to move smoothly from the get go. I noticed early on if I was the one handling a complainant, he didn't interrupt. If he had something to say, he'd wait until I was finished and speak with me on the side. When he was the one leading the way, he acted like a professional, treating the street people with the same respect and dignity as one would with a complainant from Bergdorf Goodman.

The following week was our squad's turn to work the overnight shift—an assignment given once every six weeks. The "zombie shift," as I called it, went by without any fanfare for the first several nights. Chris, having worked the shift steady for a few years, gave me a few tips on keeping my energy up. Tip number one was limiting my sugar intake and number two, was doing push-ups. His self-imposed quota was 300 push-ups over the course of our shift. Every hour, the two of us would get out of the RMP and knockout fifty pushups.

The tips worked because it was the first time I worked the shift without feeling like crap.

On our last scheduled midnight tour of the week, everything was going accordingly. A Daily News truck driver pulled up next to our RMP and handed us the morning paper.

The blue-collar drivers and the police always had a good rapport with one another. Besides the occasional complimentary newspaper and us looking the other way in the middle of the night if they took a right on red, the drivers saw things we couldn't in our marked police vehicles.

After giving us the newspaper, the driver told us he thought something suspicious was going on around the block on Madison Avenue. Chris asked him what he had seen, and the driver explained that there are at least six guys dressed like maintenance workers walking in and out of the antique shop carrying bags. According to the driver, it just didn't look right.

Chris and I agreed.

I was all set to call for backup when Chris stopped me. He explained that a few weeks back while working one of the overnight shifts, a team of cat burglars were caught on Forty-Seventh Street in possession of police scanners. The professional thieves were monitoring the department's radio frequency in an attempt to stay one step ahead of the good guys. Unfortunately for them, the bungling burglars forgot to charge the batteries to the scanners, rendering them useless.

Like a ghost ship, Chris slowly backed the RMP down the block. When we reached the corner, we saw two men carrying duffle bags out of the shop and proceed to walk in the opposite direction from us. Without being noticed, Chris then pulled the RMP onto the sidewalk and drove right up to the storefront to block the entrance. I then exited the RMP and caught up to the two men with the bags. With my gun drawn, I told them to get down on the ground. While the first man complied, the second individual made a transmission over the radio he had in his hand. He spoke something in Russian and then joined his cohort on the cement. The next thing I heard, but could not see, was the sound of a vehicle screeching away from around the corner. I was certain the radio transmission from the perp helped tip-off the getaway vehicle.

Chris, having the other perps trapped in the store with nowhere to go, then called for back-up.

Soon after, a few squad cars were on the scene and we were able to round up the rest of the perpetrators—five in all. Unfortunately, the vehicle I heard taking off was able to make a clean getaway.

As Chris and I were sorting things out, a man in a robe and slippers appeared asking what was going on. The individual, Jeff Steigman, was the owner of the building/store and lived in the apartment directly above the business. After informing him that his store was burglarized, he immediately wanted to take inventory.

The store specialized in antique art, jewelry and furniture. Inside the artifact filled establishment, the owner immediately started to announce missing items. I informed Mr. Steigman that some of the merchandise might still be in one of the duffle bags that were retrieved. The owner disregarded with what I thought to be good news and still insisted the pieces were missing. That's when I realized the owner wasn't upset but rather calm and calculated.

The dishonest businessman saw an opportunity and decided he was going to use it to his advantage.

By the time we finished the report, there was over three hundred pieces missing at a cost of over eight-hundred-thousand dollars. Something told me his insurance company was going to be receiving a phone call in the very near future.

As for the five Chris and I apprehended, we took them back to the precinct to process the arrest.

There was a good chance the five perps were part of the Russian mafia. This meant that in all probability, they wouldn't cop a plea and the case would go to trial.

Ever since the influx of Russian immigrants in 1989, organized Russian crime had skyrocketed. One of the unwritten rules for them was to never accept plea deals regardless of how strong the evidence was against them. The reasoning behind it was because once they had a criminal record, they'd be kicked out of the gang and in all likelihood, be sent back to Russia. All five of the perps arrested had clean records and they would fight to keep it that way.

Besides the great collar and a possible commendation medal, there was another potential benefit for all the good police work.

Over the past several months, I had processed numerous collars down at the Manhattan's District Attorney's office without seeing the girl I met on the steps at Saint Patrick's Cathedral. I inquired about her with the other assistant district attorney's but with no luck. My best guess was that she worked in a special unit within the DA's office. I was hopeful with every visit to the courts that our paths would once again cross.

When most officers went downtown to finish writing up the complaint with the ADA's, they'd pack as if they were going camping. With the process taking anywhere from ten to sixteen hours, many would bring a lounge chair, a blanket, a cooler filled with beverages, and anything else to make themselves comfortable, while the wheels of justice moved at a snail's pace.

As for me, I'd rather volunteer to do escorts during the downtime than be crammed into the police waiting area. The assignment consisted of escorting prisoners in a paddy wagon from central booking to the courts. There was nothing glamorous about it but it did help pass the time while I waited to see the ADA.

After meeting with an assistant district attorney, I would then have to wait for the criminal complaint to be typed. I'm not exactly sure who typed these complaints, but it was safe to say they weren't professional typists. Waiting for the two-page complaint to be typed could take half the day. Knowing I had an abundance of idle time at my disposal, it was at that point I'd treat myself to a good meal around the block in either Little Italy or Chinatown. Depending on the time of day, I'd either go to Angelo's or the twenty-four hour Wo Hop's.

Once the complaint was finished being typed, the arresting officer was called over the loud speaker to report to the clerk's office so they could sign the finished document. At that point, the inefficient gravy train of overtime stopped and the tour would officially be over.

The slow-moving process was going as scheduled. I finally finished speaking with one of the ADA's around noon. It was now time to get something to eat while I waited for the "speed-typing" to be done. This was probably going to be the biggest decision I'd make all day—Chinese, Italian, or a dirty dog from the vendor next to Columbus Park.

I walked out of the back of the court building onto Baxter Street. Across the way in the park, I observed the older Chinese men and women doing Tai- Chi. I'd been up for over thirty hours straight and could barely make myself walk, and these people, who were probably three times my age, were exercising their body's as well as their minds. I was so tired I couldn't bring myself to look away. My stomach wanted food, my body wanted sleep, and my brain was simply too tired to make a decision. It was during this inner tug of war I heard someone say hello. I was half-asleep and wasn't sure if the hello was meant for me or not, but I kept on hearing, "Hello, Officer." When I finally realized the greeting was being directed toward me, I turned my head to see who was trying to get my attention—it was Kim.

I'd wanted so much to see her since we first met and now I could barely put a coherent sentence together.

"Hey, it's you. How it goes, are you."

"I'm doing well, are you all right?" she asked.

As I rubbed my eyes in an effort to better focus on the stunning brunette, I explained to her that I had been working midnight's the past week and was just a little tired.

"It's good to see you," I told her.

"Well, it was good to see you again, Officer Simpson. Be sure to get some rest."

And just like that, the girl I'd been waiting months to see, walked away toward the side entrance of the courthouse.

It was like watching a car wreck in slow motion. My brain was telling me to stop her, but my mouth couldn't move. I finally snapped out of my mini-trance and ran to the entrance. I called her name several times until she finally turned around and walked back toward me. With everyone in the lobby now staring at me as if I was crazy, I felt some much-needed adrenalin pumping life back into me.

I told her I was sorry for screaming like that but I wanted to get her attention. With a grin, she let me know I succeeded.

"Maybe this isn't the best time for me to ask you this. I haven't slept since yesterday, I could really use a hot shower, and I look like crap. But that withstanding, I'd really like to take you for lunch if you're not busy."

Kim looked at me with that same breathtaking smile I had remembered from our first encounter and said, "How can a girl turn down such an offer? Give me five minutes and I'll meet you back down here."

When Kim returned, I took her to Wo Hops. The old Chinese restaurant was two blocks away on Mott Street. It was one of Dad's favorites when he worked down here in the Fifth Precinct and now had become one of mine.

The basement restaurant was a tight fit, with tables and chairs crammed together. The walls displayed pictures of previous customers, while the rude Chinese waiters made no effort to ingratiate themselves to their customers. However, the lack of good service and no-frills decorations are soon forgotten once the food arrives. Simply put, it's the best Chinese food one will ever eat!

I could tell Kim was a bit surprised when we started walking down the stairs to a restaurant in a basement.

"Where are you taking me?" she asked.

I told her not to worry and to keep an open mind.

For the next forty minutes, Kim and I ate, laughed, and shared stories about our families. I showed her a picture displayed on the wall of Dad in uniform with his partner Lenny next to their old black and white squad car. The yellowed photo had been there for more than thirty years. Kim commented on how handsome he was and then asked if he was the reason I became a police officer. I explained to her how I used to listen to my dad tell his police stories to my mom when he'd come home from work.

"After listening to those stories, I never thought about being anything else," I told her.

"How does your mom feel about you being a police officer?"

"My mom past away when I was young, so I don't know, but I like to think she'd be proud of the person I am and the career I've chosen."

Seeing an opportunity to make my intentions clear, I told her that I thought our first date was going well.

"Officer Simpson, who said this was a date?" Kim snickered, as she looked at me with that same smile she shot me down with months earlier.

After making my argument to the barrister that this was indeed our first date, we continued with our lunch.

When we were done, I walked Kim back to the court building, being sure to get her phone number this time. As I watched her enter the same brass doors I retrieved her from less than an hour earlier, I couldn't help but wonder if the feeling I was experiencing was love. The flow of energy that was going through my body was something I'd never experienced before in my life. I was no longer tired or thinking of sleep. I was alive and ready to run a marathon.

There was a time after Francis's death I didn't think I'd ever smile again. I was numb for the longest time, and if not for the distraction of work, I probably wouldn't have gotten out of bed in the morning. But as time went on during 1989, there were two new relationships forming in my life. One was at work with Chris and the other with Kim.

Every chance we had, Kim and I were together. It was the simple little things I looked forward to the most, such as taking a stroll through Central Park or keeping her company on the ferry back to Staten Island. Everything was new and exciting, and I loved every minute of it.

The feelings I experienced on that first day outside the courthouse were confirmed—I was madly in love with Kim. Being that it was still early on in the relationship, and not wanting to scare her off, I decided to keep my feelings under wraps. But all that changed after taking her to a Broadway show.

Kim and I went to go see Les Misérables.

After watching Victor Hugo's character, Jean Valjean, come to life in the heartfelt story of a French peasant, I fell in love with the theater. The entire production, from the orchestra to the actors, was a performance I'd never experienced before.

With my senses heightened and love overflowing in my heart, I could no longer contain my true feelings.

After the play, as the two of us walked across Schubert Alley, I stopped, gave Kim a passionate kiss and told her that I was in love with her. Kim responded back in kind, telling me she was relieved I felt the same as she did.

At twenty-two, and still a neophyte when it came to life itself, I simply assumed my good fortune was going to last forever. However, the combination of time and loss would eventually teach me the costly lesson that life isn't about keeping things the same but rather a constant flow of changes that come in waves of good and bad. For the moment, this wave was seemingly perfect.

Kim lived in Staten Island with her college roommate, Janet. Both had attended Fordham Law School in the Bronx and soon after graduation were assigned to the Manhattan's DA's office.

The attractive blonde, and sometimes outspoken Janet, wasn't shy about asking me to set her up with any cute single police officers that I knew. Not wanting to play matchmaker, I suggested that she might do better finding someone in the district attorney's office.

"They're married, gay, or bad guys that I'm trying to put in prison," she told me. "Not much of a choice."

I reminded her about John John (John F. Kennedy Jr.) who was working at the DA's office at the time. Both Janet and Kim let out a huge sigh of contentment with the thought of reining in *People* magazine's 1988 "sexiest man alive." I suggested to both women to take a cold shower.

In private, Kim asked if my partner Chris was single. I informed Counsel that I objected to the question and perhaps it was time to take a recess. Not one to give up easily, Kim simply smiled at me until I gave in.

After convincing Chris that it wasn't a blind date—which, of course it was—I picked up four tickets to a Ranger game at the Garden.

When I arrived at Kim's apartment to pick her and Janet up, I knew there was going to be a problem. Janet was wearing a Pittsburg Penguins Mario Lemieux jersey. I tried explaining to her that it wasn't a good idea to be wearing the opponent's jersey while sitting in the "blue section" of the Garden, but the strong-minded Pittsburg native chose to ignore my concern.

We were to meet Chris in front of the Midtown South Precinct. The command was a block away from the "World's Most Famous Arena" and provided us with a nice little perk in Midtown Manhattan—free parking with our police issued placard.

Chris arrived wearing his number 35 Mike Richter jersey. He then looked over at Janet's jersey, rolled his eyes and said, "This should be an interesting evening."

The four of us started to walk to the Garden when I heard someone from behind in a deep voice say, "This parking is for police personnel of Midtown South only."

Technically, the person was right. However, the professional courtesy was usually never an issue. Before I could turn to discuss it with the officer, the individual continued to say, "Midtown North hair bags aren't welcome here."

The practical joker was none other than my good friend Anthony Dwyer. I hugged the burley officer and then introduced him to everyone.

"I think Officer Dwyer is just trying to get even for being the brunt of a practical joke some time back," I explained to the group.

"We both know you weren't smart enough to pull that off—I'm sure it had to be Eddie," the smiling Anthony retort.

The girls were curious about the details of the practical joke when Anthony interrupted and told me that if I wanted to keep my parking spot, I'd think twice about repeating the story.

It was good to see my former "Untouchable" partner. After a quick catch up with one another on our current police assignments, we parted ways. Before leaving, I told Anthony to have a safe tour.

He removed his medal of Saint Michael, kissed it, and replied that he was well-protected.

On the way to the Garden, I explained to Chris and the girls how Anthony and I were fortunate to have worked with Eddie and Sergeant Ryen in a plain clothes assignment during the holidays. I told them it was the best six weeks a rookie could've ever wished for.

As for the game, Chris and I were pleased with the results. The Rangers won 4–2 and unbeknownst to me at the time, Chris won a side bet he made with Janet. The wager was for the loser to buy the winner dinner. Chris being the gentlemen he is, still picked up the check and in time corralled his future wife and mother of their three children. To the best of my knowledge, all three kids became Penguin, Steelers and Pirate fans.

The next day, Monday October 16, 1989, Chris and I began our four-to-twelve tours for the week. We'd been looking forward to the start of the evening shift because that's when we were to finish our softball league that we started earlier in the summer. After the shift, we were to play the Seventeenth Precinct in the championship game at Clinton Park on the west side of our precinct. One of the guys in our squad had a brother-in-law in charge of the Parks Department, so we had unlimited access to the park and lights after midnight.

The league was a great opportunity to get to know the other guys in Midtown North. After all, there were two-hundred and fifty of us assigned to the command and sometimes it was difficult to get to meet everyone. There were several guys on our team that played in the minor leagues, and the rest of us were pretty good athletes that played high school and college ball. My sport was basketball. I couldn't hit a softball if it was on a tee; however, I could field better than most so I became the shortstop.

I invited Kim but being that the games didn't start until well after midnight, and she had to be up at five, there was a zero chance of her coming. However, there was one surprise spectator sitting alone on the wooden bleachers—Janet. At first, I wasn't sure if it was her, but then I noticed the Pittsburg Pirates jersey. I looked over at Chris and he just grinned. I guess I was too busy watching the hockey game the previous evening to have noticed the two had hit it off.

The game was blowout and the unofficial championship was ours. We won 24–7. Being that we still had a half of keg left and nobody was in a rush to leave, we played another game but this time we mixed the teams together. Chris was inconspicuously absent for the second game along with Janet. We were to play until the keg was finished or the sun came up. Never one wanting to see a sunrise after drinking all night, I was doing my best part to help in finishing the keg quickly.

At around three thirty in the morning we finally finished off the keg, and with that, the second game was officially over. A few of us remained to retrieve the equipment, shut down the lights and finish whatever beer was left in our cups.

During the course of the night, several squad cars had stopped by to say hello and watch some of the game. Just as we were finishing, Mike Burke pulled up with his partner, Keith Cerbone.

Although we worked in the same command, I rarely saw my former Third Division coworker. He was on steady midnights with his longtime girlfriend, Beth. To my surprise, the two were still together and now living with each other out on Long Island.

While we were all standing around Mike's RMP shooting the breeze and finishing the last of our beers, a call came over the radio that makes every cop stop what they're doing and take notice. The call was from an officer in a foot pursuit of a suspected burglar inside a building located in Midtown South. While we listened to Mike's radio, it was clear from the transmission the seriousness of the situation. All the guys present had been in foot pursuits before and knew firsthand the risks involved.

Ninety-nine percent of all foot pursuits in Midtown are on the street. As a rookie, I was in so many foot pursuits on Forty-Second Street that I use to refer to it as the "the track." However, none of those pursuits were ever in a building. A building pursuit amplifies the dangers tenfold. Every hallway corner, staircase, and door an officer goes by can be an ambush waiting to happen.

As we listened intently to the foot pursuit and the other officers in the South responding to the location, something absolutely horrific occurred—the pursuing officer let out a bone chilling scream over the radio. It wasn't clear what just transpired, but hearing the continuing agony in the officer's voice, it was obvious that he was in excruciating pain and needed immediate medical attention. At that moment, Mike and his partner sped-off in their RMP.

I said a prayer to the unknown officer and headed to the North stationhouse to see if there was an update on the situation.

When I entered the precinct, I could see several officers gathered around a radio by the front desk. It had been over ten minutes since the scream of agony came over the radio, and to my astonishment, the officer was still being heard. I couldn't figure out why the officer was still transmitting over the radio and not being rushed to a hospital.

While I listened to the harrowing events unfold over the radio, I could overhear the desk officer on the phone explaining the details to someone down at One Police Plaza.

Apparently, the officer that was in pursuit of the burglar had chased the perp onto the rooftop. When the officer made it to the roof, he was ambushed by the suspect and pushed off. The reason the officer was still transmitting was because while he laid wedged in-between the two buildings in an air shaft, his speaker button on the radio was stuck in the on position.

An attempt was now being made to lift the severely wounded officer out of the air shaft but it proved to be an impossible task. Each time emergency workers attempted to move the officer, an excruciating scream echoed over the radio. The Emergency Service Unit was now on the scene and decided the only way to extricate the officer was to break though the adjoining wall.

Nearly forty minutes after his fall, the officer was removed and rushed to Bellevue Hospital. The radio transmission had finally stopped.

For the next several minutes, time seemed to stand still. No one said a word. The stationhouse that was always buzzing was as quiet as a church. Like my colleagues, I was left wondering about the welfare of the seriously injured officer. I bowed my head and prayed to Saint Michael to once more look over one from his flock.

While I stood there praying, I felt the presence of someone standing directly in front of me. As I looked up, I could see that it was Beth. I couldn't understand why she was standing there. Beth and I hadn't spoken to one another in nearly two years. Now she stood in front of me not saying a word. Her eyes began to well up as her hands and face began to tremble.

As she began to speak, her voice started to crack, "Mike just paged me. It was... it was Anthony. He didn't make it."

There was only one Anthony she could've been referring to but I had to ask to make certain.

"Dwyer?"

With a nod of her head, she confirmed the grim reality that it was our former coworker from the Third Division.

As the two of us embraced one another, the first thought I had was not of Anthony but of his parents and the hell they were about to endure.

Anthony, twenty-three, was yet another young officer lost to the senseless violence brought on by an abominable underworld of thugs and cowards. When Mike gave me the news of Eddie, I was in shock and filled with sorrow. Upon hearing the tragic news of Anthony, I wasn't saddened or reflective—I was mad. The circumstances hadn't changed, only my emotions. This wasn't a game we were playing— this was a life or death situation, with the bad guys getting to live, while the good, ill-fated guys received a ceremonious farewell.

The circumstances behind the tragic night were made clearer over the next few days. Four men had smashed the glass door of a McDonald's in Times Square. A maintenance worker inside heard the noise and was able to escape. He ran to the Deuce and found Anthony, along with Sergeant Flanagan and Officer Labrecht. After explaining to the officers what had just occurred, the three men responded to the McDonald's.

Flanagan and Labrecht captured one of the suspects in the basement while two of the suspects ran to the roof. Anthony gave chase and as he stepped out onto the roof was pushed off by one of the suspects, Edward Matos, twenty-one, from Coney Island, Brooklyn.

Within a week, all four suspects were apprehended and eventually convicted of second degree murder.

On the ride out to Long Island to attend Anthony's funeral, I was still consumed with anger. I knew my thoughts were wrong, but I still couldn't help fantasizing about throwing the four bastards into the same air shaft that ended Anthony's life and let them suffer the same fate. Instead, the four would receive a twenty-five to life sentence, and just like the thugs in Eddie's case, be eligible for parole.

I believe in God. I had believed prior to becoming a police officer and continue to believe in my Lord and Savior more than ever. However, what I wasn't aware of, and didn't fully appreciate prior to joining the force, is the existence of evil. It's real and it's powerful. Evil's sole purpose is to create chaos and destruction. There's no room for good and evil to coexist. The good is fooled by evil and believes that it can be changed. It can't.

To think that the killers of Anthony and Eddie can entertain the idea of breathing as free men outside a correctional facility in this lifetime can only bring a smile to Satan's face.

When the hell will this madness end?

CHAPTER 9

Life's Curveballs

The best laid schemes o' Mice an' Men oft go awry.
—"To a Mouse" by Robert Burns, 1785

As a young man, I often wondered why my dad would get nervous when I spoke of the future as if I had all the answers. I guess as I look back, I see how inexperienced and naive I was when it came to life. It was that blissful ignorance that allowed me the ability to feel as though I was in complete control of what I was doing and where I was going. But as for Dad, he experienced firsthand life's brutal unfairness and understood that at any moment, things could change without notice and without apologies.

It took time to appreciate the good things in my life after Francis's death. Although I was still angry with his tragic decision, I was no longer blaming God for it. In fact, I thanked the good Lord every day for blessing me with a father that loved me unconditionally, a partner at work I could trust, and a girlfriend I was very much in love with. At twenty-four, my life was heading in an upward trajectory with no curveballs in sight.

Kim and I had been dating for nearly two years when I made the decision to ask her to marry me. I could barely contain my excitement at the thought of getting on one knee and asking her for her hand in marriage. I decided to pop the question on her upcoming birthday—Friday, December 14.

Upon sharing my intentions with Dad, he expressed how happy he was for me. He asked if I had purchased a ring yet, and I told him I was going to the diamond district the next day to pick one out. With that, he excused himself and returned with a small ring box. "Maybe this is something you might consider," he said as he handed me the box. "This is the ring I gave your mother over thirty-five years ago when I proposed to her."

I never saw the ring before or at least I hadn't remembered it. The Victorian-style setting was laid in platinum with a round, sparkling diamond. The ring itself was absolutely perfect, but I was hesitant to accept such a generous gift. Dad, sensing my unease, assured me that Mom would've wanted me to have it.

My plans were set. The night of Kim's birthday was the same evening as the precinct's Christmas party. I thought it to be perfect. I'd pick up Kim at her apartment in Staten Island and take the ferry over to Manhattan. There, as we crossed the bay with the city skyline in the backdrop, I would propose to her. Afterwards, we would go to the party and share the good news with our friends.

The past several weeks leading up to Kim's birthday had been hectic for both of us. We hadn't seen much of each other due to me finishing up my final semester at John Jay College and Kim's overflow of high profile cases. There were some weeks our schedules conflicted so much that the only chance we had to see each other was over lunch down by the courts. We'd sit on the benches across from the courthouse, enjoying a couple of hot dogs and sharing a diet cola. It was there I'd listen to Kim discuss one of the many cases she was working on. As she spoke, I'd pretend to be interested, but truthfully, all I could think about was the night I was going to propose to her.

The night finally arrived.

I picked Kim up at her apartment and began to drive down Bay Street toward the Staten Island Ferry Terminal.

As we took the ferry across the harbor, my thoughts were so preoccupied with my proposal that I failed to realize Kim hadn't spoken a word yet. All I could think about was how seemingly perfect the evening was. The dark December night had illuminated the city skyline like a postcard, while the echoing waves hitting the side of the vessel sounded as though a harp was being played in the background.

The time I'd been waiting for had finally arrived. However, just prior to getting down on one knee, Kim blurted out, "Dean, I need to talk to you."

It's funny how the brain works. I immediately knew from the serious tone in her voice that those words could only mean one thing—it was over. I desperately hoped my instincts were wrong, but she went on to confirm my worst fears.

She explained to me that she met someone at her office and was fairly certain she was in love with him. He was a senior district attorney that she'd been recently working cases with. She told me she loved me and always would, but simply didn't see a future together.

The roles where now in reverse from moments earlier. I was now the quiet one as she did all the talking. Kim begged me to say something but I truly was lost for words. I didn't know if I should be upset at being dumped or relieved that I never popped the question. While I sat there staring out at the city lights reflecting off the water, I came to the realization that I was no longer in control of what I wanted. However, there was one thing I was in control over—my emotions.

I remained amiable, and after taking a few minutes to recover from the core shaking news, I finally began to speak. I told Kim that from the moment I met her, I knew she was special and how I very much wanted her in my life. Speaking from my heart, I told her I never before felt the way I did and now wondered if I could ever trust my feelings again.

I never did make it to the Christmas party that night. I took the ferry back to Staten Island to retrieve my car and then drove directly home. After explaining to Dad that it simply wasn't meant to be, I gave him back the ring. He then said something I'd carry with me for the rest of my life. "Son, everything happens for a reason."

He had no way of knowing it at the time, but those prophetic words would have profound meaning by the next day.

As for the rest of the evening, I joined Dad across the street to watch my ten-year-old cousin Benjamin play in a CYO (Catholic

Youth Organization) basketball game. This was certainly not the Friday night I had envisioned. Instead of being at a party introducing Kim as my fiancé to my friends and co-workers, I was in a poorly-lit basement gymnasium watching a bunch of kids trying to be the next Michael Jordan.

I guess Dad thought the game would be a good distraction for me—and he was right. I was surrounded by the people closest to me in my life: Dad, Father Gerald, Aunt Gwen and my cousins. Without having to ask for it, God seemed to put me in the right place at the right time.

During the game, I saw Father Gerald by the concession booth. I walked over to say hello and noticed he was holding a white foam cup. Knowing it wasn't coffee, I pressured the jolly pastor to share some of his refreshments with Dad and me by telling him, "Doesn't it say somewhere in the Bible that if you have two shirts to give one to the poor? And you call the Protestants cheap."

"The sinner calling out the sinner," he quickly quipped.

After instructing one of the girls from behind the counter to fill-up two more cups from his "private stock," he continued: "That verse your referring to has to do with shirts and food for the poor, not my Johnny Walker Blue. By the way, Dino, you look like the wrong end of the sheep."

"Well, thanks Padre. My night wouldn't have been complete without those kind words. By the way, I'm wondering how a boy from Crossmaglen knows what the wrong end of a sheep looks like? I'm guessing some cold nights and warm sheep… baa, baa."

After the back and forth banter, I went on to explain to Father Gerald of my hectic schedule as of late for being the cause of the dark rings under my eyes. I then told him just prior to my arrival that I had the love of my life rip my heart out and skewer it like a shish kabob. "Besides that, I'm terrific," I facetiously told my pastor.

The girl came back with the cups and handed them to Father Gerald along with an extra cup for me. As she handed me the cup, I realized it was the girl I met months earlier, Diana.

"Hola, Senorita," I said.

She smiled and quickly walked away.

Father Gerald, not one to miss a thing, questioned my improved Spanish. I explained to him that for my final semester, I had to fulfill a foreign language requirement and happened to choose Spanish.

The skeptical priest laughed as he handed me the cups by saying, "You just happened to choose Spanish, my ass."

I thanked my friend for the refreshments and returned to my seat. I gave Dad one of the cups and told him I shamed Father Gerald into sharing his hooch with us. When I opened the extra cup that Diana gave me, there was a slice of an orange in it. The inside joke brought something I didn't think was possible just hours earlier—a smile.

The next morning, I went downstairs to have breakfast with Dad. He was sitting in his usual spot at the dining room table, but instead of reading the morning paper, he was intently listening to the radio. I could hear the commentator finish the report by saying the case was under investigation by the District Attorney's office and Internal Affairs. Dad then turned off the radio and began explaining what had transpired.

Last night, at around two in the morning, two men were beaten in midtown. The victims stated they hailed a cab in front of the Carnegie Deli when five men approached them, told them they were police officers and were commandeering the vehicle. When the two men refused to get out of the cab, the alleged off-duty officers beat the men and dragged them from the taxi. The victims state their assailants called them "fags" and found it difficult to believe they could actually be real police officers. After being taken to the hospital to treat their injuries, medical personnel informed authorities that both men suffered several lacerations, contusions and that the most serious injury to one of the victims was a severely fractured eye socket. Dad finished by stating that no arrests had been made as of yet.

I now understood the reason behind Dad's worrisome look. Across from the Carnegie Deli on Fifty-Fifth and Seventh Avenue is the Irish Pub, the location of the previous evening's holiday party. The question now was, did a couple of the guys drink too much and get stupid? I prayed that wasn't the case but there was one word in

Dad's recount that stood-out: "commandeer." Perp's didn't talk like that, cops did.

I knew Chris was going to the party with Janet, so I reached out to see if he'd heard anything regarding the incident but to no avail. Knowing I'd see Chris the following morning, I decided to wait until then to talk with him.

Sunday mornings at the Midtown North stationhouse were usually quiet. With less people in the Manhattan and most of the brass taking off, the shift was a nice change of pace to the hustle and bustle normally associated with midtown. An added perk to the unsanctioned downtime was Chris and I going for breakfast at our favorite French eatery—Le Brasserie. The upscale, East Fifty-Third Street restaurant had the best French toast and coffee in NYC.

Chris and I discovered the place when a customer tried faking a seizure in an attempt to get out of paying a very expensive check one evening. We were called to the scene along with the paramedics. When we arrived, Chris recognized the guy. His name was Jimmy Bata aka "Jimmy the Con."

Chris locked the petty thief up before and figured his sudden health issues may not be a hundred percent legit.

The impeccably dressed, sixty-something-year-old, had a pension for cons. To the naked eye, one would never suspect the Hungarian born Jimmy to be a simple street thief. I guess that's what made him so believable to his unsuspecting prey.

In order not to make a scene, Chris whispered in Jimmy's ear, "You have three seconds to make a miraculous recovery or when the paramedics come, I will personally use the paddles on you."

At first, Jimmy didn't budge, but once Chris told him where he'd be placing the paddles—on his privates—Jimmy not only made a miraculous recovery but was well enough to even pay his bill.

Pierre, the manager, was grateful for our help and insisted we come back any time for a meal. Following Sergeant Ryen's advice, Chris and I followed up with the manager several more times prior to accepting his gracious offer.

When I arrived at the command to start my Sunday morning shift, I could sense something wasn't right. For starters, I noticed a lot of brass in uniform behind the front desk. There was our Commanding Officer, Captain Marks, our ICO (Integrity Commanding Officer) Lieutenant Butler, and the newly promoted chief, "Don't call me a guinea bastard" Moretti.

To go along with the long-faced brass were several uptight bodies wearing suits—in all likelihood from Internal Affairs.

Something told me Chris and I weren't going to be visiting Pierre at Le Brasserie.

When I went upstairs to the locker room, I saw Chris. I asked him if he'd seen all the "happy faces" downstairs and he just nodded. Before I could talk with him any further, he was already finished getting into his uniform and on his way down to the muster room.

At muster, all the suits and brass were lined up like a firing squad in front of us. They all had a look on their face like something was stuck up their asses. That was everyone except our CO, Marks.

Captain Marks was not your typical brass type. In his early forties, the avid runner was still a street cop at heart. He'd always wear his NYC Marathon Medal the day after he'd compete. He was a fair boss that didn't look to hurt the low-level patrolmen. In the cut-throat world of the NYPD brass, that was considered more of a weakness than an attribute.

The slender-built boss informed the group of the incident that occurred early Saturday morning in front of Carnegie Deli. Without adding much more information than the local news, our CO then informed the squad that IAD was heading the investigation and needed to speak with several officers.

Marks started calling off the names of the officers that were to stay behind. After Marks was done, I realized nearly half the names on the roll were called, including mine. Captain Marks, with a look of complete despair, then dismissed the rest of the officers.

Out of thirty-two officers, only fifteen were released to their assignments. The rest of us simply stood there not knowing what was next.

Seventeen police officers confined to a relatively small area would normally create for some good banter. However, that was not the case on this Sunday morning. All the remaining officers left in the muster room seemed nervous and uptight. As for me, I knew I didn't do anything wrong so I simply stood there and waited my turn to be called.

Adjacent to the muster room was the CPOP (Community Patrol Observation Program) office. The suits took over the room and began calling in individuals one by one. Some of the officers were in and out quickly, while others took a bit more time.

After about thirty minutes, one of the suits called my name. As I entered the office, I observed two other suits behind a desk. They introduced themselves as bosses from IAD. The one suit did all the talking while the other two were glaring at me as if I had just abducted a ten-year-old girl.

"Officer Simpson, do you know why you're here?"

"No, sir."

"No clue, Officer?"

"No, sir."

While the suit was asking me questions, I noticed a pad on the desk. Although it was faced in the opposite direction, I could tell it was a copy of the list of those that attended the holiday party.

"Where were you Friday night?"

I didn't know why the suit didn't simply come out and ask me if I was at The Irish Pub—I guess he wanted to see if he'd catch me in a lie.

"Sir, from six to seven I was on the Staten Island Ferry. After that I drove back to Brooklyn and went to my cousin's basketball game. After the game, I went home and shortly after that, I went to sleep."

"You are aware we can suspend you on the spot for lying to us, and in all likelihood, have you terminated for obstructing an investigation? Maybe you'd like to try again."

"No need, sir. I'm well aware of my whereabouts on Friday evening. I have nothing to add or change."

The gray hair suit had steam coming out from his over starched collar.

"Do you take me for an asshole?" he screamed.

"Sir, I don't think there's any proper way for me to answer that question."

"Listen, you piece of dog shit, maybe I can help you refresh your memory about Friday night."

As I sat there taking the suit's crap, I wondered why they were allowed to talk to us in that manner. If I were to talk to a civilian that way, I'd have vacation days rightfully taken away. It just showed the contempt the higher-ups in the NYPD had for their own officers. Street cops were nothing more than expendable parts to the brass. We were on the front lines dealing with the real world, while the brass complained about their seat cushions not being puffy enough or how the coffee machine was on the brink again.

Dad warned me about of the gauntlet and the best way to get through it: "Get promoted, get off the street and let the pawns do the work. To survive twenty years on the street doing patrol was the most dangerous part of the gauntlet. If the street punks didn't get you, the brass eventually would."

In a calm voice, I decided to push back. "Sir, I'm not dog shit. I'm a New York City Police Officer. I'd appreciate not be spoken to that way."

"So, Mr. Proud NYPD Officer can you explain to me why you left out going to the precinct party? Did it slip your fucking mind?"

"I decided not to go, sir."

"Really? You spent $150 on two tickets and didn't go? You expect us to believe that?"

I tried never to lose my cool while on the job. However, if I ever saw this scumbag in front of me in a dark alley, I'm pretty sure I'd take pleasure in kicking his ass. At that moment, I had more respect for a crack dealer than the hypocrite sitting across the table using foul language and calling me "dog shit." This boss was nothing more than a parasite hiding behind his position and justifying his existence by treating innocent cops like common criminals. If cops were involved in the assault of the two victims, then they should suffer the consequences—but there's no need for these suits to come in here and treat good cops like shit.

Since I felt I made my position clear, I chose not to answer the prick's question. After an awkward few moments of silence (from him, not me), the suit snapped at me.

"I asked you a fucking question, officer."

In a calm voice, I asked, "Can you repeat the question?"

With his frustration level mounting, the suit tried one more time to rattle me.

"We know you were at the party, we know you were in front of the Irish Pub when the incident occurred, and now we know you're a lying sack of shit. It's going to be a pleasure taking your gun and shield."

I heard all I could hear from this idiot. I wanted to tell this suit to go to hell, but then he'd have me on insubordination and I wasn't about to make it that easy for him. So, I got up from my seat, unclipped my shield from my uniform, removed my firearm from the holster, and after emptying the six rounds of ammunition, placed my gun and shield on the desk.

"What the hell do you think you're doing?" the suit asked.

Although I knew the prick hadn't directly requested my gun and shield, I decided to call his bluff.

"Sir, you said it was going to be a pleasure to take my gun and shield. Well, here they are."

At that point, suit number 2 stepped in.

In the role of "good cop," he said, "All right, officer, holster your weapon. Nobody was asking for it. All we want to know is if you attended the party Friday night, and if you did, what time did you leave?"

"Sir, I did purchase two tickets to the party. I picked up my girlfriend in Staten Island and took the ferry to Manhattan with the plans of attending the party. My plans changed and I decided not to go. I already explained my whereabouts for the rest of the evening. What I'd like to know is when it became the department's policy to treat fellow officers like perps."

Without answering my question, he said, "Thank you, officer, you're dismissed."

When I left the room, I looked over at Chris and saw him sitting with his head down.

I started to make my way toward him when one of the suits yelled in my direction for me to leave the area. I couldn't help to wonder if my partner was all right.

I didn't see Chris until the next day. I asked him how things went with IAD and he simply grunted and said, "Okay, I guess."

I knew Chris wasn't one to talk a lot, but his reserved demeanor left me worried that he was somehow involved in the case. I knew better than to push the issue with him, so I let things be.

Over the next several weeks, the Carnegie Deli assault case, as it was now labeled, seemed to die down. The suits stopped coming around and things seemed to get back to normal. I still sensed something wasn't right with my partner, but at least now we were back into a good groove in the squad car.

Winter was in full blast. We were doing a four-to-twelve shift on a bitterly cold night in late January. It was the type of night that reminded me why I preferred to be in an RMP and not a foot post. Halfway through our shift, we received a radio call for a domestic dispute at 427 West Fifty-Third Street.

Upon arriving, we noticed a young, twenty-something-year-old female sitting on the stoop hysterically crying. I saw that she was bleeding from the lip and her left eye was severely swollen. After calling for a bus and reassuring the young lady that everything was going to be all right, I asked her what happened.

She told me her boyfriend had been drinking and was upset, so he began to hit her. I asked her if the boyfriend was still in the apartment and she responded that he was. I made a further inquiry to whether there were any weapons on the premise, and with a slight hesitation in her voice she said, "I don't think so."

After the ambulance arrived, Chris and I entered the building to confront "lover boy," aka Rick. While we walked up the five flights of stairs to the apartment, Chris asked me if I caught the girl's half-hearted response to the weapons question. I acknowledged that I had and stressed we should take extra precaution. I removed my service revolver from the holster and left it down by my side.

When we arrived to the top floor unit—because after all, all police incidents occur on the top floors of buildings that don't have elevators—I noticed the door was open enough to see the boyfriend sitting on the couch with his back to us. He was watching television and drinking a can of beer.

While staying in the hallway, I called out to him in an innocuous tone. "Hey, Rick, it's the police. Can you please step out here so we can talk with you?"

"If you want to talk, come on in and we'll have a cold one together," the woman beater said in a carefree manner.

"Rick, it's a little tight in there for my partner and me. I'd feel better if you'd come out here, so we can find out what happened tonight."

"The bitch was being a bitch, anything else?" he said with a more aggressive tone.

"We need to talk, come on out."

The once calm and cool Rick responded like the aggressive, drunk punk we already knew him to be by yelling, "I ain't fucking moving!"

Summing up the situation, I didn't like the setup. The suspect had his back to us with only one hand visible—the one that was holding the can of beer. The other hand was down by his side with the couch obstructing our view. The apartment itself was tight with a narrow opening to where the punk was sitting. Plus, we were dealing with an apparently intoxicated individual with anger issues that could very well be armed.

I suggested to Chris that we call ESU for backup. As the saying goes on the NYPD, "When people need help they call the police, when the police need help, they call the Emergency Service Unit."

Chris immediately disagreed and said, "Enough is enough, let's get him." Before I could discuss the situation further, Chris quickly entered the apartment while I trailed behind. In one single motion, the perp turned toward us from the sitting position and fired off a shot in our direction. Chris, without any regard for his own safety, rushed the perp. With my partner directly in front of me in the confined space, I had no angle to take a shot. Chris grabbed the guys hand and wrestled the two-shot Dillinger Revolver away from him. He then took out his own gun and proceeded to let loose on the guy by pistol-whipping him. After a few seconds, I realized Chris was out of control, so I pulled him off.

I still didn't know if either one of us were struck by the round the perp let off. After cuffing the punk, I checked myself and asked Chris if he was hit. Chris ignored me and just stared at the perp like he was possessed.

After a quick examination, it appeared the shot had gone over our heads and lodged above the door jam. Thank God we weren't hit, but I wouldn't go as far as to say we were both all right.

Chris and I had worked together for over two years. We had our share of close calls but this one was avoidable, as well as reckless. His actions nearly put us both in a drape-covered coffin and now I wanted answers to why my partner was seeking a death wish.

I waited until we were back at the stationhouse with the prisoner secured before I pulled Chris to the side. With my adrenalin still pumping, I tried my best to remain calm. I started by asking the obvious:

"What was that all about?"

From his silence, along with his manic body language, I could tell Chris wanted nothing to do with the current conversation but it was time to find out what was wrong with my partner.

As Chris attempted to leave the room, I grabbed a hold of him and said, "You nearly got us both killed tonight. I deserve to know what the hell is going on."

I'm uncertain if it was the weight of my words or the pressure he'd been going through, but at the moment, Chris finally broke. He put his hands over his face and began to cry. "I'm sorry, Dean, I'm so sorry. I didn't mean for any of this to happen."

For the next few minutes, Chris explained to me the events surrounding the night of the Christmas party.

At around two in the morning, with the party dying down, Chris decided to call it a night. When he walked outside the pub, he saw several partygoers outside having a smoke. He told the guys to have a good night and to get home safe. He then walked around the corner to retrieve his car.

"It's unbelievable," Chris said with his head sinking into his shoulders. "Janet had to fly to Pittsburg that morning because her ailing father took a turn for the worse. If she's with me, there's no way I'm still at the bar until two in the morning. When I drove back around the corner, that's when I saw the four off-duty cops I just left were now in some sort of ruckus. I stopped because I thought the guys needed my help. One of the four told me everything was under control and for me to go on my way. When I left, the two individuals were still in the cab with some loud arguing going back and forth. The dragging of the guys out of the taxi and assault happened after I was gone. It wasn't until the next day when I heard the incident on the news that I realized things had escalated out of control."

Chris found himself in a no-win situation. He didn't want to be labeled a rat, but at the same time he risked going down with them if IAD discovered he was at the scene. To top it off, a witness saw a dark colored Nissan Pathfinder leaving the location, and as luck would have it, he was the only one in the command that had that type of vehicle.

I couldn't imagine the pressure Chris was feeling as Internal Affairs was closing in. The past several weeks must've been pure hell for my partner. He had nothing to do with the assault but by being in the wrong place at the wrong time, he now had the weight of the world hanging over his head.

I now understood why IAD backed off the case. They wanted to let the pressure build on the guys involved—knowing one of the five would eventually break.

Chris didn't tell me the others' names nor did I wish to know. He did ask me what I would do and I told him the truth. "I don't know."

I later asked Dad the same question and he told me what I already knew, "One of them is going to cut a deal and the others are going to be paraded for the 'perp walk.' The guy who turns will be considered a rat and the others are jail bound. He's screwed either way."

IAD didn't have to wait long to get their rat. Within another week, one of the four finally caved and ratted everyone else out. The rat was Josh McKenna, a real Irish drunk if there ever was one. I had the displeasure with working with the twitchy officer several months earlier when Chris was on vacation. The ten-year veteran was the quintessential hag-bag. He complained about everything and thought somehow the world owed him. His appearance was an embarrassment to the job. His uniform was always dirty and wrinkled while his breath smelled like a saloon at closing time. The officer that physically resembled more like a snake than a rat, was nothing more than a loud mouth punk that screamed trouble.

Josh decided to do what most cowardly rats did when they were cornered—save his own ass. In the process, he gave up all the other officers present at the time of the incident, including Chris.

Before long, two of the other officers caved in and admitted to their role in the assault. From everyone's account of the occurrence, it was Josh that started the altercation.

The four decided to hail a cab when they decided to go to another bar. The two victims that were directly across the street happened to be hailing a cab at the same time. The cabbie decided to pick up the two across the street instead of the four intoxicated, off-duty cops. This sent Josh into a rage. He ran across the street to confront the cabbie and the two men that were now in the back seat of the taxi. When the men wouldn't leave the cab, Josh took out his badge and identified himself as a police officer. He then told the cabbie he was commandeering the vehicle. That's when Chris stopped to see if everything was okay. Shortly after Chris left the scene, the situation escalated. Josh began to drag the two men out of the taxi as the other three guys came over to break it up. Three of the four involved in the altercation agreed to the events that evening except for one—Josh. He swore he was only trying to break-up an argument between the two victims and the three off-duty officers he was with. According to him, it was the three off-duty cops that were to blame for the assault.

There was one thing all four could agree upon—Chris's role in the incident. They all agreed that he stopped to see if they needed assistance and when he was told everything was under control, he continued on his way.

The victims couldn't identify the assailant, but their stories were more in line with the three off-duty officers than Josh's. But since he was the first rat to the cheese, he brokered the best deal. He was transferred to IAD, while the others were immediately suspended and soon thereafter terminated from the department. In return for his cooperation, Josh was given immunity by the District Attorney's office. Two of the other officers involved accepted plea deals. Only Andy Gustello and Chris decided to take their chances in front of a jury.

Andy had been a good friend to the rat and couldn't believe the manner in which he was now being repaid.

Years earlier, Josh was going through a divorce when the good-natured Andy let him stay with him. The "temporary" arrangement lasted for six years until the back-stabbing best friend recently moved out. During that time, Josh would cry poverty due to his divorce and child support. He'd tell Andy that he felt bad about not contributing to the expenses of the apartment, but he still made no effort and offered no money. From an outsider, it was easy to see that Josh was taking advantage of his partner's kindness, but Andy didn't see it that way. All he could see was a friend in need.

Andy's years of loyalty was rewarded with perjured testimony from a rat. With the help of his best friend, Andy was convicted on the assault charges and was sentenced to two years at Rikers Island.

If not for the media attention, Chris's criminal case in all likelihood would've been thrown out. Everyone involved, including the victims, admitted he had nothing to do with the assault. However, the vindictive DA's office wanted to make an example out of him for not cooperating with the investigation. It wasn't enough that he lost his career, now they wanted him to do prison time.

Chris was acquitted on the felonious assault charges but was found guilty on the lesser charges of official misconduct and obstructing governmental administration. He was sentenced to six months.

Over the years, I tried staying in touch with Chris but time and distance eventually created an innocuous rift between us. Years later,

I bumped into him and Janet in front of Madison Square Garden. The circus was in town and the Channing parents were taking their children to see "The Most Spectacular Show on Earth." Chris apologized for not returning my phone calls and then confessed that it simply was too difficult to keep in touch with anyone associated with the job. I told him I never took it personal and would always consider him my one and only partner.

As unfortunate as the Carnegie Deli assault caper was for Chris, it did have a few silver linings. For starters, Janet stayed by Chris's side when a lot of other people would've left. Their relationship had gone through a fiery furnace and now was as strong as steel. As for his post NYPD career, Chris became a successful businessman.

Janet helped Chris get back on his feet by filling a need down at the courts. There was a demand for drivers to escort witnesses and late-working ADAs home, so after completing his six-month debt to society, Chris began his new career behind the wheel of a Lincoln Town Car. After a short time, the resourceful Chris saw an opportunity and decided to buy several more cars and start his own operation. Not long after, Chris's company dominated all of Lower Manhattan, including the business district. Last I heard, my former partner had a fleet of over two-hundred cars, limos, and shuttle buses and a net worth well north of seven figures.

With Chris's departure from the department, I was now in need of a new partner. For the next several months, I searched but to no avail. I compared everyone I worked with to Chris and that's when I realized I'd never be able to replace him.

Rumors had been circulating that the department was going to be announcing the next promotional exam any day. I was now at a crossroads in my NYPD career. I felt it was time to move on from patrol—but to where? Even if the sergeant's exam was the next day, which it wasn't, it would still be months, if not years, before I was promoted.

I decided to discuss the matter with the recently assigned Administrative Lieutenant, Vasos Stamotopoulos, or as I nicknamed him, Lieutenant Alphabet.

I happened to know the lieutenant from playing together in a winter basketball league run out of the basement of a Greek church in Bay Ridge. He played center for one of the opposing teams and had put me on my backside on more than one occasion.

I went to the second-floor office and knocked on the lieutenant's door. Upon entering, he quickly recognized me and gave me a warm welcome.

"Hey, shooter," the lieutenant said, referring to my basketball skills.

"Hi, Lew, I wanted to wish you well in your new position in the North. By the way, I'm a little surprised you were able to recognize me standing upright," I told the able-bodied boss.

The lieutenant let out a laugh and then explained how he didn't like faster players than himself coming into his lane.

After telling him I'd make a mental note of it, I then went on to explain to the lieutenant my desire to leave the squad car in pursuit of a detail within the command—Anticrime, Robbery, Community Affairs, or anything else that might be available.

"I checked everyone's numbers in the precinct prior to taking over. There's no question your activity shows you deserve to get into one of those details, but simply put, there's nowhere for you to go until guys either retire or get promoted. However, I might have something that could work for both of us. Our Highway Safety unit consists of six guys that have become lazy in their cushy detail. I'm looking to shake things up and could use a guy that's willing to do more than simply take jumpers from the outside."

It was clear to me from the lieutenant's basketball metaphor that he wanted a worker and not someone simply settling for the easy way out.

After telling the lieutenant I was interested, he went on to explain the particulars of the assignment.

I'd be responsible for the entire West Side Highway within the Precinct. If there were any accidents, I'd respond to investigate them and file the proper reports. When there weren't any accidents, I'd be responsible for ensuring the safety of the highway—another way of saying I'd be doing a lot of car stops and issuing citations. I was to report only to the lieutenant, would have weekends off, and the best part—I worked alone! And, as long as I produced the numbers (citations), I had free rein.

The assignment sounded almost too good to be true. I'd still be in a squad car but instead of being married to a partner and a dispatcher, I was to be my own man.

I told the lieutenant I was in and thanked him for the opportunity.

It wasn't until I told Dad of my news that I felt a slight concern. The wiser street cop was quick to point out how dangerous car stops were and how I was adding to the risk by working alone. What he looked at as a liability, I had been looking at as a blessing. I already worked with one corrupt partner in John Buchannan and had zero luck finding a replacement after Chris's departure. I explained to Dad that I'd rather be alone than take the risk of getting a partner that was going to get me jammed-up, or worse, killed.

However, I took Dad's advice to heart and promised I'd be on my toes.

The new assignment quickly proved to be a godsend. The steady hours and weekends off brought back a luxury I hadn't enjoyed since my rookie days in the Third Division. I now had a "normal schedule" with the added bonus of not having to adjust my body for the dreaded overnight shifts. Another perk to my new schedule was the ability to make myself available to Father Gerald and the newly formed fifth-grade girls' basketball team he wished for me to coach.

It didn't take long to understand the lieutenant's issue with the hag-bags currently assigned to the unit. Everything about their work and appearance showed complete apathy toward the job and the people they swore to serve and protect. They were a group of malcontent blowhards counting the days before they could put in their retirement papers and relocate to Boynton Beach.

As for the detail itself, I knew it was only going to be a pit stop prior to getting promoted to sergeant, but for the time being, I loved my newfound freedom of flying solo in the squad car. There was only one problem about that promotion to sergeant: there still wasn't any news of exactly when the next exam would be. Months turned into years as the rumors and misinformation continued to swirl about an exam that never seemed to get scheduled. I knew eventually I'd have my opportunity, but until then, I was enjoying my Highway-Unit assignment.

Grandpa Frank wasn't your stereotypical grandparent. He was a tough Irishman that had been worn down by a life full of hardship and unwanted travels. Of course, as a six-year-old, I couldn't understand why this man with hands of stone and a face with more lines than a TripTik book, was so unhappy.

I can remember as a young child telling my Pall Mall, chain-smoking grandfather that one day I was going to be a police officer. I was going to have lots of medals like my dad and drive in a big police car around New York City. I would think most grandparents would've encouraged a child's dream—but not grandpa. In his thick Irish brogue, he said, "So, you have it all figured out, do you? We'll see, young man. Life might just throw a few curveballs between now and then."

The Irishmen's sour words never departed from my memory. At the time, I took his hurtful remarks to mean that he doubted my abilities to achieve my future goal. It wasn't until later in life that I realized his words weren't about me or my abilities at all. Rather, it was about him and the adversities he faced during the course of his life. For Grandpa Frank, he had two that would forever change his path: the fleeing of his beloved Ireland and the loss of his daughter Margaret.

But I was certain my life would be different. I wasn't about to let life's little curveballs get in my way. I was in control of my future—or so I thought.

The heavy rains were remnants of a winter nor'easter that was still pounding the eastern seaboard on that first Tuesday of 1996. My 0600 hours shift started like so many prior. After signing out a radio and getting the keys to RMP 3338, I was on my way to the Westside Highway. The only slight variation this morning was the retrieving of a few extra "Accident Reports" from clerical. Between the wet roads, diminished visibility and commuters rushing to work, the combination was ripe for multiple vehicular accidents.

As I entered the clerical office, I saw a face I hadn't seen in a while. It was that of Mike Burke. Mike had been assigned to the steady midnight shift ever since we came over as rookies. My day tour shift and his overnight shift overlapped each other by a little over an hour, so on occasion we'd run into one another. But as of late, I hadn't seen my fellow Third Division alum at all.

After saying hello to Mike, I asked him where he'd been hiding. That's when he told he'd been reassigned to the Ceremonial Unit.

The detail's primary use was as pallbearers at police funerals. Most of the funerals were for the older, retired members of the service. Although it's not the full fanfare of an inspector's funeral, the service is a nice offering by the department to pay their final respects to one of its members. Always looking sharp in uniform and strong enough to lift those heavy caskets, I thought Mike was a good fit for the unit.

When there weren't any funerals scheduled, Mike was to report back to the North. He explained that for the past several months, the Ceremonial Unit had been so busy that this was the first day he didn't have a funeral to report to. He sounded so disappointed in the notion that as I said goodbye to him, I sarcastically told him that I was sorry nobody died. Mike then responded with a wise crack of his own: "Well, if you feel that bad, maybe you can do something about it."

I knew Mike's comment was an off-the-cuff, harmless banter between two officers. Unfortunately, Mike had no idea at the time that in less than fifteen minutes his, words would nearly come to fruition.

Like a creature of habit, I drove my RMP down to Fifty-Fourth Street and the Westside Highway. I chose this concealed location to help view motorists without being detected. However, there was one drawback to my tucked away location and that would be the proximity to Clinton Park.

The steep staircase that led into the park was directly behind where I normally positioned the RMP. I was concerned with this blind spot and made certain to check my rearview mirror often to ensure nobody approached from the rear without me knowing.

Over the years, I'd become friendly with many of the residents that frequented the park. Most would either walk their dogs or use the open green space to exercise in the early morning hours. We were all familiar with each other's schedule. In fact, if I were to show up later than 6:15 a.m., Ann, a local dog walker, would tease me for being late.

On this particular morning, the rain was so heavy that all the people I'd usually see were not out yet. However, as I backed-up the RMP, I noticed two men at the top of the stairs that looked out of place. They were both wearing hoodies over their heads and neither had an umbrella. Once the two men noticed my RMP, they turned away and began walking back into the park. I was uneasy at what I just observed. Maybe it was nothing but my instincts were telling me the two men were up to no good. With my back to the park and the two mystery men somewhere behind me, I decided it would be a good idea to investigate what was going on.

I shut off the RMP and proceeded to walk up the granite flight of stairs. Between the heavy rain and the sun still an hour away, visibility was difficult. If not for the dimly-lit lampposts along the pathway, I wouldn't have been able to see a thing. When I reached the top of the staircase, I looked to see where the men went off to. Not seeing anything, I began making my way into the park. In the distance, I saw one of the men take off running.

The man had done nothing wrong, but his furtive actions raised my suspicions to the point that I was about to call for backup. It was at that point I noticed the second man come from behind a tree that was only a few feet to my left. He had his head tilted down with the hood of his jacket covering nearly all of his face. I couldn't see his eyes or his hands, so I began instructing the individual to stop and take his hands out of his pockets.

I knew I was in trouble once I saw how close the perp was to me. I had neither my radio or gun at the ready and found myself at a tactical disadvantage—all of which was avoidable if I called for backup and had my firearm in my hand instead of still being in its holster.

There's an arbitrary safety zone an officer likes to keep between himself and a possible perp. This space is critical in keeping an officer safe and buying him time to make a decision. The more the space is compromised, the less options and more dangerous the situation can become.

As soon as the individual came out from behind the tree, his proximity had already breached my safety zone. In that split second, I could surmise a confrontation was imminent and that I hadn't time to do anything but defend myself with my hands.

With the individual a few feet away and closing fast, I could see him remove his hands from his side jacket pockets. In one hand, I observed a small shiny firearm being raised in my direction.

I was in no man's land with only one thought—I'm screwed.

Knowing I couldn't get to my gun in time, I decided to charge the perp and close the gap between us as quickly as possible. The perp was able to get off one shot before I was able to get to him. With my adrenalin in survival mode, I still hadn't a clue if I was shot or not. In the ruckus, I was unable to tell where the nozzle of the gun was pointing. Since I had my bullet proof vest on I was trying to keep the gun in my midsection, while still wrapping my hands around the assailant's hand that was holding the firearm. Within a few seconds, the perp was able to get a second shot off.

There were two shots fired at close range and still I wasn't certain if I had been hit or not. At that point, my sole concern was to hold onto the gun for dear life. I began to feel a burning, numbing feeling in my hand and became concerned I was going to lose control of the firearm. With the assailants one free hand, he began punching me in the side of the head. I stayed in a crouch position in an attempt to limit the blows. With the perp having only one hand on the gun, I could feel myself starting to gain control of the firearm. Just when I thought I had full possession of it, I felt the perp's knee connect with my midsection. The thrusting blow relinquished any control I had over the gun, along with any air in my lungs. Now with the perp in full control of the firearm, he began hitting me with the butt of the gun to the side of my head.

As a youngster, I played sandlot football on a field that overlooked the Verrazano Bridge. Francis was the one that introduced me to the game by giving me a football one year for Christmas. With the temperature well below freezing, he took me outside and showed me how to throw the oddly-shaped ball for the first time. After that, I was hooked. Every chance I had, I played catch with Francis or anyone else who was willing to chase down my errant passes. One day in school, I saw I flier on the wall for a new Pop Warner football league that was forming for young boys. I immediately signed up. When I was asked by the coach what positioned I wished to play, I responded without hesitation, "Quarterback." He laughed and then asked me what my second choice was. I asked him if I could throw the ball once before giving him my second choice and the coach agreed. I never did have to tell him what my second choice was.

For the next several years, I played quarterback and loved every second of it. For me there was nothing more beautiful than a tight spiral flowing through the air. During one game, I called a play for my flanker, John Pickerel, to run a post route. I could've thrown the ball sooner but I purposely waited until John was well down the field before I let it go. I was watching the football travel through the air when I felt someone hit me from my blind side. In an instant, the air had left my lungs and I was keeled over, unable to breath. It was the closest I ever felt to dying in my life. The coach came out to check on me and explained that it was just the wind getting knocked out of me.

It had been nearly fifteen years, but as I lay face down on the wet, cold pavement gasping for air, it was that childhood memory that popped into my head.

The fight was over and I lost. The only question left was whether or not my nemesis was going to put a bullet in the back of my head. I desperately attempted to roll on my back, not for any tactical purposes, but because I wanted to look my executioner in his eyes before he doled out his evil.

By the time I rolled over, the assailant was gone.

I heard what I thought to be sirens in the background but couldn't be certain. The perp's last round was fired just inches from my right ear and I was experiencing a deafening ringing noise.

I would learn some time later that the security guard assigned to Pier 96 heard the shots from across the highway and dialed 911. The 10-13 code immediately went out over the radio and within moments, several units were on the scene.

If not for the security guard's 911 call, and the blaring of the sirens that precipitated, there's no doubt in my mind the perp would've finished what he'd started.

By the time the first officers arrived, I was still gasping for air but had at least made it to my knees. When I looked over at the one officer, I could see his lips moving but couldn't make out what he was saying. As the officer was checking to see if I was shot, I tried telling them I was all right but found it difficult to speak. They were worried about the blood coming from the side of my head from where I was pistol-whipped. I wasn't concerned with the contusion but rather the throbbing feeling that was now intensifying in my hand. I looked down and noticed blood coming out of a hole from my police issued, grey leather glove. I had been shot in the right hand during the struggle but hadn't realized it until just then.

I was now in the back of an RMP heading to the hospital. With my hearing popping in and out, I was still having a difficult time understanding what the officers were saying. The only words I could make out were, "St. Claire's Hospital." It took most of my strength, but I screamed, "No, take me to Roosevelt."

I never forgot how I was treated by the staff at St. Claire's Hospital after being pricked by a needle on Thanksgiving Day. Although the hospital was much closer, I made certain the officers took me to where I knew the staff would treat me with some kindness and dignity.

By the time we arrived at the hospital, the adrenalin that had been masking the pain was wearing off. My hearing was still going in and out, which only added to the surreal feeling I was now experiencing.

Within minutes, several other officers from the precinct arrived at the hospital. Amongst them was Mike. He had a look of guilt on his face that I assumed was for the earlier banter between us. I know I was the one laying on the gurney, but at that moment, I think the poor guy felt worse than I did.

He came over and started apologizing when I explained to him if not for my terrible police tactics, neither of us would've been in Roosevelt Hospital on this crappy morning.

By the time Mike and I finished talking, I could see the color come back to his face. I thought besides Dad, Mike might've been the next most devastated person if I was killed. That's when I realized—Dad!

I didn't want my poor father receiving another early morning visit from the brass regarding one of his sons, so I thought it be best to call him before someone in the department was dispatched to make the notification.

I was in no hurry to know how bad the injury was to my hand, so I still hadn't removed the glove yet. One of the nurses came over and told me it was time to take a look at the injury. I politely told the female nurse that she had a wait a minute because I needed to make a phone call.

"But, Officer, I really need to take a look at the hand in order to assess the injury," the motherly nurse told me.

"Ma'am, I need to call my father before someone else notifies him of what happened this morning. Give me two minutes and then I'm all yours."

The understanding nurse told me to wait while she retrieved a cordless phone for me to use. After returning with the phone, she closed the drapes to give me some privacy.

As I dialed the number, I could feel my stomach begin to do somersaults. All things considered, I was okay, but nobody wants to tell someone they love they've just been shot. This was going to suck.

Before allowing it to ring a second time, Dad picked up.

"Hey, Dad, it's me," I tried saying in a positive tone.

In a calm, cool voice he asked, "What's wrong, son?"

I thought to myself, *Amazing.* I said all of four words but I should've known his instincts were too good to be fooled.

I tried holding back my tears but that only made me choke-up more. For the second time that morning, I was unable to speak.

That's when he told me to relax and exhale.

"Dean, take it easy. It can't be that bad. Whatever it is, we'll deal with it."

I finally composed myself enough to tell him what transpired. At the end, I assured him I had nothing more than a flesh wound to the hand and that I'd be fine. He continued to stay calm and told me he'd see me shortly.

How I wish I never had to make that call.

The nurse had been patiently waiting on the other side of the curtain playing defense to anyone who wanted to see me. Once I was finished with the call, I asked her to come back in. I knew it was time to remove the glove and see exactly what the injury looked like.

There was a small entrance and exit wound that didn't seem to look overly severe. I thought a few stitches on each side would do the trick and I'd be on my way. I was sadly mistaken. The small caliber round had shattered several bones in the hand, and an operation to repair the damage was scheduled for later that morning.

After two days at Roosevelt, I was finally released. Dad came to pick me up, and soon after, we were on our way home. I was happy to be out of the hospital and in the comfort of my own bathroom, shower and bed. It wasn't until I went to sleep that first night out of the hospital when I realized something wasn't right.

I started to become so dizzy that my stomach turned and I began to get sick. I was sweating one minute and freezing the next. At first, I thought I might've caught a bug while in the hospital. The entire night I was unable to sleep. In the morning, I went downstairs to see if Dad was awake. He wasn't up yet, so I decided to lie on the couch. Within a few minutes, I was sleeping like a baby. The cycle continued for several weeks until I finally resided in the fact I was better off living downstairs with Dad.

It didn't take long for me to realize that it wasn't a virus my body was fighting but rather something mental. I feared being alone so much that there were times I wished I was back in the hospital just so I could be around people. I don't know what I would've done if it hadn't been for my dad staying by my side.

The detectives handling my case informed me they were tracking some leads that directed them to a drug dealer from the Dominican Republic. He was known for being a ruthless crack distributor from Washington Heights who was trying to expand his turf from uptown to midtown. He'd been linked to several homicides in New York, Miami and the Dominican Republic, but none transpired in any convictions. Unfortunately, if they did find this guy, it was going to be difficult for me to make a positive identification since I wasn't able to get a good look at the assailant's face.

I started to notice a trend whenever I would discuss the case with anyone. That evening, I would have the worst nightmares. The theme of the dreams was always similar. I was paralyzed and unable to get away from the imminent danger that was coming toward me. In some of the dreams, I would have my service revolver out but as hard as I would pull on the trigger, I wasn't strong enough to fire the weapon. Each dream would end with me gasping for air right before I'd awake in a lather of sweat.

In the same speed the bullet pierced through my hand, my life had been turned upside down. The routine I'd come to love and enjoy prior to getting hurt had been replaced with fear, anxiety, and nightmares. No longer did my schedule include work, basketball practice and getting together with friends, but rather a docket that included endless doctors' appointments, shrinks, and my favorite— weekly interviews with the police surgeon so he could evaluate "my progress."

Out of all of them, the visit to the police surgeon really pissed me off the most. The insensitive, bureaucratic paper pusher—otherwise known as the police surgeon—had one concern: how fast he could get me off sick leave and back to a modified assignment. Every week was the same question: do you feel well enough to answer phones and do some clerical duties? And, every week I'd give the same answer: "As soon as I can wipe my own ass, I'd be more than happy to play secretary."

However, until then, I had no plans in returning to work.

I knew I was playing a game of fire with the egotistical Police Surgeon, but I still had one advantage over him: I was a police officer recovering from a gunshot wound. True, the wound wasn't as severe as some other line of duty injuries, but mine had been in the media. If not for that, I was certain he would've taken me off sick leave and put me on desk duty in a heartbeat.

So, the police surgeon and I played a little dance. He tried pushing me back to work, and I kept saying no. I didn't feel like playing Mrs. Wiggins (Carrol Burnett's clueless secretary character) just because some police surgeon wanted his "sick leave numbers" to look better. I knew I couldn't hold him off forever, so when I was ready, I'd go back.

A month had gone by when I told my dad I thought I was ready to go back to the command and suffer some papercuts. My hand and whether it would recover its full range of motion were still in question. I was undergoing physical therapy twice a week, and a decision regarding whether I needed a second operation to stabilize some of the fractured bones was still being considered by the hand specialist. I would inform the police surgeon of my decision at my next scheduled visit.

When I arrived at the police surgeon's office in Lefrak City for the appointment, I was ambushed by the commanding officer, Sergeant Jones and the surgeon himself, Doctor Reynolds. Before I could speak, both men were informing me that I was to be taken off sick leave immediately and put on modified assignment. I had to assume my "ass wiping comment" hadn't gone over well with the surgeon on my previous visit and he decided to play hard ball with me. The sergeant went as far as to tell me if I refused, he'd have me suspended.

Call it nerves, PTSD, anxiety, frustration or simply tired of dealing with stupidity, but I had a moment most would consider a breakdown. I couldn't believe I was being threatened with a suspension by a sergeant whose biggest contribution to the NYPD was determining how many paper clips he needed in the next clerical supply order, and a doctor who was so bad that he couldn't open up his own medical practice.

Up to this point, I hadn't complained about a thing. I took a little over a month to recover and, although I was still having issues sleeping, I thought going back to work, answering phones and pushing papers might actually be helpful. But being threatened into going back wasn't going to work for me.

I got up from my seat and told both men to go to hell.

"Who do you guys think you are? I was the one laying on the ground sucking wind while you two desk jockeys were in this heated office playing god with people's lives. So, go ahead and suspend me, but don't dear ever threaten me again."

As I walked out of the office, the sergeant was screaming back at me, "You're hereby suspended, Simpson! You're done!"

I tried calming down as I walked the two blocks to the subway station, but my anger was getting the better of me. To be treated with such an impervious attitude by the doctor and sergeant had me less concerned about the consequences of my actions and more about whether it was time to leave the job I once said I'd work for free. I knew I wasn't in the right state of mind to be making any rash decisions, so I decided it was best to go home and calm down.

However, life stepped in one more time and threw me my final curveball as a member of the NYPD. While standing on the subway platform, I lost conciseness and fell to the pavement.

Aside from the day I was born, I had never been hospitalized before. Now, twice in the last month, I'd be admitted to a hospital.

Several tests were conducted and the diagnosis was a temporal bone fracture in the inner ear. In all likelihood, I suffered the injury when I was pistol whipped by the assailant. The news explained why I had been dizzy and suffering from vertigo-like symptoms the past several weeks.

I never did return back to work, nor was I ever suspended. The decision whether or not to stay on the job was no longer mine. The injuries to the hand and the newly-diagnosed vertigo were permanent. In less than a year, I was processed out of the NYPD, given a disability pension and a plaque from my fellow officers.

Irony being what it is gave me one last shot across my bow the day after I retired. Mike Burke called me to wish me well, and on a side note, informed me that the department officially announced the next sergeant's exam for later that spring. I couldn't help but laugh since I waited my entire career to hear that news and know it meant absolutely nothing to me.

Then Mike wished me well in whatever it was I was planning on doing post-NYPD. That's when it hit me that I truly wasn't a police officer anymore. At that moment, I wasn't sure what should be more concerning to me: not knowing what I was going to do next or not caring.

I was now thirty as I pondered my empty outlook on life. I could hear Father Gerald's voice in my head echoing the words he'd tell his students at assembly. "An idle mind is the devils play ground."

CHAPTER 10

The Lone Blue Shoe

In three words, I can sum up everything
I've learned about life: It goes on.

—Robert Frost

The summer of 2001 had all been but a blur. Between Dad's passing and the continuous void left from leaving the force early, I now had little gumption and absolutely no direction in life. I hadn't planned on being a self-pitied drunk by the time I was thirty-five, but the truth was that's exactly what I'd become. Without work or love in my life, I struggled to find a reason to want to get out of bed in the morning.

My dad was my mentor, my rock, and my best friend. The thought of not being able to share his company any longer saddened me greatly. However, given the selfish choice of having him still around or laying him to rest, the choice was easy—he fought the good fight, it was time for him to rest.

Dad had a nagging cough most of the winter but chose to ignore it. After finally convincing him to visit a doctor to run some tests, we awaited the results. It was on Saint Patty's Day when he broke the news to me.

"This will be it for a while," he said lightly, referring to the scotch he was sipping on. "Chemo starts tomorrow."

The bravest man I ever knew was diagnosed with Non-Hodgkin's Lymphoma. The debilitating blood disease had two grades; high and low. Sadly, Dad was diagnosed with the more aggressive high-grade.

For the next several weeks, the two of us drove into Manhattan to Sloan Kettering Hospital for his chemotherapy treatments. This was the same Sloan Kettering he stayed in years earlier when he was having his "supposed" heart attack. How I wish this was only a charade too.

The serene view from the treatment facility was full of sun light and panoramic views of the East River. If not for the unpleasant purpose of the visit—having poisoned pumped into one's body—the visit would otherwise have been pleasant.

The staff from top-to-bottom was professional in every way. They continuously encouraged their patients and understood the importance of a positive attitude. They made family members feel a part of the process by suggesting we donate needed blood, platelets, and double red cells.

At any given time, there were over a dozen other outpatients receiving their chemotherapy along with Dad. Each session could take up to three hours with televisions, magazines and friendly interaction between patients helping the time go by.

On many occasions, Dad would hold my hand during the chemo treatment, squeezing it and letting me know how much he loved me. He'd always seemed guarded with his words and wasn't big on showing his sensitive side, but after the diagnosis, something changed in him. He went out of his way to let people he cared about know how much they meant to him. He shared his kindness with anyone willing to listen—nurses, doctors, and most of all his fellow outpatients. He'd let them know that together they were going to "kick cancer's ass."

While he reflected on his life, he told me he wished he'd been a more patient and loving person. I told my best friend that I loved him for who he was, not for who he wanted to be. However, he felt his time was short and it was important to make peace with the things in his life he would've liked to have done differently. Here was my dad riddled with a disease that was going to take away his life, and his primary concern was desperately trying to be a better Christian.

Those days at Sloan Kettering had become some of the best days I ever spent with my dad. I know that may sound crazy under the circumstances, but I thanked the good Lord for giving me that precious time with him.

He opened up to me like never before, sharing intimate stories of his life. Each visit to the cancer center was a journey back in time. Some days he'd discuss his childhood, while other days he'd tell stories about when he was in the army. But it was his stories about being a police officer that captivated me the most—just like they had when I was a child. While telling his tales to me, Dad would stop to ask if he was talking too much, to which I'd reply, "It's about time."

When he was too tired to talk any longer, I'd read the Bible to him. He told me my voice was comforting, and the word of God was like food for his soul. Being a strong spiritual man, he never blamed God for his infliction but rather thanked Him for all His blessings.

Three months after being diagnosed, James Michael Simpson passed away on June 20, 2001. During his life, he had many great accomplishments but none greater than being my dad.

As the days past after Dad's death, I began a slow and steady decent into depression. Unlike the common cold or flu, where the symptoms are clearly present, this ailment is much less overt to the inflicted. Without a healthy routine or something in my life to care about, I began to drink heavily during the night and sleep throughout the day. I'd reached a point that I either wanted to be intoxicated or unconscious—anything else had become pure hell.

It was the evening of September 10 when I made my usual evening trek to The Wicked Monk to partake in my over-indulgence in alcoholic beverages.

"The Monk," as the locals affectionately referred to it as, had become my sanctuary away from my dreaded, empty apartment.

The watering hole was a brain storm by three guys from Cork County, Ireland. The three—Paul, Devlin and Bryan—were disgruntled employees at another Irish Pub in the neighborhood named Peggy O'Neil's. When the time was right, they pooled their resources, scouted for a location, and opened the most unique pub in all of Brooklyn. The wood, stained glass, pews and altars were all part of a church back in their hometown. When they were informed that the church was to be demolished, they decided to have as much of the old sanctuary sparred and shipped to Brooklyn. The finished product resembled an Irish Gothic Monastery—right down to the confessional booths.

Everyone seemed to have their own favorite part of the pub. For some, it was the restored wood used to build the bar, and for others, it was the cathedral-shaped, stained glass windows erected behind the taps. The sinners favored the confessional booths, but as for me, I loved staring at the mural painted on the ceiling directly above the bar.

Most patrons didn't know it existed until they'd look up to see what I was staring at. The oval-shaped work of art displayed a group of monks gathered around in a gala of drink and wickedness. Perhaps, the thirty-foot long mural wouldn't have been worthy of a Saturday Evening Post cover, but I would think even Norman Rockwell would've appreciated the meticulous detail in the artist's work.

The barkeep was a childhood friend named Scott "Scotty" Whelan. We played basketball together for the church when we were in grade school. Although we lived in the same neighborhood, I lost touch with Scotty over the years. It wasn't until about a year before when I stopped in at The Monk to see what all the fuss was about that we rekindled our friendship. The tall, charismatic barkeep was a perfect fit for any bar, especially an Irish one. Scotty had the wit to keep up with the cantankerous old geezers and the charm to woo many of the young, female patrons.

When I told Scotty I was no longer with the NYPD, he offered me a position working the door on the weekends. I didn't think of myself as much of a bouncer, but Scotty assured me it was more for show than anything else. So, with nothing better on the horizon, I accepted.

Within a few weeks, I pretty much knew everyone. The position wasn't exactly stimulating my intellect, but it gave me something to do on Friday and Saturday evenings. In all likelihood, I would've been there drinking anyway, but at least now I was making a few bucks while getting splinters in my ass. On occasion, some young filly would try sneaking in with a fake driver's license, or some intoxicated patron would need to be escorted to a taxi. But otherwise, I was nothing more than a body sitting on a barstool.

I didn't know how Scotty kept up with all the women. He'd have them scattered strategically along the bar and would bounce from one to the other, while never missing a patron with an empty glass. He'd even remember to send a few Wild Turkey and cokes my way throughout the night.

Monday nights were a bit different from the weekend crowd. For starters, the hard drinking, blue-collar clientele on the weeknights were less concerned about appearances. We were there to drink, and if something should entertain us in the process without interrupting our goal, then that was okay, too.

This Monday happened to be a little more special than usual. It was the start of the NFL season for the New York Giants. They were playing the Broncos in Denver. The game wasn't too good for us homey's. Denver spanked the Giants 31–20.

Despite the defeat, I found myself being appreciative for the distraction.

For the entire game, I uncharacteristically nursed three beers and hadn't touched the shot of Jack Daniels poured for me by Scotty. This had been the soberest I'd been in months.

After the game, a few of the guys asked me to play darts.

Before working at The Monk, I never picked up the spear throwers but as it turned out, I was a natural—rehabilitated hand and all. We'd play for a few bucks a game, but I was just happy to do something besides drink.

On my first throw, I nearly hit the ceiling. My second throw hit the wall two feet adjacent to the dart board, and I didn't bother throwing my third. I hadn't been drinking, and my coordination wasn't used to doing anything sober. I walked directly over to Scotty and ordered a tall Wild Turkey and coke with a double chaser of JD. By the time I sucked down all three, my coordination was back.

I knew my alcohol consumption had increased the past several months, but I simply didn't care. Mind you, just because I was intoxicated didn't mean I acted like a drunk. For me, there was a huge distinction. I'd grown to despise loud, obnoxious drunks, so I was the quiet, reserved type that only spoke when it was absolutely necessary.

After the issue with the darts, I'd come to the realization that I was no longer in control of the alcohol, but rather the alcohol was in control of me. This epiphany on my part didn't scare me straight or sober me up. It simply showed that my descent reached a new low.

A few hours after the football game had ended, Patrick, one of the owners of The Monk, came in with his friend, Leroy. I never met Leroy before but I could see that the overweight, black man thought he was a cowboy or at least wanted to be one. He had the boots, jeans, the oversized belt buckle and, of course, the cowboy hat. Patrick graciously bought everyone a shot at the bar and introduced his friend.

It wasn't long after I heard Leroy challenging for the dart board.

"I'll play anyone for a hundred bucks," the intoxicated, wannabe cowboy uttered.

I could see the guys looking over at Leroy like a bunch of hyena's eyeing an easy mark. I reminded the boys that the individual was a guest of the owner and it would be better to let things be. No sooner had I corralled the wolves when Patrick walked over to me.

Patrick was in his early thirties and the youngest of the three owners of The Monk. Although we never socialized together, I knew the leprechaun-resembling Irishmen to be a bit of a jokester. He enjoyed bar-hopping, always making The Monk his final stop.

"Dean, how goes it tonight?" Patrick mumbled in his thicker than molasses, Irish brogue.

"I'm still on the right side of the dirt," I politely replied.

"Grand, that's grand. I have a favor to ask of you. My friend is a bit of an ass and I'd like to teach him a lesson. We just come back from the city where we were hustled for every dime we had because my cowboy buddy over there couldn't hit the side of a barn if he was leaning on it. He hasn't a nickel in his pocket and now he wants to challenge you for the board. Play him and beat the sorry ass son-of-a-bitch."

I knew it was late and everyone present was well past the witching hour. I tried being diplomatic to Patrick's request but he wouldn't hear of it. He wanted his buddy beaten and what's more, he knew exactly what he wanted me to play him for.

"Play him for that ridiculous hat. I want to piss in that damn thing. Do you have any idea what it's like to walk around Manhattan with Fat Albert and Roy Rodgers all rolled up into one? I had enough of Fat Rodgers for one night, so please, go whip his ass and bring me back that hat."

I played Leroy one game of Cricket—my hundred for his cowboy hat. Less than three minutes later, I was the proud owner of a Stetson ten-gallon, ridiculous looking, cowboy hat.

Leroy went to give me the hat but I told him to keep it. Leroy was drunk and as Patrick told me, "couldn't hit the side of a barn." I was drunk too, but the difference was I functioned better that way. The only way the match would've been fair is if I played sober while he played in his inebriated state. That would've been some ugly dart throwing.

The jolly Leroy was thankful for my gesture, but insisted I take his hat. I told him to buy me a drink and we'd call it even. He finally agreed and said, "You're a real mensch."

Having never heard of the term before, I asked him what it meant, to which he replied that it was a Yiddish word meaning that I was one of the good guys.

I thanked Leroy for the compliment and then told him that I never thought I'd be in an Irish pub being called something in Yiddish by a black guy. We both had a good laugh and headed to the bar.

I apologized to Patrick for not taking the hat and explained how I didn't feel right about it. Patrick didn't seem to mind and told me he was glad the spanking at least quieted down his impetuous buddy.

Now it was time to do shots.

The spirited, young owner loved doing shots of After Eight's—a mixer of Bailey's and Kahlua, with a splash of Peppermint Schnapps filled in a cocktail shaker over ice and served neat.

After Scotty's vigorous one-handed shake and spin of the silver shaker, he flawlessly poured the concoction into the symmetrically aligned shot-glasses on the bar. Patrick then doled out the shots as if he were a priest celebrating the Eucharist. Then Patrick raised his shot-glass and gave a toast to Leroy, "To the most uncoordinated black man I know."

After downing our shots, Patrick proceeded to take the hat off Leroy's head and put it on. The hat was about three sizes too big for the frail Irishmen. As Patrick started dancing, something between the Irish jig and the two-step, the hat kept dipping over his eyes. The comical sight was enough to make me burst out laughing. Then Patrick started with the commentary.

"Look at me… I'm a black cowboy from New York City. I can't throw a dart in the ocean if I was standing on Ellis Island."

Thanks to Patrick, and a good-sported Leroy, I enjoyed a brief moment of levity.

It was now after five in the morning. A few minutes earlier, I noticed Scotty discreetly excuse himself to the basement with one of his young, female companions. With the front door now locked and the bartender preoccupied, one might think the bar was closed but that was far from the case.

Patrick took over behind the bar, and from the looks of things, none of the patrons seemed eager to call it a night. That is, except for me. It was time for this vampire to get back to his cave before the sun came up. I wished the men a goodnight-morning and headed on my way.

When I arrived home, I kept to my routine. I disconnected the phone, shut the blinds, and inserted my earplugs. My goal was to sleep until at least the afternoon. To my displeasure, I missed my goal and woke up at ten thirty. I knew I wasn't going to be able to get back to sleep, so I decided it was time for me to once again attempt to go through Dad's papers.

I found the task to be daunting. Dad's entire life was jammed into two tall filing cabinets and an oversized roll top desk, and now it was left to me to do the purging.

There was Dad's diploma from graduating kindergarten dated 1937. Why he was still holding on to that, I hadn't a clue. He had receipts and copies of taxes going as far back as 1950. There was an entire drawer of the cabinet filled with love letters to and from Mom. In another drawer, he had pictures from when he was in the service. Many of the photos were with Dad and several of his army buddies. Never before had I seen him look as happy as he did in those pictures; a young, strong man with his entire life ahead of him.

Out of everything I had to go through, the pictures proved to be the most difficult. They showed a man full of life and hope where now, neither existed.

I decided it was time to take a break from the purging. I walked up the block to get a coffee and the paper. As I made my way to the corner, I noticed an eerie quietness on the streets. The day was beautiful without a cloud in the sky, but there were hardly any cars or people out and about. The few people I did see were entering the church. For a second, I thought it might've been Sunday but thanks to Monday Night Football, I knew that wasn't the case. I was still half asleep with a Red Sea splitting headache but had enough sense to know something wasn't right.

I entered the produce store where I worked as a youngster, and there on the television behind the counter, I could see why the people were flocking to the church. I took off my ultra-dark sunglasses to see what was being broadcasted: The World Trade Center buildings were no longer.

While I watched in horror, I struggled to comprehend exactly what was transpiring.

I walked across the street to the church hoping to find Father Gerald. I needed someone to explain to me what was going on.

When I entered, I could see him talking with several of the parishioners. When he was finished, he walked over to me and said, "It's not good." I knew my mentor a long time and never once saw him look this troubled. As I hung on his every word, he continued,

"Entire company's from the NYFD were in those buildings when they went down. The overall death toll is going to be staggering."

I sat in a pew and looked up at Jesus on the cross behind the altar. I begged Him to take my life in return for sparing the innocent. There were people that needed to get home to their loved ones. They had children to raise, spouses to love, and memories to still make. While I sat there trying to explain to God that my life had less meaning than those He was taking from their families, I already knew my offering was in vain.

Without knowing exactly why, I decided to go home and change into my police uniform. While putting on the navy-blue trousers and sky-blue shirt, I realized for the first time how much weight and muscle mass I lost since I left the job five years earlier.

I remembered when I was on the job getting dressed in my NYPD uniform how it made me feel as though I was indestructible. However, as I got dressed, I felt anything but confident. I felt vulnerable and woefully unqualified to be wearing a uniform meant for "The Finest."

I started to second guess my decision, when I heard a reporter on the television say something profound. He said this was our generations Pearl Harbor. Hearing those words and understanding the tragic events of December 7, 1941, I knew I had to get myself down to ground zero.

I could see on the news that both the Manhattan and Brooklyn Bridges were filled to capacity with civilians walking across its spans. Needing an alternative way to get into Lower Manhattan, I decided to take my chances with the Brooklyn Battery Tunnel. When I arrived at the Brooklyn side of the tunnel, I quickly realized I wasn't the only first responder to figure out the alternate route into the city.

The Tunnel Authority Police had closed the tunnel for vehicular traffic but were still able to assist uniformed members in getting to the Manhattan side.

I jammed into one of the police vans with about a dozen of the other responders. One could hear a pin drop as the officer began to make his way through the tunnel.

After about a minute, the veteran MTA officer that was driving the van spoke. "It's spooky, guys. The only part of either building that remains is a portion of the exterior, metal framing. Everything else is gone."

The driver dropped us off just outside the tunnel on the Westside Highway—three blocks from where the Towers once stood.

Once I exited the vehicle, I better understood the officer's simple, but accurate description by what he meant by "spooky." The area seemed to be suspended in time. The once bright and sunny day had been eclipsed by a powdery haze. The sounds one would normally experience in the bustling area were absent, except for the occasional siren or radio transmission. Office papers filled the narrow lower Manhattan streets, while the gray, thick dust clung to everything in sight.

As a group, we started walking north toward the largest crime scene in US history. When we reached what was once the South Tower, we could see for the first time the massive devastation.

Through the debris cloud, I could make out the remnants of the outer metal columns. What once stood over thirteen-hundred feet in the air, was now splintered like an erector set to no more than sixty or seventy-feet high.

While looking around at the enormity of the devastation, I thought of the line from Dante's Inferno:

"Abandon all hope, ye who enter her."

The first several days was a continuation of the non-stop bucket brigade that had begun on day one. The goal was to systematically remove the smaller debris in hope of finding survivors. There were the occasional calls for silence by other rescue workers when they thought they'd heard a possible tapping noise or a muffled yell for help. We'd all concentrate the dig around those areas only to come up empty each and every time. Before long, the realization that there weren't going to be any rescues started to become a reality. After a few weeks, the odor of decaying human remains became more prevalent as our mission tragically converted from a rescue, to a recovery.

I hadn't touched a drop of booze since the night before all this hell started. It was as if I turned the alcohol switch off in my head.

My focus had been shifted away from self-pity to wanting to help others. With nowhere else to go and nothing else to do, I spent all of my waking hours down at the pile. I dealt with my spells of dizziness and lack of coordination as best I could. When I needed to, I sat down and took breaks. It was on one of those breaks I saw a fireman that I thought to be a childhood friend of mine. With his back turned to me, I noticed on the bottom of his NYFD jacket the last name "MCMANUS" printed in large fluorescent lettering.

Taking a chance, I called out his first name, "Brenden."

Having turned to see who it was, I realized it was indeed my grade school friend Brenden McManus.

Although Brenden moved away from Bay Ridge to Flatbush after we graduated Saint Patrick's together, we'd still bump into one another over the years. Once the two of us were of legal age, we'd see more of each other while bar-hopping in the Ridge.

In a world filled with so many jerks and sinners, Brenden was definitely one of the good guys. The Cary Grant lookalike never bragged or boasted about his feats. He was a humble individual that always had kind words to share with friends and strangers alike.

After recognizing it was me, Brenden, walked over to say hello. "Hey, Dino, how's it going?"

"How's it going for any of us?" I rhetorically responded back. I then asked him what everyone else was wondering. "How bad do you think the number is going to be (referring to the death toll for the NYFD)?"

Brenden bowed his head and said, "Too many. We have guys on the job down here looking for their sons, brothers, fathers... not good, not good at all. There's going to be a lot of funerals to attend the next couple of weeks."

I asked him if he was aware of any recoveries thus far.

Seeing Brenden more at ease, I knew he had some good news to share.

"On day one, I heard there were six guys from Ladder 6 that made it out alive after the building collapsed. They're reporting the group was saved by some sort of "safety pocket" but I'd call it a "pocket of miracles.""

Hoping to hear more similar stories, I asked Brenden if he knew of any other rescues.

While holding onto his Halligan bar, he bowed his head in dejection and said, "No, but we're all still praying there's still a few more miracles to be found up there," as he pointed toward the pile of what was once the North Tower.

Unknown to the two of us at the time, there were several other rescues made within the first twenty-four hours; twenty in all. Sadly, there wouldn't be any other miracles discovered in the pile after that.

Prior to Brenden leaving to catch up with his company, he told me to say a prayer for a mutual friend of ours, Jimmy Riches. Brenden let me know that he was still amongst the hundreds of missing Firefighters.

Brenden and I knew Jimmy from a bar in my neighborhood, "The Cantina." The young, Irish-American was a well-liked bartender in the Ridge's watering hole. Always sporting a smile and an easy-going demeanor, the rugged-built, neighborhood kid took the path most of us did when deciding on our career, he followed in his father's footsteps. So, after trading in his barkeep apron for a firemen's pick and ax, Jimmy was now proud to be part of the same fraternity as his Dad—New York's Bravest.

Jimmy's firehouse was the closest in proximity to the World Trade Center. Thus, his house was the first of the first responders to answer the call. These were the guys that had one mission in mind: climb the stairs and keep going up until they found those in need of assistance.

People outside of New York City are sometimes fooled into thinking that a small-town atmosphere can't exist within a big metropolis. In reality, that's exactly what New York is—a bunch of small communities wrapped up into one big apple. Before all was said and done, every community throughout the city, or within a fifty-mile radius of ground zero for that matter, would know someone that perished on 9/11. Jimmie's loss would be the first of many that would be felt by our small Brooklyn community.

Each day as I entered the pile, there were ordinary citizens lined along the barricade thanking me, a stranger, for my service.

Hundreds of ordinary men and women giving their support in the rescue by handing out bottles of water, gloves, masks and anything else they thought could help in our efforts. The humanity continued down in the pile where I saw grown men cry like babies, while their brethren comforted them with a hug.

Yes. There was a time one would be hard pressed to differentiate New York City from Mayberry.

As the days turned into weeks, I tried my best to keep up with the younger, stronger volunteers on the bucket brigade; but to my dismay, I could feel my body starting to weaken.

One afternoon while working at the pile, my right eye started to twitch. Having gone through the episodes before, I knew at a minimum I was about to have a vertigo attack, or at worst, a panic attack. Neither one was pleasant, but the panic attacks were extra horrifying since I felt like I couldn't breathe. Having never seen what I looked like during one of these episodes, I could only imagine how scary it was for others to witness my melt down. I desperately looked around to see if there was a place for me to sit and ride it out, but my vision was blurred. That's when an angel in the form of a fire-man approached me and asked if I was all right. I quickly told the unknown rescue worker that I was about to get sick and needed to find a place to sit asap. The fireman took me by my arm and escorted me a few feet away to where there were some cases of water stacked high enough for me to sit down. He then left me for a few seconds and came back with a wet towel. I put the towel over my head and shielded my eyes from the sunlight. I told my guardian angel I was feeling better and insisted he move on, but being a stubborn first responder, he insisted he wasn't going anywhere until he was satisfied that I was all right.

As I sat there feeling like a horse's ass, the fireman introduced himself to me as Jimmy.

"Jimmy, thank you for your help. I'm Dean."

"Do you live in Bay Ridge, by chance?" the brawny, middle-age gentlemen asked.

Now realizing that the individual must've known me, I strained my eyes to see if I recognized him, but to no avail. I then asked him if we knew one another from the Ridge.

"I recognize you from the jogging path by the bridge (Verrazano). You're a runner, right?"

I told him I use to run the path several times a week, but in recent years hadn't been down there as much.

I took the towel off my head and once again thanked Jimmy for his help. Having seen the color come back to my face, I was finally able to convince him I was going to be all right. While I shook the rugged fireman's hand to say goodbye, I couldn't help but feel that I knew the individual. Maybe it was from the jogging path but I felt like I was looking at someone I knew, not someone I glanced at in passing. I thought to myself he must be a lookalike for someone, but the truth was I didn't know a lot of guys in their fifties. Who knows, maybe it will eventually come to me or maybe I'm simply tired and need to get some rest. Either way, it was time for me to call it a day.

The Miracle of Ladder Company 6

With the single greatest death toll in the department's history—343 firefighters—if it hadn't been for a grandmother named Josephine Harris, the number could've been worse.

It was Firefighter Mike Meldrum who first dubbed Josephine Ladder Company 6's guardian angel. Call it luck, a miracle, or the work of a guardian angel, but something occurred in the North Tower that defied physics on that clear blue Tuesday morning.

The sixty-year-old Josephine had started the long descent down the narrow staircase from the Seventy-Third floor when she crossed paths with Captain Jonas and the other five members of Ladder 6. From that moment on, the fate of Ladder Company 6 and Josephine would be forever linked.

The captain, "Captain Jay," instructed the strongest member of his team, Bill Butler, to assist the struggling Josephine down the remaining flights of stairs. One problem, Josephine felt like she couldn't go another step. That's when Josephine stopped where she was and sat down.

Firefighter Tommy Falco, knowing the South Tower had already collapsed and time was of the essence, reassured Josephine that there was no way they were going to leave her behind. So, as a group they waited on the stairwell between the third and fourth floors for the exhausted Josephine to rest. The hope was that the short rest would enable Josephine to finish the last few flights of stairs and as one, walk out of the lobby of the North Tower together. The group would never get that chance.

The sound of the rumble and the reverberation throughout the stairwell precipitated everyone's greatest fear: the building, along with millions of pounds of cement, steel, and debris was heading their way.

In an interview eleven days after 9/11, Firefighter Sal D'agostino, a member of Ladder 6, recalls that exact moment with Stone Phillips of NBC.

"I got on my side and crawled to the doorway, and then I just lay there. And waiting for it to come. This is it. This is horrible, and this is it. And I said a prayer…"

As hell itself came showering down over the group, they were tossed around between the second and fourth floor staircase. Miraculously, none had been crushed to death and were saved due to an adamant Josephine Harris, who decided she couldn't go one more step.

I would think the iconic writer Rod Sterling of the Twilight Zone would've been proud of the irony presented due to Josephine stopping exactly where she did. If she stopped on a higher floor or continued further down, as the firemen pleaded with her to do, there is little doubt they all would've perished. However, because of Josephine, they were exactly where they needed to be at exactly the precise moment they needed to be there.

During that same interview with NBC's Stone Phillips, Matt Komorowski reflected on being a firefighter.

"I think being a fireman runs through your core. And even if stuff happens around that core, you always have that core."

Firefighter Komorowski's words can ring true for all first responders; firefighters, police officers, paramedics and EMT's alike. It takes a unique individual willing to put their own life on the line in order to save a perfect stranger. I believe it's that "core" Komorowski was referring to that showed the world on 9/11 something most people living in the five boroughs already knew—that our men and women truly are the Finest and Bravest.

The recognition and praise the media bestowed upon the first responders was well overdue to say the least. Unfortunately, it took the sacrifice of over four hundred of those first responders to garner such attention.

During those weeks I spent down at ground zero, I remember thinking there was only one thing I could be certain of and that was time. Time would keep marching on the way it did after Pearl Harbor was attacked and when Hiroshima and Nagasaki were abruptly introduced into the atomic age. Time doesn't have an agenda, a religion or a purpose. In some ways, time is like the wind—one can't see it, but if you wait long enough, you can see the effects of it.

In time, the rubble will be cleared away and some monument and/or museum will be erected, and possibly another building will be built. One year will turn to five, five to ten, and eventually someone will be laying a wreath at the base of some statue to commemorate the fiftieth anniversary, the way President George H. W. Bush did at Pearl Harbor on December 7, 1991.

However, waiting for that time to pass will not be easy for those that were directly affected. For them, I would suspect they'd probably like to fast-forward time, but we all know time doesn't work that way. It will no doubt be an arduous task to clean up and rebuild, but with time, that's exactly what will happen.

Police, firemen and volunteers came from across the country to offer their support. Everyone was praying and digging, hoping to find more miracles. However, it didn't take long to realize there weren't going to be anymore feel-good stories coming out of the pile.

I'm not sure when the official word came down that the operation was moving from a rescue to a recovery, but it was becoming clearer with every passing day that's where things were heading. With sons, daughters, mothers and fathers still buried in the debris, no one wanted to give up hope. But eventually, the operation had to start moving from a bucket brigade to a big machine operation.

With so many volunteers operating in a confined area, it was only a matter of time before we (the volunteers) were more of a hindrance than a help.

The ornery Iron Workers were becoming increasingly impatient with trying to work around the hundreds of cops and firemen. Finally, after three weeks of going a hundred miles an hour and exhaustion starting to seep in for everyone, emotions finally reached a breaking point one evening.

The confrontation between the two sides erupted the way most do: someone didn't like the way someone else was addressing them. The overworked Iron Workers were, by nature, a tough, strong-minded group of blue collar hard-hats, while the police and fire guys weren't used to civilians giving them orders. All it took was one hard-hat yelling in the direction of the first responders to "get the hell out of the way" for a war to nearly erupt. The spat was quickly extinguished by calmer heads, but the reality was clear that it was time for the big boys with their big equipment to take over and make some headway.

I'd been down at ground zero for twenty days and nights straight. After the confrontation between the volunteers and Iron Workers, I decided it was time for me to leave and not return.

While I began to walk away from the pile, I turned back to take in one last overview of the men and women desperately attempting to undo Satan's handy work.

As the work lights illuminated the darkened sky, I could see hundreds of workers moving like an army of ants, each feverishly working, not for themselves, but for the greater good of a larger cause.

The last object I saw before walking away was a lady's blue dress shoe. The single piece of footwear was missing its counterpart, as well as their rightful owner. With dried blood scattered upon it, I couldn't help but notice the lone shoe was the same color the sky was on the morning of September 11. The orphaned, sky-blue shoe rested on the side of one of the piles of rubble. I allowed my mind to wonder and speculate the significance of what ordinarily would've been a very insignificant shoe. I wondered how the shoe found its way to the pile and what might've been the fate of the owner. I speculated how the blood could've made its way onto the shoe. Maybe the owner tripped and cut herself while she fled to safety, leaving behind half of her favorite pair of shoes. I prayed the only thing the owner lost on that horrific morning was that lone, sky-blue shoe.

The truth is I don't know the last moments of the blue shoe's owner or of the thousands of souls that perished prior to the buildings collapsing. One thing I did know was life as we knew it, for everyone in NYC and throughout the country, was never going to be the same.

I took in one last deep breath through my nostrils and scanned the pile. The smell of charred debris, death, and a blue shoe would be my last reminders of ground zero.

Over the next several weeks, it started to become painfully apparent that no one in the city was immune to the tragic events of 9/11. Whether it was a direct loss of a family member, a neighbor, childhood classmate, or someone from their congregation, everyone knew someone that had suffered a loss. When Dad died, it was sad but certainly not tragic. These deaths, young and old, were all tragic because they shouldn't have happened.

It didn't take long for the procession of funerals to start. There was a teammate I played Pop Warner football with as a youngster—the girl I took to a dance back in high school—one of my cop buddies that recently rolled over from the NYPD to the NYFD, becoming one of New York's Bravest. Then there was my friend from college who went on a job interview at Cantor Fitzgerald. His interview wasn't scheduled until nine that morning but he heard about the legendary wait times with the elevators, so he decided to give himself a little extra travel time and reached the 103rd floor office a little after eight thirty. The first plane hit the North Tower, home of Cantor Fitzgerald, sixteen minutes later.

Over the coming months, I would learn of more childhood friends, acquaintances, friends of friends, and people I met in passing over the years that, for whatever their reason, were in the wrong place at the wrong time. I didn't suffer the personal loss so many others throughout the city had. I couldn't imagine their pain or the difficulty they faced trying to comprehend the events that unfolded on that day.

I decided since I was no longer spending time down at ground zero, I'd do my best to attend as many funerals as I could. I remembered how comforting it was to me when I saw those attending my father's funeral and I wanted to offer that gesture, as small as it was, to the victim's families.

The lucky families—if I dare call them that—didn't have to wait long for a funeral, finding their loved ones remains early on. However, after six weeks, only 425 people had been identified out of 2,780. For the less fortunate families, they had the agonizing ordeal of waiting to hear from the Medical Examiner's office. After one year, only half of the victims had been positively identified—predominately through advance DNA testing. When all the different numbers and statistics were tallied and logged, there were two that stood out to me—300/1,100. Only three-hundred bodies were found intact, while over eleven-hundred victims were never found or identified.

The look etched in the faces of parents having to do the unthinkable, burying one's child, had become all too frequent the days following 9/11.

I heard the grief in a parent's voice when Grandpa Francis expressed his broken heart to Dad when Mom died. At Eddie's funeral, I witnessed for the first time the distraught look in a parent's eyes the day they were to bury their son. Anthony's parents endured the same excruciating experience on their unthinkable day. With so many young people perishing in the terrorist attack, there were now countless parents having to go through something they never thought they'd have to—attend their child's funeral.

It was late March when I received a phone call from my fireman friend Brenden McManus. "They found his body," he told me, referring to Jimmie Riches.

On the day of Jimmie's funeral, I had already envisioned the look on his parents faces. I pictured in my mind the scenario that I'd seen play out all too many times before. However, on this early April morning, I'd be in for a few surprises.

The mass was held at Saint Patrick's Cathedral. My first surprise came when I saw Jimmie's father, Battalion Chief Jim Riches. I met Mr. Riches months earlier down at ground zero. The chief had been the one to assist me when I was feeling ill. I recalled thinking of how I couldn't place where I'd seen him before but now it was clear. With the chief's rugged round face and hazel eyes, I was looking at an older version of his son.

The second surprise at the funeral had to do with the mood. Yes, there were the tears and the sorrow for a life seemingly cheated from a young man, but there was also something rarely witnessed at a funeral—a sense of relief. Jimmie's family had been waiting over six excruciating months to put their son's body to rest, and believe it or not, they considered themselves the fortunate ones. With so many families still waiting to be notified of the recovery of their love one, at least the Richeses could now give their son a proper burial.

After 9/11, all three of Jimmie's brothers—Timmy, Danny, & Tommy—followed in their older brother's footsteps and became New York City Firemen. As for the ironman patriarch of the family, Chief Riches nearly died from Acute Respiratory Distress Syndrome attributed to breathing in the toxic air every day for the seven months he was down at ground zero. During that time, the chief was desperately digging to find the remains of the hundreds of firemen that were still buried in the debris, including his son.

Jimmie's mom, Rita Riches, in an interview with FOX 5 New York articulated living with the loss of her son:

"You have to go on the best you can. You put your best face on but your heart is broke."

Broken heart or heavy heart, everyone in the New York area was trying to figure out how to move on.

That fall, we as a country were glued to our televisions and radios—desperately seeking to make sense of a day that made no sense to any of us. No one was outwardly asking, but many were thinking, when would it be all right to laugh again or enjoy an autumn walk through Central Park? Or go to a ball game without feeling guilty?

The three major television networks were in a similar conundrum. They had the delicate task of figuring out when to resume their normal programming, which included the comedy-filled, late-night talk shows. Finally, on September 17, nearly a week after our country was attacked, CBS aired, *The Late Show with David Letterman*.

I had the privilege of meeting Mr. Letterman on several occasions. First was when he was working for NBC at 30 Rockefeller Plaza, and then later when he moved to CBS and broadcasted his new show from the landmark Ed Sullivan Theater. Both were in the confines of the Midtown North Precinct with the Ed Sullivan Theater being just up the block from the West Fifty-Fourth Street stationhouse.

Mr. Letterman always had a kind word to say to the men and women in blue and seemed to genuinely love the city. One day, Chris and I were parked on West Fifty-Third Street in our RMP, just west of Broadway, when the backdoor of the Ed Sullivan Theater opened and Mr. Letterman came walking out. He hadn't seen us parked across the street, and for the moment, no one noticed the incognito celebrity wearing a tee shirt, glasses and a worn-out baseball cap. Finally, a child no older than ten tugged on her mother's jacket and said, "Mommy, there's David Letterman, can I get his autograph?" The mother gave her daughter permission as long as she promised to be polite while asking. With still no one in the fast-paced city aware of the celebrity's presence, the young girl politely asked Mr. Letterman for his autograph, which he graciously provided. After receiving the famed signature, the excited girl with her autograph book in hand ran back to her mother screaming, "I got it! I got it!" The entire time, Mr. Letterman watched the reaction of his simple act and the impact it had on the young child. Without cameras present or onlookers to witness, Mr. Letterman signaled for the mother to return with her daughter. He then whispered something in the ear of one of the stagehands standing nearby, and within a few seconds, the worker returned with an 8 ×10 picture of the host. Mr. Letterman signed the picture and gave it to the appreciative young fan.

The entire encounter of providing the girl with two autographs lasted no more than a minute, but the impression would last with me—and I'm sure with the mother and daughter—a lifetime.

Mr. Letterman's actions weren't of an overpaid, pretentious snob but rather of a good-natured individual looking to make a stranger's experience a little more memorable.

So, on the Monday following 9/11, I anxiously waited to hear from the replanted mid-western man to see how he was going to grapple with the events that occurred over the past six days in his adopted hometown.

In a somber tone, Mr. Letterman opened the show sitting at his trademark desk and talking into his old RCA DX77 microphone. With a model of the very skyline that had been targeted days earlier being displayed behind him, the host when on to share his thoughts and feelings:

"In the past week, others have said what I will be saying here tonight far more eloquently than I'm equipped to do, but if I'm to continue to do shows, I just need to hear myself talk for a couple of minutes, and, so that's what I'm going to do here. It's terribly sad here in New York City. You can feel it, you can see it. It's terribly, terribly sad…"

The host of the Late Show then openly questioned if he should even be doing a show and then gave the reason behind why he decided to go forward—it was because of Mayor Giuliani.

"Very early on after the attack… Mayor Giuliani encouraged us, and here lately, implored us to go back to our lives, go on living, continue trying to make New York City the place that it should be… I want to say one other thing about Mayor Giuliani. As this began… and you're watching and you're confused, depressed, and irritated, and angry and full of grief and you don't know how to behave, you're not sure what to do because we've never been through this before, all you had to do is watch the mayor. Watch how this guy behaved. Watch how this guy conducted himself. Watch what this guy did. Listen to what this guy said. Rudolph Giuliani is the personification of courage…" (the audience as one erupts in applause to show their

appreciation for the herculean work undertaken by the man that will forever be considered America's Mayor).

During the applause, I noticed the late-night host taking deep breaths and at times looking as if he may break down at any moment. However, Mr. Letterman courageously continued with his nearly ten-minute opening monologue, which was unlike any he had given before.

Then Mr. Letterman addressed the first responders:

"Fortunately, most of us don't really have to think too much what these men and women do on a daily basis. And the phrase New York's Finest and New York's Bravest, did it mean anything to us personally firsthand? Well, maybe, hopefully but probably not, but boy it means something now, doesn't it? They put themselves in harm's way to protect people like us and the men and women from the Firefighters and the Police Department who are lost are going to be missed by this city for a very, very long time… and my hope for myself and everybody else, not only in New York but everywhere, is that we never ever take these people for granted, absolutely never take them for granted."

That evening, while listening to the man I'd grown to admire from afar, I couldn't help but become emotional. He spoke from the heart with eloquence that the self-deprecating host earlier declared he was deficient in. And with one last anecdote to Mr. Letterman's monologue, he concluded with a story of the American spirit and hope.

"There's a town in Montana by the name of Choteau, it's about a hundred miles south of the Canadian Border (population) 1,600 people. It's an ag-business community, which means farming and ranching. Montana has been in the middle of a drought for… three years. If you got no rain, you can't grow anything; if you can't grow anything, you can't farm; if you can't grow anything, you can't ranch because the cattle don't have anything to eat. And that's the way life is in this small town. Last night at the high school auditorium… they had a rally… for New York City; not just a rally for New York City, but a rally to raise money for New York City. If that doesn't tell you everything you need to know about the spirit of the United States, then I can't help you, I'm sorry…"

Thanks to a wise-cracking, gap-toothed comedian speaking from his heart, the process of healing had begun.

CHAPTER 11

My Promise

That which does not kill us, makes us stronger.
—Friedrich Nietzsche

As the autumn leaves gave way to the arctic cold air, the realization was that the holidays, whether I felt festive or not, were soon going to be upon me.

This was going to be my first Thanksgiving and Christmas without my dad. I knew things would be difficult but not nearly on the same magnitude for those families that were affected by the events of 9/11. Several months had passed, and still hundreds of families were waiting to hear if their loved one's body had been found. It was going to take a lot more than Donna Reed and Jimmy Stewart to get into the holiday spirit this year. In fact, this was one year I think most New Yorkers would've preferred skipping right over the holiday's all together.

I was back in my routine at The Monk, which also meant I was back to my heavy drinking. As it was, the events of September 11 had done nothing more than hit a pause button on my inevitable descent toward self-destruction.

When I came in to work the door the Saturday before Christmas, Scotty waved me over to the bar. He informed there was a party of four patrons having dinner, and one of them had inquired about my whereabouts. "He was wearing a white collar," Scotty informed me.

It wasn't difficult for me to surmise that it must've been Father Gerald doing the inquiring.

I looked around the jammed pub, but between the multitude of patrons and the oversized Christmas decorations, I was unable to spot the padre.

I grabbed a stool from the bar, along with my pint glass of Wild Turkey and coke that Scotty discreetly left off to the side, and positioned myself at the front door. It was just after nine, which meant soon I'd be wishing the older, more cultivated dinner crowd a good night, while welcoming in the younger patrons.

While sitting there, I started to get a bit anxious. I hadn't seen Father Gerald since that fateful morning on 9/11. I all but gave up on going to his weekly, Saturday evening sermons and had completely abandoned my coaching responsibilities.

So as I leaned against my stool contemplating how the conversation between the two of us may go, I heard a familiar voice wishing me a Merry Christmas. The friendly greeting was coming from Mrs. Strahan. After giving a hug and reciprocating her well wishes, I inquired where Father Gerald was hiding. She explained that he was retrieving their belongings from the coat-check room.

Moments later, Father Gerald appeared, and in his Irish brogue gave me a taste of his sharp wit by saying, "My Lord, it's been so long I nearly didn't recognize you, my son."

After kissing the padre on both cheeks, he proceeded to introduce the young man standing beside him as Shawn.

While shaking Shawn's hand, I couldn't help but notice a deep sadness in his eyes. He tried to smile during our introduction, but I could tell the effort was a strain. Knowing Father Gerald and his kindness, I surmised that the young man was going through some crisis in his life and the good Priest invited him out for dinner.

Waiting behind the two men was a beautiful young lady. The smiling brunette was festively dressed in a red sweater and a pair of black riding boots that rose just above her plaid skirt. I was attempting to figure out the stranger's relationship to the group when I finally recognized the bonita to be Mrs. Strahan's assistant, Diana. With her hair down and the apron gone, the once diamond in the rough was now sparkling.

Diana was no sooner saying hello before Mrs. Strahan was whisking her away. After all, this encounter by Father Gerald wasn't by chance and it was now time for him to have a moment—one-on-one with me.

However, before Diana left, she handed me a folded program. The pamphlet was for the following evening's midnight mass. In her soft Colombian accent, she whispered to me that she hoped I could join her for the sermon. Diana then quickly turned and left with Mrs. Strahan and Shawn.

Father Gerald had been fussing buttoning his black overcoat in what looked more like a delay tactic than anything else. Now that the others were waiting for him outside and the two of us were alone, Father Gerald had what he came here looking for—me. Never one to miss anything, he started by pointing to the program in my hand and expressed that my presence at the mass would make a grand Christmas gift to him and the Lord.

Then Father Gerald began to speak to me in a tone I was unfamiliar with. Having been around the priest for as long as I had, I knew his many different ways of communicating. He had his sermon voice, his wise cracking voice, his stern voice, and his drinking voice. In what now could best be described as a serious, but compassionate voice, the padre asked me if he needed to worry about me. I told him the truth—I wasn't sure but to please keep me in his prayers.

"My son, you're always in my prayers. The issue for me is I don't know exactly what I should be asking God to help you with. I feel as though one of my sheep has run astray and I'm desperately trying to find him before Satan does."

The words touched me because I knew them to be true. I was lost, and now my priest knew it as well. My eyes started to well up, as I could feel the emotions run through my body. Father Gerald then began to tell me about his guest, Shawn.

"The young man I introduced you to earlier is going through a rough patch. He was married over the summer to a woman he thought he was going to spend the rest of his life with. They very much loved each other, planning their future children's names and what schools they'd attend. I guess it's safe to say with both being Villanova alum, they already had the college picked out. That all changed on September 11."

I now better understood the look on Shawn's face. A look of someone trying to be happy but simply was incapable.

Father Gerald went on to explain how they still hadn't found the twenty-eight-year-old Cantor Fitzgerald employee's body and the torment her young husband was now going through as the holidays approached.

"As bad as things appear to be for Shawn right now, I'm not worried about him," Father Gerard said. "He'll get through this. He'll always love his wife and miss her dearly, but because of Shawn's strong faith in God and his will to live, he will persevere. He'll find that path because whether he realizes it or not, he's looking for it."

Before Father Gerald left to meet up with his three guests, he asked if I would come to the Rectory and visit with him. Unable to speak, for fear that I may start to cry, I nodded my head up and down in agreement to his request, knowing I had no intention of doing so. It wasn't that I didn't want to see my mentor, it was that I didn't want the help I knew he was graciously going to offer.

Before leaving, Father Gerald posed the question again to me regarding what he should ask God to help me with. I didn't know how to respond, so I simply stood there motionless. Realizing I hadn't an answer, he interjected by saying, "Not to worry, I'm sure between the three of us—as he pointed upwards—we'll figure things out."

For the rest of the evening, all I could think about was the padre's visit and his question that I was unable to answer.

I was thankful the shift at The Monk had been an uneventful one. In other words, no fights to break up or drunks to throw out. My body was at the pub but after talking with Father Gerald, my mind was elsewhere.

I grabbed my trusted pea coat jacket, along with my gloves and Scottish cap and proceeded to walk home. The late hour, along with the arctic chill in the air, put me alone with only my thoughts to keep me company.

While I walked along the desolate sidewalk, I could hear the wind blowing through the alleys of the apartment buildings. As I turned the corner, I found myself stopping for no apparent reason to look at the grocery store I once worked at as a youngster. Across the street from the store was my church, fully decorated in Christmas lights. There was a time I considered both these places an extension of my home—an extension of me.

I can't help but think of how seemingly perfect everything once was. Those days of delivering groceries and my duties as an altar boy had given me something I've been lacking for quite some time: a meaningful purpose.

My life was so much simpler and kinder back then. I had purpose, responsibility, friends and one other thing that goes along with such remembrance—happiness. I had a brother that protected me from the neighborhood bullies, and a priest that taught me how to shoot a jump shot. I had a dad who made sure I had a roof over my head and a hot meal for dinner every night. There are so many things I took for granted. Perhaps nothing greater than how perfect life once was.

As another strong arctic blast of wind twirls down the street, it snaps me out of my brief trek down memory lane.

I've passed the church and grocery store every night on my way home from the pub, never giving either a second thought. Why then tonight did I choose to stop and be reflective? I knew the answer, as well as the trigger to all the thoughts flooding into my head. It was Father Gerald.

He was in a quandary of wanting to help but not knowing how. We both were aware that I was lost, but what my friend wasn't aware of was that I didn't wish to be found or saved.

In a moment of clarity, I thought to myself the awful irony that stood before me. Dad wished nothing more than to live but died, where as I stand here living but wish I was dead.

I continued walking home with only one thought in mind—to end my life. I hadn't a reason to live. Father Gerald's visit proved to me how unhappy I'd become. In his attempt to help me, the padre inadvertently magnified how truly lost I'd become. To accept his benevolence would mean I cared, which I no longer did. I cared about nothing or nobody—least of all myself.

After arriving home, without a lot of thought or planning, I decided it was time to end my life. I removed my .38 Ruger Revolver from my waistband holster and put the barrel of the gun to my temple. With enough force as to move the hammer ever so slightly, I began to pull the trigger. I continued to put slight pressure on the mechanism and then I'd release it. I desperately sought a reason, any reason, for why I shouldn't complete the task at hand.

It was then I had a flashback of Francis's suicide. I never saw the scene after Francis took his life, but I could only imagine the horrific site left behind. So, while I sat there on the edge of my bed scratching the barrel of the gun to my temple, I decided I'd pull the trigger—but not here.

For a brief moment, I had a reprieve on my suicide, but it didn't last for long. A voice inside me, maybe from one of the demons that wasn't pleased with my decision to put things on hold, spoke to me. The voice told me if I couldn't come up with a reason to live, then I should simply pull the trigger regardless of the mess I'd leave behind. After all, why should I care? I looked over at the clock that was hanging on the wall and saw it was ten minutes before five. I made a deal with the demon. If I couldn't derive one reason to live, I'd pull the trigger when the clock struck five—bloody mess and all. All parties concerned agreed and the clock began ticking.

The first minute had come and gone without anything coming to me. I needed something, anything, but my brain wasn't cooperating. I started to think of Aunt Gwen, along with my cousins, to see if my living would make a difference in their lives; but the truth was besides the initial shock and sorrow of my departure, their lives would not be affected. I then thought of Father Gerald and came up with the same conclusion.

The clock was ticking faster now. As I watched the second hand go around, I was now down to five minutes. I thought of everyone I could. I even thought of the bar I just left. It didn't take long for me to come to the conclusion that my absence at The Monk would hardly justify a reason to live.

It was now less than a minute to go, and I decided to stop trying to think of a reason to live and concentrated on the task at hand. I chose to clear my thoughts and yield to the inevitable. I once again positioned the gun to my temple and asked God for his forgiveness. It was at that precise moment I had vision.

The vision was of a couple I met as a rookie, Mr. and Mrs. Washington. The parents had lost their daughter in a Midtown apartment house fire. Out of the tens of thousands of people I interacted with as a police officer, this couple left an indelible impression on me. I met them under the worst of circumstances but because of their faith and love for one another, they were thanking God at a time when most people would've been blaming Him.

However, I found it disturbing that the couple from Queensbury, New York should be in my last thoughts and not Mom, Dad and Francis.

The harder I tried to suppress the vision, the stronger their image appeared to me. I finally yielded and thought back upon that cold, miserable January afternoon when I met Mr. and Mrs. Washington at the Medical Examiner's office.

It was my last day at the Third Division. I had no idea at the time, but those previous six months would prove to be my most enjoyable time while on the NYPD. I felt so fortunate to have worked alongside Eddie and Anthony, and to have been mentored by Sergeant Ryen. Due to the fatal fire, the last day wasn't the kumbaya most of us were hoping for.

I recalled my inner reluctance when Sergeant Gooden entrusted me with the task of reporting to the Medical Examiner's office for the notification process. At the moment, I wished that the sergeant hadn't such confidence in me and had chosen someone else. But shortly after meeting with the Washington's, I realized that the task was not a burden—it was a privilege.

I was still struggling to see why the Washington's were in my thoughts when I remembered the promise I made to Mr. Washington. I gave him my word that one day, I'd make the trek to Lake George and climb his beloved Black Mountain. It had been many years, and during that time I hadn't once thought about Lake George or the promise I made. But as I sat there with no other purpose left in my life, I felt compelled to go climb a mountain in the dead of winter. So, after writing into my journal for the final time, I left for Upstate New York.

The view from my Amtrak seat is one I hadn't experienced before. The northern scenic route hugs along the Hudson River, passing towns I've heard of but had never visited. The further north the train traveled, the less appearance civilization existed. The trees had long lost its leaves, only to be replaced by snow and icicles. Having spent all my life in the overpopulated, overdeveloped NYC, I'm surprised to see how much is still left untouched.

The train ride had become an unexpected, but calming influence on me. I started to think of my previous actions hours earlier and strangely found myself at ease with the fact that I nearly ended my life. I'm convinced that I will find a better location in the secluded mountains to finish what I previously started.

I hadn't been paying much attention to the other riders. Ever since the train left Penn Station, my eyes were fixated on the passing landscape. In fact, it wasn't until the women across from me tried getting my attention that I realized the railcar was near capacity.

At first, when the middle-aged female said something, I hadn't realized she was directing her words toward me. It wasn't until she repeated herself that I became aware she was trying to get my attention.

"Beautiful," she said again, referring to the passing scenery.

I tilted my head forward in her direction and politely replied, "Yes, yes, it is."

I had a sneaky suspicion the full-of-sunshine commuter wasn't through with the conversation.

My instincts were quickly confirmed.

The well-dressed passenger continued in her piercing, high-pitched voice to say, "I travel into the city at least twice a week. I just love the city, don't you?" Without stopping to give me an opportunity to answer or for her to take a breath, she continued. "I love the change of seasons. I love walking through Central Park as much as I love shopping at Bergdorf Goodman's. I love, love, love the Broadway shows and all the fine restaurants. I love going to the Russian Tea Room after a show for a nosh and to people watch. I know I said I love all the seasons in New York, but truthfully, I'd have to say that this time of year (Christmas) has to be my favorite. Is there any place better to be than Rockefeller Center and seeing the Christmas tree? I saw A Christmas Carol last night at Radio City. I go every year. Have you ever seen the show?" I gave a simple nod of the head to indicate that I had and also to allow her to continue without interruption.

While the Gucci-toting woman continued to tell me all about her love affair with New York City, I recalled the evening Sergeant Ryen took his "Untouchables" to Radio City Music Hall to see the Rockettes.

The Sergeant told us the day before not to report to the command but instead, we were to muster at the north-east corner of Forty-Ninth Street and Sixth Avenue. He instructed the three of us to wear a suit because as he put it, "We were going deep undercover."

Eddie, Anthony, and I met at the assigned location and waited for Ryen to arrive. We all speculated what the big assignment could be. Anthony thought we were going to raid some high end social clubs, while Eddie thought it might have something to do with a sting operation. When they asked me what I thought, I told them I hadn't a clue, but I was lying.

I knew the sergeant better than anyone in the squad. I knew he loved being a cop and sharing his knowledge with us greenies. I further knew how sentimental our boss was when it came to the city. Nobody appreciated the culture and everything the Big Apple had to offer more than Ryen.

So, with the three of us standing in front of Radio City Music Hall, and only a week before Christmas, I surmised there was a good chance our boss was taking us to see the show that was boldly displayed above us on the marquis—"A Christmas Spectacular."

Shortly afterwards, a festive Ryen arrived sporting his trademark Scottish cap and navy-blue pea coat. Our good boss, with a smile ear to ear, then proceeded to lead us into the theater.

While walking into the lobby, I could feel the electricity in the air. There were people young and old, from near and far, to take in the holiday spectacle.

The stunning art deco foyer was being lost on most of the anxious guests scurrying to their seats, but not me. The prism-designed light fixtures that hung from the forty-foot ceiling softly illuminated the waiting area below. And in the spirit of the holidays, a bright, white chandelier in the shape of a Christmas tree hung in the center of the room, while the strategically placed green-lit wreaths gleamed as they dangled throughout the lobby. I noticed how the brass banisters leading up to the mezzanine popped against the rich, crimson-colored walls and carpet; reminiscent of the Plaza Hotel's elegant entrance.

With so much to take in, I was finding it difficult to keep focused on any one single item. That is until I spotted the mural on the second level. Covering the height and width of over twenty feet in each direction, the masterpiece had a spiritual sense to it. The question for me was not in the beauty, which for a non-art critic was abundantly clear, but its meaning. The picture told a story that took place over time, but it was that story I was having difficulty in understanding. I found it much less daunting to simply admire the beauty of the composition than try to make sense of it. That's when Ryen observed my interest and quickly educated me on the art work.

"That mural is the story of a man's life," Ryen began to explain. "It begins showing the young man filled with hubris and vanity, and then finishes with the inevitability—getting older and dying."

After Ryen's narration, and a further intensified observation of the details on my part, I couldn't help but find the Oregon Indian chief depicted in the mural to be a tragic figure. He squandered his youth only to make a futile attempt at the end of his life for atonement.

Before going to our seats, I asked Ryen if he happened to know the name of the angelical painting. Always the teacher, he responded, "The Fountain of Youth."

Seeing I was having difficulty discerning the title, Ryen explained, "Dean, as we move on in life and the end comes closer, there's nothing in the world one wouldn't do than to be young again. For the Indian chief, he'd give anything to turn back the clock, and in the process, live his life differently."

As my boss continued staring at the mural, I sensed he related more to its meaning than this twenty-year-old rookie.

The show itself did not disappoint. After some persuasion by three ghosts and a sickly Tiny Tim, Scrooge changed his ways. The long-legged Rockettes then took over and choreographed some amazing, high-kicking, toy-soldier maneuvers.

After the show, Ryen had arranged for us to go backstage to meet the cast. Anthony saw a few of the Rockette girls off to the side and decided to pull them into a photo op. Not content with a few snap shots, Anthony persuaded the girls to do their legendary eye-high leg kick. With two girls on each side of the barrel-chested rookie, they began their own chorus line. The sight of the novice-dancing Anthony trying to keep pace with the professional dancers was comical to say the least. Even now as I think back upon the evening, I can't help but openly chuckle.

My ill-timed laughter breaks the rhythm of my new acquaintance and has her asking, "I'm sorry, did I say something funny?" I shook my head to indicate that she hadn't. However, my actions had exposed the fact to her that I wasn't paying attention. In the attempt to reel me back into her conversation, she asked a question that couldn't be answered with a simple head gesture.

"So, what do you love most about New York City?"

While still looking out the window, I responded to her question in a cold and insensitive tone.

"I love the anonymity." After a slight pause to allow for an anticipated interruption, which never materialized, I continued. "I love the fact that nobody cares about me and that the feeling is more than mutual. I love that in a city with over eight-million people, I can go for days without talking to a soul and not feel as though I missed out on a single thing."

Not certain if I made my point, I turned my head to face the once-cheerful lady in order to deliver the final death blow to our budding encounter. With complete sincerity, and looking directly into her eyes, I said, "The thing I truly love most about New York City is being left alone."

I turned my head back to look out the window in anticipation that I could now go back to my solitude. However, being an Irish Catholic, I quickly began to feel guilty over my rude behavior. The stranger wanted nothing more than to kill some time by engaging in some small talk, and I chose to have nothing to do with it. I'd become so depressed and miserable that I couldn't engage in a simple conversation without being a complete jackass.

My insensitivity toward the stranger only strengthened my resolve to finish what I started hours earlier. All I wished for now was getting to the lake, climb the mountain Mr. Washington referenced, and find a secluded spot where I could finally make my peace.

With no louder than a whisper, I could hear the once cheerful lady say, "No, that's not true."

I could've pretended not to hear her and continued in my alternate universe, but I was actually relieved that my insensitive remarks hadn't deterred her from continuing to talk.

I immediately turned and apologized for my rudeness. Not wanting to accept my apology, she informed me that she was the one that was sorry for interrupting me. She then turned her attention to the magazine she had on her lap.

Not satisfied, I then put my hand out and introduced myself. "My name is Dean, Dean Simpson."

With a bit of trepidation, she extended her hand and introduced herself as Erin McNaughton.

I hadn't paid much attention to the blue-eyed, black-velvet hair commuter earlier, but now as I look into her eyes, I can feel my actions had clearly disturbed her.

With the roles reversed, me the pursuer and she the reluctant participant, I asked what she meant when she said, "No, that's not true."

"I just don't believe anyone truly wishes to be alone," she replied. "I simply think it goes against nature." She paused for a moment, clearly to think of what she wanted to say next. "I've been without my husband for the past seven years. One of the reasons I enjoy going into the city as much as I do is to interact with the people. Maybe I should realize that not everyone shares in my enthusiasm."

She then smiled, while looking at me, implying that I wasn't one of those enthusiastic people. I chuckled at the zinger and then apologized again for being less than a gentleman.

With the tensions eased, I politely asked what had happened to her husband.

Erin told me she was living a fairytale life. Her husband had a successful medical practice in their hometown of Saratoga, while she put her practice on hold to raise their daughter.

"Everything was perfect," she said. "And then I received that phone call. He had a brain embolism and three days later, he was gone."

"Those phone calls really suck, don't they?" I rhetorically asked.

Picking up on the fact that I'd experienced a similar call, she asked, "What was yours like?"

To my surprise, I began to tell her about the call I received at four forty-four, Christmas morning. I explained to Erin the guilt I felt for not going with Francis that night and the task of going to tell my father something he already knew.

It was just moments earlier that I dismissed the stranger as an irritant, but now, as I sat there feeling vulnerable, I opened up to her as if she was my closest friend. I could feel my emotions starting to rise as they had earlier with Father Gerald, so I tried my best to deflect the conversation in another direction. I asked her about her daughter, but Erin ignored my inquiry and pressed me on my earlier comment regarding wanting to be alone. I once again attempted to reroute the conversation by asking why she hadn't remarried.

"All right," she said, "I'll answer your question and then you'll answer mine. My husband was the love of my life. Not just in words, but truly my soul mate. We did everything together. I miss him so much that I get angry sometimes, but then I remember the thirty-two years God blessed me with him and my anger is replaced with gratitude. I have friends, a daughter, and two grandchildren I can dote over—but there can only be one love of my life, and that's why I'll never remarry. So, why do you seek solitude?"

The seemingly innocuous question started an emotional chain reaction from within. My body became numb, my throat dry, and my eyes filled with tears. Moments earlier, I hadn't the desire to speak, and now irony took its revenge upon me by not allowing me to put two words together.

Erin took notice and asked as only a mother could, "Are you all right?" I nodded my head that I was, but my body language was telegraphing an entirely different story.

I could feel the sweat pour out from my pores as every nerve in my body tingled. All the while, Erin continued reassuring me everything was going to be all right. In the middle of this indefinite panic attack, I couldn't help but feel for the imposition I was putting this poor woman through.

It took several minutes and the comfort of a stranger, but I was finally able to regain my composure. I began to explain to Erin how my life changed after my brother's death.

"I don't think I was ever the same after that phone call," I told her. "I'd seen many horrific things as a police officer, but nothing in the world could prepare me for that call. When I was a cop it was always someone else's family, not mine… Francis should still be alive."

The compassionate stranger tried convincing me that I was allowed to be free from the guilt. I heard similar words from Father Gerard years earlier, but what neither understood was if I went with Francis that night, "it" wouldn't have happened.

Erin agreed by saying, "Dean, maybe that's true. Maybe what happened in the bar doesn't occur, but maybe it does. Who knows exactly? One thing we do know is that at some point, your brother would've been by himself still contemplating the same decision, under the same circumstances. This was his choice, and whether you believe it or not, you're not responsible for other people's actions."

I knew what Erin was saying made sense. However, Francis's suicide was but one of the many demons still clasping at my soul.

Both being New Yorkers, it was simply a matter of time before the conversation diverted to 9/11.

I explained to Erin how I was sleeping off a night of binge drinking when our country was being attacked.

"Good people, better people than me died that day," I told her. "The world is full of evil and I'm tired of being a part of it. That is yet another reason why I seek solitude. Call it a prophylactic for evil, but the less I expose myself to the world, the less chance I have of being consumed by it."

In a low but defiant tone, Erin disagreed.

"No, Dean. Don't you see it's just the opposite? By closing out everyone, you end up keeping the good out. And believe me, there's much more good in this world than evil."

For the next two hours, Erin and I discussed life, love, and the trials and tribulations that went along with each. We couldn't have been further apart on the spectrum—Erin, with her Pollyanna outlook on life and me, Mr. Doom and Gloom.

Erin asked me if I was acquainted with the Greek mythological Pandora's Box. I told her that I was familiar with the story and the devastation unleashed by Pandora when she opened it; not unlike Eve when she ate the apple from the Tree of Knowledge. She then asked me if I was aware of the last thing left in the box. Acknowledging that I was unaware, she responded by saying, "Hope."

"If not for hope, then all else is lost. I have to hope that good will prevail over evil, that love is stronger than hate. Don't ever give up hope."

I explained to Erin the reason for my trip to upstate was because of a couple I met years earlier. I told her of the tragic event behind the death of the Washington's daughter and the unique courage they showed under the worst of circumstances.

"It was Mr. Washington that made me promise I visit Lake George and climb Black Mountain," I finished telling Erin.

A stickler for details, Erin inquired why I was fulfilling my promise now, after all these years.

Not wishing to share my true intentions, I half-jokingly told her I had nothing better to do today and thought it might be fun to hike a mountain in the middle of winter.

Over the loudspeaker, I could hear the conductor inform the passengers that we'd be arriving into the "Albany–Rensselaer Station" in ten minutes. Erin then excused herself to go use the restroom.

While she was away, I thought about her words and the pleasantness of her company. I couldn't help but wonder if God put the eternally, optimistic grandmother next to me to show how life can go on if we choose. It's the first positive thought I had since putting the gun to my head.

When the train came into the station, Erin handed me a folded piece of paper and said, "I don't even know if the trail is open and you certainly don't look like you're dressed for a hike, but I want you to read this when you get to wherever it is you're going."

After a short embrace, I put the paper in my pocket and then the two of us parted ways.

During the thirty-minute cab ride to Black Mountain, I could see parts of the Adirondack mountain range in the not so far off distance. The row of offsetting mountains went as far as the eye could see. I asked the cabbie where the mountains in the distance were located and he told me they were in Vermont.

"You should've been up here a few months ago," the local cabbie told me. "In all the forty-eight years I've been here, I'd never seen such vibrant foliage like that before. It was as if God came down and painted them himself. Truly magnificent."

My only knowledge of the area came from Mr. Washington and a few things I recalled from my sixth-grade Social Studies class. I knew the region had its history dating back to the Revolutionary War, but in modern times, the tranquil Adirondack's had become an escape for city dwellers looking to get back to nature.

I had the taxi driver drop me off in the parking lot at the base of the mountain. It was now noon, and although the sun was shining bright against the crisp blue sky, it was proving ineffective against the unrelenting winter air. My one bit of luck in regards to the elements was the absence of snow.

It took me less than two hours to ascend the 2.5-mile trail to the summit. When I turned around to take in the view of the thirty-six-mile-long Lake George and the boundless mountain ranges behind it, I felt an overwhelming sense of appreciation. Perhaps the way one might feel about the artwork of a Da Vinci or a Michelangelo. However, this magnificent artisanship could not be credited to a mere mortal, for this was truly the work of God.

As I looked at the white caps on the lake below, I said a prayer. I asked God for his forgiveness and for the first time in a long time, His guidance.

At the summit was an abandoned campfire, long extinguished and full of ashes. Next to it was a log. I sat there and took out Dad's Bible.

Dad was never without his Bible, reading from it every day. He said it was with the word of God during those most trying and difficult times during his life that gave him the strength to continue on.

So, as I sat there on top of Black Mountain, a place where Mr. Washington so accurately described as heaven on earth. I opened Dad's Bible in the hope that I too could be filled with the strength of the Holy Spirit.

Upon opening, I noticed a small piece of paper with a list of several scriptures written on it. On the top of this makeshift bookmark, Dad had written the words, "Inspirational Scriptures."

I started down the list and began to turn the pages to find each scripture he noted. The more I read, the more I realized the scriptures Dad had chosen were like a road map leading me closer to God.

The next scripture on the list was 1 Corinthians 10–13.

There are numbers in life that will forever follow us. Some of these numbers are associated with a positive occasion, such as a birthday or anniversary. And then there are the numbers that will forever haunt us. For those, I have a set of three—9/11, 4:44, and the police call for help, 10-13. The last time I uttered those numbers, I was laying on the ground in the pouring rain gasping for air. It's been several years since I was shot in Clinton Park, and although my physical injuries have long healed, my mental scars are as fresh as the day it happened.

With my hands trembling, I open the Bible to 1 Corinthians, scripture 10, verse 13.

> No temptation has overtaken you that is not
> common to man. God is faithful, and he will not
> let you be tempted beyond your ability, but with
> the temptation he will also provide the way of
> escape, that you may be able to endure it.

The impactful words let me know I wasn't alone in my affliction. The Lord was with me and through Him, I could find the one thing I desperately sought—peace.

Thinking I had but only one option to rid myself of my demons, I was led to the cusp of my being. But as I continue to pray for the salvation of my soul, it became clearer with each inspirational scripture that I could be free of the darkness without having to end my life to do so.

So, on Christmas Eve 2001, with the Adirondacks as my backdrop, I retrieved a pen from my coat pocket and wrote down the following pledge:

> I pledge these words in the hope of saving my
> soul and with God as my witness:
> I will never allow the demons to control my life
> again.
> I will no longer indulge in the drink.
> I will dedicate my life to helping others in the
> darkness.
> And I will live through the principals of the Bible.

Before heading back down the mountain, I took the folded piece of paper Erin gave me earlier out from my back pocket. The note read:

> Dean, life is a gift meant to be shared.
> Don't ever give up hope!

> Merry Christmas,
> Erin.

Just hours earlier, these words would've landed on deaf ears; but now, with my pledge in hand and my heart open, I relish in the profound note.

Like a man with newfound hope, I descended down the mountain, only stopping once when I came across a narrow ravine. I emptied the chambers of my .38 Ruger, scattering the rounds down the sliced opening. I then took one last look at the firearm that I had since I was a rookie and tossed it into the abyss. Having come so close to misusing my trusted sidearm, I no longer felt I had the privilege in allowing myself to ever carry it again. I said my goodbyes and then continued down the mountain.

By the time I reached the bottom, darkness had already set in. It was almost five in the afternoon and I was two-hundred and fifty miles from home. I had one goal in mind: get back for Father Gerald's Midnight Mass.

I began walking along the side of the isolated road, knowing at some point I would need a little assistance from above if I were to get home in time. A short time later, a state trooper vehicle pulled up alongside me. The young trooper asked if I was in need of some assistance, to which I replied, "Absolutely."

The young trooper's name was Raymond Long. He was tall with wide shoulders, blonde hair and looked like he just graduated from the academy. In what sounded like a southern drawl, the officer asked me how I got to be where I was. I told him it was a long story but simply put, "I was on the wrong road."

I explained to Trooper Long that I wanted to grab a taxi in town, and from there to the train terminal in Albany. He began to laugh and said, "You won't get a cab tonight. Don't you realize it's Christmas Eve?"

With that he picked up the radio and called into dispatch. "Central, I have to drop a package off down at the trooper barracks in Albany. Will advise when done, 10–4."

The trooper looked over at me with a grin and said, "Looks like you're my package."

For the next thirty minutes, the full of life young man began to tell me about his exciting pending news. Tonight, when his shift ended at midnight, he was going to ask his girlfriend of four years to marry him.

"I have it all planned," he said. "Later, I'm going to surprise her at church. I already spoke with her father and he gave me his blessing. I have the ring, the blessing, and all I need now is a little snow to make it perfect."

As the young trooper told me more about his childhood sweetheart, I think of the beautiful future that awaits him and his soon to be fiancé. I can hear the excitement in his voice with every detail he shares. It's an excitement that comes from being in love and having a future filled with hope.

It's that hope that has me anxiously wanting to get back home.

When we arrived at the train station, I thanked Trooper Long for the ride and wished him all the best with his plans. He no sooner pulled away when the first snowflakes of the season began to fall.

The next scheduled train to New York City was to depart in less than an hour. I grabbed some dinner from a vending machine and then waited patiently on the platform.

By the time I boarded the south bound Amtrak train, I was officially exhausted. Between the lack of sleep and the emotional rollercoaster ride of the past twenty-four hours, I finally hit a wall. All I remember was leaning against the window seat, and the next thing I knew a conductor was giving me a poke to inform me that we'd arrived at the final stop: New York City.

I felt like I slept for days but it had been no more than two hours. Now with my batteries recharged and spirits high, I was off to Brooklyn.

It was just a little after eleven as the taxi drove over the Brooklyn Bridge. Thanks to the Lord and a rookie trooper, I was going to make it back in time for the mass.

When I arrived at Saint Patrick's, the cabbie, seeing the logjam of cars in front of the church, decided to drop me off across the street. When I exited the taxi, I couldn't help but notice that I was standing in the exact location I'd been the previous evening. Although the spot was the same, my outlook was completely different.

Before entering the church, I made my way to the Mother Mary statue. The life-sized statue stands outside upon a pedestal between the walkway of the church and the Rectory. It was here, dressed in my dark suit and white carnation, that mother and I stopped for a photo just after I received my First Communion at age seven. For years, I would come to this very spot and pray to her. I'd let her know how much I wished she was still with us and how much I love her.

The night before, I saw the statue and thought of crossing the street to say a prayer, but I couldn't bring myself to do it.

However, tonight is different. I'm different. Filled with hope and the desire to live, I willingly kneel down in front of the statue and begin to pray.

"I know it's been awhile, Mom. I can still feel you with me even though you've been gone for quite some time. I know you've been busy with Dad and Francis, and I pray the three of you are at peace. As for me, I've been floundering for too long and have decided it was time to start living my life again. I've had some demons that I know I still have to face, but at least I'm not afraid anymore. When I'm done here, I'm going inside to see Father Gerard. He more oversees the masses than performs them these days. Time is catching up to our good friend. Mom, there's someone else I hope to see tonight. She told me she'd be saving a seat for me. I hope she does. Well, it's time for me to go. I'll talk to you tomorrow—Merry Christmas!

Epilogue

It was a few days before Christmas in 2014 when a punk by the name of Ismaaiyl Brinsley decided he was going to kill two New York City Police Officers. Boasting of his intentions on social media, the career criminal drove from Baltimore to Brooklyn to fulfill his deranged proclamation.

The two officers, Rafael Ramos, forty, and Wenjian Liu, thirty-two, sat in their blue-and-white squad car, probably discussing their families or some local sporting teams the way cops usually do to pass the time, when they were assassinated in a hail of gun fire. The officers never had a chance.

The inexplicable, heinous act brought me back twenty-five years earlier when Eddie was killed. The two executions were similar in every way except one—the motive.

In Eddie's case, it was about a drug kingpin trying to intimidate cops and witnesses in the attempt to protect his lucrative empire. It was greed along with a lust for power that seduced the killers into doing Satan's handy work.

However, the killings of Ramos and Liu weren't about money, drugs, or retaining power. The sadistic, ideology attack was on an institution and its principles of law.

The deranged gunman wanted to kill two cops, because in his words, "I'm putting wings on pigs today. They take one of ours… let's take two of theirs. #ShootThePolice #ErivGardner."

The punk was referring to the death of a black man named Eric Gardner at the hands of a New York City police officer. So connected was the gunman to the Staten Island resident that he didn't even know how to spell his name correctly. However, that didn't stop him from taking the law into his own hands and acting as judge, jury, and executioner to two officers that had nothing to do with the Eric Gardner incident.

In my opinion, this new, insidious enemy to the men and women in blue has the potential to be far worse than the crack dealers of the '80s. Drug dealers know killing a cop is going to be bad for business so they are less likely to put out a contract hit. However, those individuals that are motivated by hate in their hearts, evil in their minds and a warped sense of justice have but one motivation—and that is to kill.

As 2014 came to a close, I couldn't help but wonder if this latest tragedy was an anomaly or something far worse, an opening for other delusional, copycat offenders to act out their demented fantasies.

Around this time, the anti-police sentiment was gaining traction throughout the inner cities. There was a new organization stoking the flames by using several disturbing chants at their rallies, such as:

"Pigs in a blanket, fry 'em up like bacon."
"What do we want? Dead Cops! When do we want it? Now!"

In Dallas, during the summer of 2016, another deranged individual that shared the same hatred values as the NYC shooter, declared war on the police by shooting twelve officers, killing five of them—the worst loss of life of law enforcement since 9/11. A man by the name of Micah Johnson, twenty-five, a veteran who served in Afghanistan, was the cause of the carnage.

During the standoff, the African American male, protested recent shootings of black men by white cops. He stated that he wanted to kill white people, especially white officers.

It was becoming clear there was a new problem for officers to be on the lookout for—people that wanted to kill cops simply because they were cops.

After the killing of the five police officers—Lorne Ahrens, Michael Krol, Michael J. Smith, Brent Thompson, and Patrick

Zamarripa—the soft-spoken Dallas police chief, David Brown, said, "All I know is that this must stop—this divisiveness between our police and our citizens."

In a news conference held the Monday after the nightmare, Chief Brown articulated a sentiment felt by most—if not all—officers throughout the country:

"We're asking cops to do too much in this country. Every societal failure, we put off on the cops to solve…"

After listening to the chief's words, I decided it was time to wipe the dust off my journal and share my story.

I pray that by telling my story, those that might have negative feelings toward the police might actually gain some understanding and empathy for the job we do. We're human. We're no different when it comes to how we feel or the effects of the pressure that goes along with such a profession. Yes, there're some bad apples, but 99.9 percent of cops start their tour wanting to do the right thing. They'd much rather help a citizen then lock one up.

As for my fellow brethren, keep your eyes open. See the signs for depression and don't hesitate to seek professional help. Most of all, remember God loves you.

The bloodshed and twisted steel that galvanized us as a nation on 9/11 has been replaced with divisiveness, anger, and violence. I pray we can recapture our unity as one country under God before we destroy ourselves.

As long as one doesn't give up, there's always hope.

—DD Simpson

CPSIA information can be obtained
at www.ICGtesting.com
Printed in the USA
BVHW03s2236110918
527246BV00001B/11/P